Adventures in Internationalism

A Biography of James Brown Scott

Adventures in Internationalism

A Biography of James Brown Scott

George A. Finch

Edited by
William E. Butler

The Lawbook Exchange, Ltd.
Clark, New Jersey

ISBN 978-1-61619-165-8 (hardcover)
ISBN 978-1-61619-166-5 (paperback)

Lawbook Exchange edition 2012

The Lawbook Exchange, Ltd.
33 Terminal Avenue
Clark, New Jersey 07066-1321

Please see our website for a selection of our other publications and fine facsimile reprints of classic works of legal history: www.lawbookexchange.com

Library of Congress Cataloging-in-Publication Data

Finch, George Augustus, 1884-1957.
Adventures in internationalism : a biography of James Brown Scott / by George A. Finch ; edited by William E. Butler.
p. cm.
Includes bibliographical references and index.
ISBN-13: 978-1-61619-165-8 (hardcover : alk. paper)
ISBN-10: 1-61619-165-1 (hardcover : alk. paper)
ISBN-13: 978-1-61619-166-5 (pbk. : alk. paper)
ISBN-10: 1-61619-166-X (pbk. : alk. paper)
1. Scott, James Brown, 1866-1943. 2. International law--United States.--History. 3. Law teachers--United States--Biography. I. Butler, William Elliott, 1939- II. Title.
KZ3178.F56 2011
340.092--dc23
[B]

2011018759

Printed in the United States of America on acid-free paper

CONTENTS

EDITORIAL FOREWORD

The present volume contains an integrated version of several manuscripts of a biography prepared by George A. Finch for and of his mentor and superior, James Brown Scott. The manuscripts repose in the Manuscripts Division of Georgetown University Library, to which institution they were donated ca. 1967 by Eleanor Finch, the daughter of George Finch who, like her father, was closely linked with the management of the American Society of International Law. I am grateful to Nicholas Sheetz, Curator of Manuscripts, and to the Georgetown University for permission to publish this biography and for their many kindnesses in supplying copies of relevant materials from the Scott archive.

Although the obituary of George Finch published by his close friend and colleague, Lester H. Woolsey, mentioned that ". . . at his death Finch had, unfortunately, not completed Dr. Scott's biography . . . ,[1] the extent to which he had progressed and the whereabouts of the manuscript were not mentioned. I discovered the manuscripts among the Scott Papers at Georgetown when preparing introductory articles for some of Scott's books being reissued by The Lawbook Exchange, Ltd. So far as I could determine, the Scott Archive had not been mined by other international lawyers and did not figure in the centenary history of the American Society of International Law.[2]

Scott and Finch had agreed sometime earlier in their friendship that Finch would undertake Scott's biography, rather in the manner that many decades earlier Scott had produced a biography of his State Department colleague, Robert Bacon (1860-1919).[3] Indeed, Scott made Finch his literary executor in his will. There are in fact several manuscript versions of the Scott biography. Each is un-

---

[1] "L. Woolsey, "Editorial Comment", *American Journal of International Law*, LI (1957), p. 755.

[2] In his history of the American Society of International Law, Kirgis makes reference to an interview with Eleanor H. Finch on 16 May 1994. She retired from the American Society in 1972 and presumably did not disclose the existence of the Scott Papers at Georgetown University.

[3] See J. B. Scott, *Robert Bacon: Life and Letters*, intro. Elihu Root. Foreword by Field Marshall the Rt. Hon. Earl Haig (1923).

dated. Most contain emendations and corrections in the hand of George Finch. Some are plainly first copies; others are carbon copies, but there are annotations in hand on all versions. A certain amount of cutting and pasting was done among the versions to make inserts or ensure deletions. In integrating them for the purposes of this book, I have preferred inclusion to exclusion of material. I suspect that at some point Finch (or his daughter) decided to streamline the account and began to reduce the amount of detail. One can well understand how in the interests of readability and even marketability he might have inclined in that direction.

But the aim of the work has changed. Now it is an archival treasure rather than a fresh appreciation of a major figure in international law intended to appear not so long after his death. The detail is interesting, not otherwise easily obtainable by the modern generation, and beyond our memories. In style and substance the biography is decidedly well within the bounds of political correctness and professional discretion. Finch will have known Scott's foibles and weaknesses better than anyone, but there is no hint of them here other than to paint his subject in the best possible light. In his obituary of Finch, Woolsey remarks that he had heard it said "at the time" that Dr. Scott "was a misfit for the Carnegie job", but that Finch replied "… it was his job to see that this did not prove to be true. And he kept his word".[4] This is the reply that would do credit to an English civil servant with respect to his Minister. There is no scandal here, no disclosures of intimate detail or State or institutional secrets, no criticism of his colleagues, and a laconic style that lets Scott speak for himself in most matters. His aim was, through Scott, to trace the movement on behalf of international law during the first four decades of the twentieth century in which Scott was a key actor and to which Scott devoted his life.

Characterizing Finch aptly from the documents in the files of the American Society of International Law, Kirgis wrote that Finch came across as

> . . . an efficient, highly competent successor to Scott as the person in charge of the Society's daily affairs. Unlike Scott, he did not stamp his personality or his vision of international law on the Society. Rather, he seems to have been characterized by his eye for detail and his acute sense of propriety. He was a cautious

---

[4] Woolsey, note 1 above, p. 754.

> person, taking great care not to overstep the bounds of authority the Executive Council delegated to him. On more than one occasion he declined to take action suggested by some prominent member, on the stated ground that he lacked authority to do so in the absence of a decision by the Executive Council. Even if on some of these occasions he was using the ostensible lack of authority as an indirect way of declining to do what he was not inclined to do anyway, the impression remains that he interpreted quite narrowly how far his writ ran ... What he may have lacked in vision, he supplied in diligence.[5]

Those are all qualities present in this treatment of Scott in this book.

Also in evidence here is the close relationship between Scott and what in modern times would be styled the "East coast foreign policy establishment", which seemed to take changes in Presidential administration routinely in stride. According to this version of events, the commitment over the decades to mechanisms for the peaceful settlement of international disputes within that establishment is formidable. So too is the close linkage between undertakings of the Carnegie Endowment, the American Society of International Law, and sundry other non-governmental organizations and societies, on one hand, and the Department of State and other agencies of the United States Government, on the other.

In integrating the multiple versions of the biography, I have corrected typing errors and added some details of publication to the footnotes but not otherwise annotated the text, despite temptations to do so. Nothing has been excised from the manuscripts. The last Chapter, entitled "Fragments", consists of what I believe to be brief essays by Finch that he intended to interpolate somewhere but never got around to doing so. The designation of sub-sections within lengthy chapters has been made by me; Finch had not gotten around to this, although doubtless he would have done so. No doubt Finch would have polished and completed the footnotes in more systematic form had the manuscript been completed.

The "Notes on Principal Personae" and the Index have been supplied by me.

Turning to George A. Finch (1884–1957), he gives his own account of how he came to be associated with James Brown Scott.

---

[5] F. L. Kirgis, *The American Society of International Law's First Century 1906-2006* (2006), pp. 86–87.

After graduating from the Georgetown University Law School in 1907, he took a position as a law clerk in the United States Department of State and was there when Scott was appointed Solicitor to the Department of State.[6] As Finch recounts herein, he was present when Scott received by post the invitation to join the newly-founded Carnegie Endowment. It was, according to Finch, at that very moment that Scott secured Finch's commitment to join him at the Endowment and, for all practical purposes, in all of his ventures thereafter.

Finch served as secretary to the United States Commission to Liberia in 1909 and was then assigned to the office of Counselor of the Department of State when that post was created. When Scott left Government service to join the Carnegie Endowment, Finch followed, as agreed. Woolsey described Finch as "the power behind the throne at the Endowment and also in the American Society of International Law.[7] As between the two commitments, the Carnegie Endowment took the greater portion of his time. Prior to 1940, Finch served as assistant Secretary and then Assistant Director of the Division of International Law at the Carnegie Endowment. Upon Scott's retirement in 1940, Finch was elevated to the posts of Secretary and Director of the said Division and elected a Trustee of the Endowment.

During the First World War, Finch acted as an expert on international questions attached to the War Industries Board in 1918. When the United States entered the War, he joined Scott with the State-Navy Neutrality Board, which gave opinions on various issues for the Secretary of State. In 1919 he was appointed Assistant Legal Adviser to the American Commission to negotiate the peace at Paris, also joining Scott.

Although in this book he only occasionally refers to his own role in matters, he too was a delegate of the Carnegie Endowment at the Second, Third, and Eighth Pan American Scientific Congresses and at the Conference of American States in Lima, Peru. In 1929 he was a representative of the Endowment to the Orient. His

---

[6] According to Scott, they first met on 1 April 1906: "After an intimate association and collaboration with Mr. Finch of over thirty years – to be precise, thirty-one years to the day …", as related in Scott's Foreword dated 1 April 1937 to Finch's lectures on the sources of international law. See note 7 below.

[7] Woolsey's obituary of Finch is also the best biography extant of Finch and has been relied upon extensively here. See note 1 above, pp. 754–757.

interest in Latin American affairs was no less than Scott's, recognized by being made Knight Commander of the Order of Cespedes (Cuba) and of the Order of Balboa (Panama). The University of Thessalonika (Greece) awarded Finch an LL.D. (Hon.).

Following Scott's death, Finch acted as consultant to the United States Delegation at the Conference on United Nations Organization at San Francisco in 1945. For many years he served as the President of the Inter-American Academy of Comparative and International Law[8] and as a member of the Curatorium of The Hague Academy of International Law. Just as Scott had done, Finch lectured at the School of Foreign Service of Georgetown University on subjects of international law. He was a member of the American Bar Association, including service as Vice-Chairman of the ABA Committee on Peace and Law through the United Nations, member of the Advisory Committee of the Inter-American Bar Association and of the Research in International Law of the Harvard Law School; and a member of the American Law Institute; Associate of the Institute of International Law, Corresponding Member of the Panamanian Academy of International Law; and Honorary Collaborator of the Hellenic Institute of International and Comparative Law.

His services to the American Society of International Law were immense. From 1909-1924 he served as Secretary of the Board of Editors of the *American Journal of International Law* and Assistant Secretary of the American Society of International Law; managing Editor of the *Journal* and Secretary of the Society from 1924 to 1943; Editor-in-Chief of the *Journal* and Vice President of the Society from 1943 to 1953; Honorary Editor-in-Chief of the *Journal* and Honorary Vice President of the Society from 1953 to 1957. Just as Scott, he contributed dozens of editorials, leading articles, and addresses at annual meetings to the *Journal* and the *Proceedings* of the Society.[9]

---

[8] Finch's range was considerable. He lectured at the Inter-American Academy on "The Punishment of War Criminals", "The International Control of Atomic Energy", "Sovereignty over Polar Areas", and "Sources of International Law".

[9] His major monograph, drafts of which were used in Summer Sessions from 1932 at the University of Michigan Law School, is G. A. Finch, *The Sources of Modern International Law* (Washington, Carnegie Endowment for International Peace, 1937). He delivered the substance in French at The Hague Academy of International Law in summer 1935. My own copy is autographed by Finch and bears the manuscript and rubber stamp ex-libris, together with annotations, of Mr. Justice

A proper appraisal of the role of the Carnegie Endowment in shaping the development of international law during the lives of Scott and Finch has yet to be undertaken, especially of the publications issued during this period. While some are mentioned in this volume, among them many obscure accounts, reports, and compilations deriving from support of the Institute of International Law and the American Institute of International Law, Finch does not begin to account for the full range of Scott's and his own contributions in this regard. Other dimensions of Scott's activities likewise are omitted, among them the conferences and exchanges for teachers of international law in the United States and abroad and the awarding of scholarships to study international law. These I have tried to address in some measure in my own introductory article which follows.

It should be observed that the Scott Papers held by Georgetown University may or may not be precisely the Scott Papers to which George Finch alludes in some of his footnotes. Apart from altering the style of some footnotes and adding some details to them, I have not interfered with the Finch citations. Whether items that he cites to the Scott Papers are in fact held by Georgetown, and whether they are the same copies, is a matter to be independently investigated.

It remains to express my indebtedness to Greg Talbot of The Lawbook Exchange, Ltd. for underwriting the acquisition of copies of the Finch manuscripts and for making the publication of this volume possible.

William E. Butler
Newville, Pennsylvania

W. G. Morrow, Territorial Court of the Northwest Territories, Yellow Knife, Canada.

BIOGRAPHICAL MATERIALS ON JAMES BROWN SCOTT

William E. Butler

George Finch's manuscript has been invaluable to me in writing a number of pieces to introduce various works by James Brown Scott together with other materials in the Scott Papers at Georgetown University. Nonetheless, he omits much that deserves to be said. In the interests of completeness I offer my own account of James Brown Scott in brief, and also take advantage of information not accessible to George Finch at the time.

James Brown Scott was born near Kincardine, Canada, on 3 June 1866, the youngest child of John Scott (1830–1885) and Jeannette Brown (1831–1901). His father was a stone cutter, and his mother the daughter of a weaver. Both had emigrated in 1849 from Scotland to New York, where they met and married in 1853 before moving to Canada. There were four other children in the family, three girls and a boy: Mary, Margaret, John, and Jeannette. John died in childhood, aged 15. Three years after the birth of James, the family left Canada for Philadelphia, returned to Canada in 1871, and relocated permanently to Philadelphia in 1876.

James and his sisters were provided with a good education. When their father passed away they were left with sufficient funds to complete their studies until they became self-supporting. All the Scott children excelled in their schooling and completed their education in Europe. Mary, the eldest, studied in Berlin, Vienna, and Munich after graduating from the Women's Medical College in Philadelphia; she was among the first women to be admitted to the Institut Pasteur (Paris). Upon her return to the United States, she became a specialist in children's diseases, an interest aroused by the boyhood death of her brother John.

Margaret became a professor of romance languages upon completing her studies in France and Germany at initially the University of Illinois and then Syracuse University. She outlived the other members of the family.

Jeannette, the youngest sister, studied art and followed the career of a painter. Upon graduation from the School of Design in Philadelphia, she attended the Pennsylvania Academy of Fine Arts and then studied in Europe for five years, from 1889 to 1894. Returning to the United States, she accepted a position as instructor in painting at Syracuse University, retiring in 1927 as head of the Department of Painting with the degree of Doctor of Fine Arts.[1] She was interested in women's rights and helped to finance the Inter American Commission of Women, created by the Sixth Pan American Conference (Havana, 1928), the first juridical Commission of Women ever established by governments acting in concert.

James Brown Scott completed his secondary schooling in Philadelphia and was admitted to Harvard College and graduated *summa cum laude* in 1890 with his B.A., staying on a further year to complete his A. M. (1891).[2] His career as an international lawyer commenced with his being selected for a Parker Fellowship at Harvard, which he held for three years. He did not attend law school, but instead spent a year at Heidelberg University, where he was awarded the *juris utriusque doctor*. Upon returning to the United States, he pursued the practice of law in California. He was not distracted from academic legal life for long. In 1896 he organized the Law School at Los Angeles (now the University of Southern California School of Law) and was then enticed to become the Dean of the University of Illinois Law School (1899–1903). The Columbia Law School persuaded him to come to New York (1903–06),[3] and he might have remained there had he not written a letter

---

[1] Drawn from the unpublished biography of James Brown Scott by George Finch, in the James Brown Scott Papers, Box 69, Folder 1, Georgetown University Library, Special Collections Division, Washington D. C.

[2] For biographical materials on Scott, I have had the benefit of the James Brown Scott Papers held at Georgetown University, which contain the manuscript biography by George Finch and numerous curriculum vitas prepared by Scott himself for various occasions. Among printed materials, see obituaries in the *American Journal of International Law*, XXXVII (1943), 508 (G. A. Finch); XXXVII (1943), 559–561 (F. R. Coudert); XXXVIII (1944), 183–217 (G. A. Finch); *Transactions of the Grotius Society*, XXIX (1943), vii–viii (Cecil J. B. Hurst); *Year Book of the American Philosophical Society* (1943), pp. 427–430 (P. C. Jessup); and Doris Stevens, *Paintings & Drawings of Jeannette Scott 1864–1937* (1940).

[3] While at Columbia he produced J. B. Scott (ed.), *Cases on Quasi-Contracts* (1905) and the following year, having removed to George Washington University, Scott (ed.), *Cases on Equity Jurisdiction* (1906), in two volumes; and Scott (ed.), *Cases on International Law, Selected from Decisions of English and American*

to the United States Secretary of State suggesting that a legal advisor might be appointed to the Department and that he might be considered a candidate for the position.

His interview made an excellent impression. He moved to the nation's capital, where he remained until 1940, when he retired to his summer home in nearby Annapolis. He married Adele Cooper Scott in 1901.

During the years 1905–06, he was actively involved with others in forming the American Society of International Law.[4] From 1895 to 1914 members of what many regard as the United States "foreign policy establishment" assembled each year at Lake Mohonk in upstate New York to discuss the preservation of peace and, more particularly, the perceived importance of international arbitration as an alternative to war. James Brown Scott was present at the eleventh conference from 31 May to 2 June 1905, where the American Society of International Law was conceived. He acted as one of an informal committee of three[5] which decided to put the proposal for the Society to those in attendance at the Conference and then as the secretary of the meeting of twenty-four Conference participants who supported the proposal unanimously and appointed a committee of seven to draft a constitution for the Society. When the Society constitution was ultimately adopted, Scott was appointed Recording Secretary and a member of the Executive Council of the Society. An integral part of the scheme to organize the Society was the establishment of a journal, and at the twelfth meeting at Lake Mohonk on 1 June 1906 the Executive Council appointed Scott as Managing Editor of the *American Journal of International Law*. The journal has appeared quarterly thereafter; Scott advanced from his own pocket the funds necessary to print the first two issues, being later reimbursed.

While acting as the Solicitor for the Department of State, he took a dual appointment at the George Washington University Law School (1906–11) and also lectured at The Johns Hopkins Univer-

---

Courts (1902), revised and published in 1906 by West Publishing Co., and revised throughout the interwar period

[4] See F. L. Kirgis, *The American Society of International Law's First Century 1906-2006* [(2006)].

[5] The other two members being Robert Lansing, later the United States Secretary of State, and Professor G. W. Kirchwey, sometime President of the American Peace Society.

sity (1906–16). After service during the First World War and involvement in the negotiations of the postwar settlements, he accepted appointment to the School of Foreign Service at Georgetown University from 1921 until his retirement. He acted as an exchange professor at various times at the Universities of Chile, Havana, Montevideo, Salamanca, Berlin, Frankfurt, Göttingen, Kiel, and Munich, among others.

He received seventeen honorary degrees: (Syracuse, Salamanca, Paris (Sorbonne), Universidad Mayor de San Marcos (Peru), George Washington, St. John's College (Annapolis), University of Chile, Warsaw University, University of Habana, Cambridge University, Michigan, Oberlin, Lyon, Queen's University (Ontario), Athens, Georgetown, and Southern California).

Elected an Associate of the Institut de droit international in 1908, he became a full member in 1910 and eventually served as President. He was elected to the Royal Academy of Sciences in Belgium (1919), to the Institut de France (1921), to the American Academy of Arts and Sciences (1935), among a number of distinctions of this kind. A number of countries (Belgium, Yugoslavia, Serbia, Chile, Italy, Ecuador, Romania, Netherlands, and Cuba included) conferred decorations upon him.

Having persuaded the Carnegie Institution to support his Project on the classics of international law, he accepted appointment as secretary of what became the Carnegie Endowment for International Peace and director of the Division of International Law. In both capacities for more than three decades, to borrow the apt phrase of Manley Ottmer Hudson (1886–1956), he ". . . fathered and fostered the development of international law during the greatest period of its history".[6]

Sixteenth-century Catholic doctrinal writings continued to constitute a significant portion of his scholarly writings. Not long after receiving his honorary degree from Salamanca University, he initiated measures to arrange a celebration of the 400th anniversary of Vitoria's lectures at the University, dated by common consent to 1532. In 1930 he was awarded a gold and silver plaque for his

---

[6] See the Remarks of Manley O. Hudson, in "Portrait of Dr. James Brown Scott", *Harvard Alumni Bulletin*, XXXIII, no. 14 (1 January 1931), p. 419.

original research in "establishing the title of Francisco de Vittoria . . . a Dominican priest, as the founder of modern International Law".[7]

At a luncheon of the members of the Institut de droit international in 1932 it was decided to form the International Association of Francis of Vitoria and of Suarez.[8] The 30 or so members present were regarded as charter members, with a ceiling on membership of 100 and local societies to be formed in nations accepting and abiding by the principle of international law in their mutual relations. No country could have more than ten members on the international body. Dr. Nicolas Politis (1872–1942) was elected the President and Dr. Alfred Verdross (1890–1980), the Secretary-General. The Statutes of the International Association Vitoria-Suarez were approved by the Constitutive General Assembly at Oslo on 17 August 1932 (the Association actually operating within the framework of meetings of the Institut de droit international). James Brown Scott was elected First Vice President of the Association in 1936 and recruited a number of his close professional colleagues to be elected among the maximum quota of ten in the International Association. Members of the international association were active throughout the 1930s in propagating the doctrines of Vitoria, and the association itself identified with a number of publications.[9]

Diplomacy played an important role in his career. In 1907 he was a technical delegate to the Second Hague Peace Conference. From 1914 to 1917 he was the Chairman of the United States Neutrality Board, and in 1919 acted as the legal adviser to the delegation of the United States at the Paris Peace Conference. During 1922–23 he was the legal adviser to the American delegates at the Washington Conference on the Limitation of Armaments. In 1927 he was a member of the Inter-American Commission of Jurists which met at Rio de Janeiro. The following year he served as

---

[7] Press Release, dated 5 April 1930, James Brown Scott Papers, Box 63, Folder 8, Georgetown University Library, Special Collections Division, Washington D. C.

[8] In effect this was to be an international "umbrella" association for national societies such as the Asociacion Francisco de Vitoria, established in 1928 as related by James Brown Scott, "Asociacion Francisco de Vitoria", *American Journal of International Law*, XXII (1928), 136–139. It was the same pattern he used when creating the American Institute of International Law.

[9] Among them *Vitoria et Suarez: contribution des théologiens au droit international moderne*, Preface by James Brown Scott (1939).

delegate to the Sixth International Conference of American States at Havana.

The Chichele Chair of International Law

Upon the retirement of Professor Sir Thomas Erskine Holland (1835-1926), the Chichele Chair of International Law became vacant at Oxford University in 1910. To the surprise of many, James Brown Scott decided to make application for the position. The application itself is a remarkable document—a printed booklet of considerable length setting out Dr. Scott's credentials and containing testimonials of his qualifications and character from leading figures throughout Europe and the United States.

The Scott Papers do not disclose whether Holland persuaded or encouraged Scott to apply for the position or not.[10] The electors took a considerable time to come to a view on who should be appointed, perhaps because they were divided. Scott was kept in contact with what was happening by Professor Lassa Oppenheim (1858–1919), who held the Whewell Chair at Cambridge University. On 22 November 1910 Oppenheim wrote from Whewell House in Cambridge:

> . . . As regards the Oxford chair, I have heard nothing which would indicate how matters are going on. Everybody knows that you are Holland's candidate, and people who discuss you may be divided into two camps, although everybody agrees that you are the best candidate. To the one camp belong Pollock [Sir Frederick Pollock (1845–1937)–WEB], Whittuck [Edward Arthur Whittuck (1844–1924)]–WEB], and others, with a wide horizon, who say that the best man ought to have it no matter whether he be an English subject or not. To the other camp belong a number of small minded people who say that to appoint an American would be awkward in view of the possibility of an Anglo-American conflict. Since the more influential people belong to the first mentioned class I trust that your election is certain. But so much

---

[10] Scott had persuaded Holland to edit the works of Richard Zouche (1590–1661) for the Classics of International Law series. The volumes appeared in 1911. On Holland's tenure in the Chair, see T. E. Erskine Holland, *A Valedictory Retrospect (1874–1910)* (1910).

> is absolutely certain that if you fail to be elected the only matter which bared [sic] your election is that you are not an English subject. I shall send a wire anyhow as soon as I hear of the result.

On 16 December 1910 Oppenheim wrote:[11]

> . . . I suppose that Holland provides you with news in this matter. I hear very little, but the following may be of interest: I hear from a good source that the President of the Admiralty Court who is one of the electors stands firm for Macdonnell [Sir John Macdonnell (1846–1921–WEB]. Westlake [John Westlake (1828–1913)–WEB] works hard—so Whittuck writes me—for Higgins [Alexander Pearce Higgins (1865-1935)–WEB]. There is also a rumour that Fromageot is supported by one of the electors. Another rumour is that the election is postponed on account of the political crisis, and there is also a rumour that the postponement is due to the fact that the electors have not yet come to an agreement. . .

It was perhaps the example of Professor Oppenheim which Scott followed in developing his application for the Chair. Oppenheim supplied Scott with a copy of his own application for the Whewell Chair, printed by the University Press Cambridge and dated 6 July 1908.

Scott was not elected to the Chair, impressive as his credentials were.

American Society for Judicial Settlement of International Disputes

Scott's unflagging efforts in support of the establishment of an international court of justice were pursued partly through diplomatic channels and partly through the generation of popular public support in favor of such an institution. To the latter end he played the key part in creating the American Society for Judicial Settlement of International Disputes, of which he was elected the first president. The first international conference of the Society was held at Washington D. C. on 15–17 December 1910 and attended prin-

[11] Both letters are in the James Brown Scott Papers Box 57, Folder 12, Georgetown University Library, Special Collections Division, Washington D. C.

cipally by businessmen, educators, diplomats, and federal and state legislators.

The reference to "judicial" settlement was narrowly understood; arbitration was not included, as Scott made clear in his opening remarks to the constitutive conference: The purposes of the Society are "… limited to a discussion of the judicial determination, as distinguished from the arbitral adjustment, of international controversies. It seeks to strengthen sentiment where existing, and to create sentiment where it does not exist, in favor of judicial settlement. It stands for a permanent court, as distinguished from a temporary tribunal … It stands for judicial decision according to principles of law, not compromise according to the standards of diplomacy … We are not opposed to arbitration. On the contrary, we favor it individually, but arbitration as such falls beyond the scope of our labors".[12]

There were six conferences of the American Society in all, the last in 1916. They greatly informed efforts following the First World War to create the Permanent Court of International Justice.

Court of Arbitral Justice

James Brown Scott's energies in support of the judicial settlement of disputes as the exclusive concern of the American Society for the Judicial Settlement of International Disputes reflected no disenchantment with arbitration as an alternative method of dispute resolution – to use a term in fashion today but not at the time. Having been appointed as technical expert of the United States to the Second Hague Peace Conference of 1907 after merely a year or so of service as Solicitor for the Department of State, Scott took "… a conspicuous, one may even say the leading part, in preparing and urging the adoption of the draft for a convention for a Court of Arbitral Justice, and was extremely active and useful in promoting all the conventions adopted by the Conference".[13]

Scott was selected by the Second Hague Peace Conference to prepare the official report to the Conference in respect of the draft

---

[12] *Proceedings of the Conference on the Judicial Settlement of International Disputes* (1910), p. 3.
[13] Letter of David Jayne Hill, 18 January 1917, quoted in note 27 below, p. 18.

Convention for the Establishment of a Court of Arbitral Justice. It was he who explained to the Conference what the draft intended, article by article, and urged its adoption with great eloquence. Although in the end the Conference merely recommended the draft convention to the signatory powers rather then adopting the text itself, it was felt that considerable progress had been made in the right direction. At the Naval Conference in London during 1908-09, which was to agree the law to be applied by a proposed International Prize Court, Scott urged that the United States propose the International Prize Court be vested with the jurisdiction and functions of the Court of Arbitral Justice and, when sitting, should be guided by the draft convention for the establishment of the Arbitral Court. The proposal was made, but for sundry reasons which culminated in the refusal of the United Kingdom to ratify the Prize Court Convention, the Court of Arbitral Justice never came into being. The United States did ratify, but that action did not move the United Kingdom to like action. The proposal ultimately came to an end. Scott persisted with initiatives to revive the scheme in some way. These were ultimately overtaken by the outbreak of the First World War.

The Nobel Peace Prize

James Brown Scott was nominated on at least six occasions for the Nobel Peace Prize. The first and most concerted effort on his behalf was undertaken in late 1916 for, presumably, the Prize awarded in 1917. A substantial printed Memorial, dated 29 December 1916, was submitted on his behalf.[14]

A junior Norwegian diplomat and great admirer of Scott, Gregers W. Gram, informed Scott on 2 January 1923 that he had twice proposed him for the Nobel Prize and intended to do so a third time.[15]

On 13 February 1927 the eminent French international lawyer, Gilbert Gidel (1880–1958), wrote Scott to say: "I believe that no

---

[14] See *Memorial in Support of the Nomination of James Brown Scott for the Nobel Peace Prize* [n.p., 1917]. [iv], 71 p. Copies are held in the James Brown Scott Papers, Box 59, Folder 5, Georgetown University Library, Special Collections Division, Washington, D. C.

[15] James Brown Scott Papers, Box 59, Folder 6.

one other than you deserves the Nobel Peace Prize and I shall take advantage of my right of nomination to put forward your candidacy".[16]

Professor Karl Strupp (1886–1940) wrote to Scott on New Year's Day of 1937 informing him of his nomination:[17]

> Permit me to say that I have proposed you, the father of the Permanent Court of International Justice, for the Nobel Prize; and may I dedicate to you, in the same capacity, my Commentary on the Status and Reglement of this court, which I hope to finish by the end of 1937?

Other Publications

James Brown Scott awaits his proper bibliographer. He published extensively (one would imagine well over 1,000 books, articles, reviews, and translations),[18] but both the volume and nature of his publications were skewed by his association with the Carnegie Institution and later the Carnegie Endowment for International Peace and as the principal moving force behind the *American Journal of International Law*. From 1907 to 1916 inclusive Scott published 266 editorial comments, mostly concerned with topics bearing upon international relations from the standpoint of an international lawyer dedicated to international peace, fourteen leading articles, and 58 book reviews. The series of volumes published as "Classics of International Law", all under his general editorship and many containing a learned introduction by his hand, came to twenty-two titles in forty volumes. A "spin-off" of this project was a two-volume work: Scott (ed.), *The Armed Neutralities of 1780 and 1800: A Collection of Official Documents Preceded by the Views of Representative Publicists* (1918).

He was a popular lecturer frequently invited throughout the country and Europe to deliver not merely single addresses but an

---

[16] James Brown Scott Paper, Box 59, Folder 6: "j'ai estime que nul plus que vous n'etait digne du Prix Nobel de la Paix et j'ai profite de mon droit de presentation pour poser votre candidature".

[17] James Brown Scott Papers, Box 59, Folder 6. Strupp wrote in German; Scott had the letter translated, and I have quoted the translation supplied to him.

[18] The Harvard Law School Library records more than 200 books and pamphlets under his name.

entire *cours* dedicated to a particular subject, such as the Hague peace conferences,[19] or dispute settlement. Many found their way into print as monographs or special issues of student law reviews. A number were translated into Spanish or French, usually under Carnegie Endowment auspices.

A considerable portion of his larger works comprised edited, translated, and thoroughly annotated collections of documents which in his day could not have been commercially published without Carnegie Endowment support. All without exception have retained their value for legal scholarship, as their frequent reprinting by commercial publishers demonstrates. Among the titles, usually self-explanatory if not brief, are: Scott (ed. & intro.), *Texts of the Peace Conferences at the Hague, 1899 and 1907 with English Translation and Appendix of Related Documents* (1908); Scott (ed. & intro.), *Instructions to the American Delegates to the Hague Peace Conferences and Their Official Reports* (1916); Scott (ed. & intro.), *The Hague Court Reports Comprising the Awards, Accompanied by Syllabi, the Agreements for Arbitration, and Other Documents in Each Case Submitted to the Permanent Court of Arbitration and to Commissions of Inquiry Under the Provisions of the Conventions of 1899 and 1907 for the Pacific Settlement of International Disputes* (1916–1932) in two series; Scott, *The Status of the International Court of Justice with an Appendix of Addresses and Official Documents* (1916); Scott (collected & ed.), *Judicial Settlement of Controversies Between States of the American Union: Cases Decided in the Supreme Court of the United States* (1918). 3 vols.; Scott, *James Madison's Notes of Debates in the Federal Convention of 1787 and Their Relation to a More Perfect Society of Nations* (1918); Scott (ed.), *The Declaration of London February 26, 1909: A Collection of Official Papers and Documents Relating to the International Naval Conference Held in London December, 1908 – February, 1909* (1919); Scott, *The United States of America: A Study in International Organization* (1920); Scott, *Observations on Nationality with Especial Reference to the Hague Conven-*

---

[19] See Scott, *The Hague Peace Conferences of 1899 and 1907: A Series of Lectures Delivered Before the Johns Hopkins University in the Year 1908* (1909); Scott, *The Judicial Settlement of International Disputes: Addresses at the Geneva Institute of International Relations August 16th and 17th, 1926* (1927).

tion of April 12th, 1930: A Plea for a Single and Impersonal Standard of Nationality in the Law and Practice of Nations (1931).

With particular reference to the western hemisphere he prepared: Scott, *The American Institute of International Law: Its Declaration of the Rights and Duties of Nations* (1916); Scott (ed. & intro.), *The International Conference of American States 1889–1926: A Collection of the Conventions, Recommendations, Resolutions, Reports, and Motions adopted by the First Six International Conferences of the American States, and Documents relating to the Organization of the Conferences* (1931).

His casebooks, alluded to above, dominated the teaching of international law in the United States for nearly four decades. The first edition of 1902 was succeeded by another in 1906 (with a change of publisher) and contributed to his serving for a number of years as one of the general editors of a casebook series for West Publishing Co. in St. Paul Minnesota. The last edition appeared in 1937 in collaboration with Walter H. E. Jaeger, then Professor of Law and Director of Graduate Research at Georgetown University as the junior author.

Scott's final major work of this genre appeared in two volumes under the title: *Law, The State, and The International Community* (1939–40), volume one of which constituted "A Commentary on the Development of Legal, Political, and International Ideals" and volume two a collection of quotations from the writings of those political and legal thinkers whose ideas were discussed in the first volume, all arranged in a subject order of his own making. Volume two he called in the looser meaning of the term a "codification" of political and legal conceptions influential in the modern world. His personal archive contains a large body of working papers and drafts drawn up over the years in connection with various activities, not least the preparation of *The Catholic Conception of International Law*. Whether he was able to take full advantage of this material when approaching the Vatican about incorporating international law into the syllabi of Catholic secondary and higher education or not, he made good and extensive use of these materials in this, his last, major work.

A chapter is devoted in the Commentary to Vitoria ("the founder, in the opinion of many, of the modern law of nations") and Suarez ("the prince of modern jurists"), but the influence of the progenitors of the "Spanish School" in this study is much larger when the chapter is read against the accompanying volume of documents. When Scott sent the volume to press, the Suarez works had not yet appeared in the "Classics of International Law" series and indeed were published in 1944 shortly after James Brown Scott died. But he had the manuscript of Suarez by then and was disposed to use that resource extensively: "It may ... seem, especially to those who are not familiar with Francisco Suarez, that the number of quotations from his writings is disproportionately large. And it is quite true that more passages have been drawn from Suarez than from any other writer" (p. ix). The reason for this, Scott says, is not his partiality on his part towards the Catholic jurists, but to the fact that "... in certain of his writings, especially in his great *Tractatus de legibus ac Deo legislatore*, there is summed up and blended into a philosophic whole the best of our legal and our political heritage from the ancient and medieval worlds".

The Declaration of the Rights and Duties of Nations adopted by the American Institute of State and Law at its inaugural meeting epitomizes the principles and conceptions motivating so much of James Brown Scott's activities as a scholar and practitioner of international law. He believed deeply in the American experience being relevant to all nations of the world as embodied in the Constitution of the United States and in the judicial practice of the United States Supreme Court. More eloquent an apostle of those views is difficult to identify among American international lawyers.

His turn towards Latin America may or may not have been an extension of his interest in the contributions of the "Spanish School" to the origins of modern international legal doctrine, but his deep affection for that profoundly neglected portion of the western hemisphere is transparent in all of his activities connected with the American Institute of International Law. With his departure from the scene, Latin America lost a friend who has proved to be irreplaceable.

PREFACE

Some years before his death, Dr. Scott promised a New York publisher to write a personal account of his experiences at international conferences. The title agreed upon was to be "Adventures in Internationalism". The account was never written; only a few fragmentary notes of its anticipated contents were left. The writer of this biography was an assistant and associate of Dr. Scott from 1906 in the Department of State and with the Carnegie Endowment for International Peace throughout the remainder of his life. He was asked many times by Dr. Scott to prepare the story of his life. With that desire in view, Dr. Scott designated the writer as his executor and residuary legatee, by virtue of which he came into possession of the testator's books, correspondence, and papers.

Since Dr. Scott passed away, many important changes have taken place throughout the world affecting particularly the conduct of international relations. Dr. Scott was present at the birth of the League of Nations at Paris in 1919 and during his lifetime witnessed its gradual demise. World War II had begun, the day of infamy at Pearl Harbor had occurred, and our enemies were rampant in Europe, the Pacific, and Asia at the time of his death. He had left this earthly scene when the United Nations was organized at San Francisco in 1945 to take the place of the League of Nations. The atomic bomb did not emerge from the scientific laboratories until later the same year. Dr. Scott therefore did not live to witness many vital changes in individual and national attitudes toward war and peace and the prevailing tendency to substitute politics and expediency for legal principles in the settlement of international disputes. He did, however, leave a bit of sage advice to the generations to come in the form of a rough draft of a few paragraphs for his proposed volume on "Adventures in Internationalism". They are reproduced exactly as he wrote them:

ROUGH: FOR ADVENTURES IN INTERNATIONALISM

American people are honest people. Greatness – intellectual or material – seems to be very difficult to endure. Nations which in the past have considered themselves to be the leaders in the industrial as well as in the intellectual domain have invariably felt the urge which they construe to be a duty to impose their will and their superior civilization upon their neighbors and, so far as possible, upon the world.

Greece yielded to this temptation, and actually did impose itself and its civilization upon the "barbarian" world. Rome later imposed itself upon the Greeks, and the then known world. In later times the Holy Roman Empire sought and well-nigh acquired world domination. Louis XIV spent his life until he ended in failure, in subjecting Europe to his *bon plaisir*. Napoleon laid Europe at his feet.

And we of today have been the victim of an attempt on the part of the Germanic peoples to impose their will and their culture upon their neighbors, indeed upon distant parts of the world.

Each of these modern attempts has failed, and without criticizing an ambition which seems to be inherent and whose attempted realization history pursues, I hope and pray that the unquestioned supremacy of these United States, of which I have the honor to be a citizen, will never lead their government to seek to impose their will and their culture and civilization by force of arms. We hope that Democracies – especially if they be instructed – will be more generous and less self-seeking than dynasties, that they will recognize the rights even of the most distant nations and peoples to work out their destinies and to develop themselves in accordance with their spiritual and political traditions; and that if they should be inclined to influence them, it shall be through their ideals and their pacific penetration.

1

[THE BEGINNINGS]

Sensing that it might be an epilogue, as in fact it turned out to be, to his life's work, Dr. Scott wrote on 1 April 1939 in the preface to the last of a long list of legal and scholarly volumes which bear his name as author or editor, as follows:

> For nearly half a century, from the time of entering Harvard College until the present day, I have been deeply interested in the fundamental conceptions of law and of the State; and in later years it has been my good fortune to have had practical significance with the law of the State, and especially with the law of the international community.[1]

Scholar, teacher, and expounder of the law, author or editor of some thirty separate works and general editor of thirty-five titles in series, joint editor of ten or more, writer of articles too numerous to mention, and speaker on hundreds of occasions for which he has left published or manuscript records, founder of a school of law, founder and editor of a journal of international law, co-founder of an academy of international law, advocate and successful promoter of an international court of justice, organizer of two international institutes and two societies, government legal adviser and jurisconsult, delegate to ten official international conferences and attendant at many more unofficial international gatherings, member of eight official international commissions, recipient of seventeen honorary degrees from colleges and universities in the United States, Canada, Latin America, England, and Europe, decorated by ten foreign governments – throughout his years of many-sided activities, Dr. Scott

---

[1] J. B. Scott, *Law, The State, and The International Community: A Commentary on the Development of Legal, Political, and International Ideals* (New York, Columbia University Press, 1939).

was inspired by an ideal which pervaded everything he applied his mind or laid his hands to – that ideal was *Justice*!

On the title page of one of his earliest volumes he quoted Daniel Webster: "Justice is the great interest of man on earth".[2] The justice that Dr. Scott advocated was not merely between man and man, but between men and women, or, as he expressed it later in life, "Equality in all human relationships".[3]

After a few years' experience in the practical conduct of international relations, his concept of justice evolved from the interest of the individual to that of the nation. This development in his thinking was again shown upon the title page of a volume published in 1909 which he illumined with a quotation from Albert Gallatin: "The true honor and dignity of the nation are inseparable from justice".[4] National justice, he maintained, should be measured by the same standard of morality for the State as for the individual.[5] Finally, his concept of justice expanded to global proportions, and his favorite quotation became that from the French moralist Joubert: "Might and right control everything in the world; might, until right is ready".

James Brown Scott was the youngest child of John Scott and Jeannette Brown. He was born at Tiverton, near Kincardine, Bruce County, Ontario, Canada, on 3 June 1866. John Scott was a stone cutter. Jeannette was the daughter of a weaver. Both had emigrated from Scotland to New York, where they met and married before moving to Canada. There were four other children in the family, three girls and a boy – Mary, Margaret, John, and Jeannette. John died in childhood. Three years following the birth of James, the family moved to Philadelphia. Father Scott died at fifty-four, when James was eighteen years old. The father had provided him and his three sisters with good preparatory education and left the children and their mother with enough money to complete their studies until they became self-supporting.

All the Scott children were talented students and finished their education in Europe. None of the sisters married but chose to fol-

---

[2] J. B. Scott, *Cases on Quasi Contracts* (New York, Baker, Voorhis & Co., 1905).
[3] *Proceedings of the American Society of International Law* (1931), p. 28.
[4] J. B. Scott, *The Hague Peace Conferences of 1899 and 1907* (Baltimore, The Johns Hopkins Press, 1909).
[5] See the address by J. B. Scott, "A Single Standard of Morality for the Individual and the State", *Proceedings of the American Society of International Law* (1932), p. 10.

low professional careers. Mary, the eldest, after graduating from the Women's Medical College of Philadelphia, studied in Berlin, Vienna, Munich, and was one of the first women to be admitted to the Institut Pasteur of Paris. After her return to the United States, she practiced as a specialist in children's diseases, an interest aroused by the early death of her brother John.

Margaret became a professor of romance languages after studying in France and Germany. She served on the faculties of the University of Illinois and Syracuse University. She outlived the other members of the family.

Jeannette, the youngest sister, studied art and followed the career of a painter. After graduating from the School of Design in Philadelphia, she went to the Pennsylvania Academy of Fine Arts, and then studied in Europe for five years, from 1889 to 1894. Upon her return to the United States, Jeannette accepted a position as instructor in painting at the University of Syracuse, from which she retired in 1927 as head of the Department of Painting with a degree of Doctor of Fine Arts. Alongside her teaching, Jeannette maintained her private studio at home and won praiseworthy recognition. In loving memory of his sister, Dr. James Brown Scott had privately printed a selection of her paintings and drawings, arranged by a biographical sketch by Doris Stevens. The sketch gives details of the history of the Scott family related to Miss Stevens by Dr. Scott and his sisters during their lifetimes.[6]

James attended the Central High School of Philadelphia from 1881 to 1885. The main characteristics of his life at that time were his devotion to scholarship at school and "to the Public Library where", according to his sister Jeannette, "he would frequently pass whole Saturdays", and she believed "he knew its contents as a lad better than most adults". Rummaging through second-hand bookshops was another of his pastimes and, according to Jeannette, "it was a sad birthday or Xmas if one offered him the usual gifts of gloves, cravats, etc., instead of books!" Love of books grew in him with the years. In the Department of State he was seldom seen outside his office without a well-filled green bag full of books. He made regular visits to the Department's library to inquire about

---

[6] *Paintings & Drawing of Jeannette Scott, 1864-1937*, Biographical Sketch and Arrangement by Doris Stevens (Privately Printed for James Brown Scott in loving memory of his sister, 1940). 500 ptd. At the Walpole Printing Office, Mount Vernon. Collotypes in monochrome and color printed by Arthur Jaffé, New York.

new accessions. Sometimes his prepossession for a book caused him to walk off with it without waiting to have it charged to him by the library staff. This habit and his initials ("J.B.S.") earned for him the nickname "Jimmy the Book Snatcher". Later, on frequent trips to New York in the performance of his duties with the Carnegie Endowment, he rarely failed to visit leading publishing houses and booksellers to buy the latest volumes on history, biography, art, poetry, or philosophy. His purchases were frequently by the dozen or half-dozen copies, to send as gifts to his closest friends and associates. His monthly bills often included sizable accounts for books.

Dr. Scott entered Harvard College as a sophomore in 1887. He graduated with the class of 1890 (A.B.) *summa cum laude* and continued in the Graduate School, from which he received his A. M. in 1891. Included in his studies was a course in international law given by Dr. Freeman Snow, by whom he was characterized as the "man of the iron memory". Upon graduation he was awarded a Parker Fellowship for three years' study in Europe. He specialized in international law at Berlin, Heidelberg, and Paris. He pursued the regular course of instruction for three years in Heidelberg, which included Roman Law and Constitutional Law, as well as Municipal Law. Upon graduation in 1894 he was awarded the degree of *Doctor Utriusque Juris* (J.U.D.), *insigne cum laude*:

> While in Heidelberg I had a severe attack of lung trouble, and was obliged to spend two winters in Egypt on account of health. This gave me the opportunity to travel, and I spent several months in Palestine, Asia Minor, Constantinople, and Greece, besides visiting the better known parts of Europe. As regards health I am well but must live in warm climates.[7]

On the trip to Egypt in 1893, he met Dr. Nicholas Murray Butler, then a professor on sabbatical leave from Columbia University in New York and later its President for nearly half a century. A lifelong friendship was thus begun which had a most important influence upon Dr. Scott's future career.

Following the completion of his studies in Europe, Dr. Scott returned to the United States and, attracted by the climate of Southern California, he went to live in Los Angeles. There he read law in

---

[7] Secretary's Report No. 3, Harvard College Class of 1890, p. 69.

the office of Judge Varill, was admitted to the Bar, and began the practice of law in July 1895.

The creative instinct of his nature began immediately to be manifested. Beginning with a class of students to whom he gave lectures in his law office, in 1896 he organized the Los Angeles Law School and was its dean for three years. It is now the Law Department of the University of Southern California. His services were remembered by the University in 1927 by conferring upon him the honorary degree of Doctor of Laws. A painting of him by his sister Jeannette was presented to the University.

Residence in California re-established Dr. Scott's health and gave him a breathing spell to crystallize in his mind his future life work. While laying the foundations for a career in law and legal education, he did not neglect his literary taste nor his aptitude for public speaking. His first public speech was delivered before the Sunset Club of Los Angeles in 1897. The subject was "International Arbitration". The speech revealed a basic knowledge of history, an understanding of the complexities of international relations as they changed from era to era, and reasonable conclusions concerning the probabilities of future developments. The speech on a subject that few people then seriously thought about showed a rare intellectual capacity for a young man in his thirtieth year. Moreover, it was an exposition and outline of substantially all of Dr. Scott's subsequent contributions to this field. When transmitting on 3 February 1937 the original manuscript to Judge Manley O. Hudson for deposit in the Library of the Harvard Law School, Dr. Scott called attention to the fact that the address had been delivered some forty years before and added this comment: "Between ourselves, I have been delivering that address ever since". And then, following his usual style of adorning his personal correspondence and writings with quotations from the classics or poets, he said to Judge Hudson: "As I run my eye over it, I cannot help thinking how true are Longfellow's lines, 'The thoughts of youth are long, long thoughts'. However, I am happy to say that some of the thoughts have become realities". Since that speech has never been published, it is printed in this volume from an exact copy retained in Dr. Scott's papers. It might well have served as an introduction to his last published work embodying the views matured by fifty years rich in experience—*The Law, The State, and the International Community.*

At President McKinley's call for volunteers on the outbreak of the Spanish-American War in 1898, Dr. Scott enlisted in the California National Guard and on 5 May was mustered into the Seventh Regiment, California U. S. Volunteer Infantry, as a private. This regiment remained in California. For a time he was incapacitated by typhoid fever, but he "did a great deal of work in drafting legal forms and precedents for the use of the Army".[8]

While in the military service, Dr. Scott's thoughts were apparently not confined exclusively to the art of war. In September 1898 he completed the manuscript of an edition in verse and prose of *The Rubaiyat of Omar Khayyam*, which was published in Los Angeles in the following year.[9] The work consisted of a Preface and Introduction by Dr. Scott, a reprint of Edward Fitzgerald's Omar Khayyam, and Fitzgerald's English version of the Rubaiyat with an English prose translation on opposite pages made by Dr. Scott from the French version by M. Nicolas. Dr. Scott ended the work with his own "Homage to Omar":

I.

A garden heavy with the Summer's bloom;
A warm wind laden with a World's perfume;
A River winding at his own sweet will,
'Twixt flowery banks that leave but scanty room.

II.

A clump of palms; far from the City's din
A stately mosque; a minaret, wherein
In accents faintly heard of man below
Is breathed the blessing of the muezzin.

III.

And thou, kind Master, seated in thy tent,
Untouched by Time as is the firmament,
Persuadest all who leave the noisome West,
To learn to love the drowsy Orient.

James. B. Scott

---

[8] Secretary's Report No. 4, Harvard College Class of 1890 (Cambridge, The University Press, 1903), p. 80.

[9] *Edward FitzGerald's Omar Khayyam, with a prose translation from the French of J. B. Nicolas and an Introduction by James B. Scott* (Los Angeles, C. C. Parker, 1899).

Dr. Scott was honorably discharged from the Army as a Corporal on 2 December 1898, by reason of the muster-out of his regiment.

Dr. Scott had a remarkable facility for foreign languages. He learned French and German as a student in Europe. The former he spoke as a second mother tongue and throughout his life he was an ardent partisan of its use as a general international language. Europeans were amazed at his impeccable French, which he insisted should be the only language used at the Academy of International Law at The Hague, one of his major successful projects. In 1923 he wrote a monograph in support of his deep conviction that French is and should be the modern diplomatic language.[10] He looked upon the work as a critical study in international conciliation, and an introduction to this effect was written by Dr. Nicholas Murray Butler. The work, received with great acclaim in France, was crowned by the French Academy.

Later in life, when Dr. Scott's contacts increased in Latin America and he became interested in Spanish contributions to the origins of international law, he taught himself Spanish in odd hours of leisure. He was hesitant to speak publicly in that language for some time after he acquired enough fluency for private conversation. His first attempt to speak publicly in Spanish was at the urging of his Cuban friends, who had invited him to deliver a public lecture on a solemn occasion in Habana. He wrote the address in English, had it translated into Spanish, and practiced its delivery with a Spanish teacher for several weeks before he went to Cuba. A distinguished audience, including high Government officials and university professors, many in evening attire with their ladies, was present when Dr. Scott appeared in the auditorium on the evening of the lecture. He was introduced from a platform and then escorted to a high movable pulpit and rolled to the center of the auditorium. The writer was in the audience and could observe Dr. Scott's embarrassment. His face turned a deep red, he slowly put down the Spanish version of his address, which he had arranged to be printed in advance and distributed to the audience, and took from his inside coat pocket the original English version. He asked the audience to follow his English delivery by reading the Spanish version.

---

[10] J. B. Scott, *La Français, Langue diplomatique moderne* (Paris, A. Pedone, 1924).

In Los Angeles Dr. Scott met one of his Harvard professors, Samuel Williston, who recommended him for the position of Dean of the Law School of the University of Illinois. Scott was appointed to that post in 1899. While there he met his future wife, Mrs. Adele C. Reed, a young widow taking a course in library science at the University. They were married on 1 September 1901. Due to the death of Dr. Scott's mother a few months previously, the marriage was solemnized privately at Champaign, Illinois.

The bond of affection between Dr. Scott and his mother was as strong as possible between mother and son. He literally adored her and she in turn exercised the greatest influence upon him. Annually, on the anniversary of her birthday, 18 March, he exchanged with his sisters messages of affectionate remembrance. He constantly referred to her as "our sainted Mother".

Mrs. Adele Scott was a few years senior to her husband. She came into his life soon after his mother left it. His reliance upon a woman's care, to which his home life had accustomed him, was now transferred to his wife. She looked after his health, comfort, and needs with the love and affection of both wife and mother.

Her guidance was especially needed by one of Dr. Scott's temperament. His mental concentration upon the problems of the day often caused him to overlook essential personal and physical details as of minor importance. At time he was a striking example of an absent-minded professor. When provided in advance with railroad and Pullman tickets for a trip out of the city, careful watch had to be kept to see that he did not use them for bookmarks and leave the office without them. This was an experience that actually happened. Once, when Dr. Scott and the writer were scheduled to go on a trip to New York together on business, he left by an earlier train and when he arrived in New York telephoned to Washington to inquire why he had gone to that city. On another occasion, when he left Washington for Baltimore to deliver a lecture, he boarded the wrong train, one going westbound for Chicago. He discovered the error in time to get off at a small town in Western Maryland, where he had to remain several hours for another train to bring him back to Washington.

Dr. Scott's duties in the Department of State, and later with the Carnegie Endowment for International Peace, and the many calls upon him for lectures and speeches, required him to make frequent trips about the country and abroad. From the Second Peace Conference held at The Hague in 1907, which he attended as an official

Technical Delegate, until the outbreak of World War II in September 1939, Dr. Scott went abroad practically every year except when transportation was not available because of war conditions. In some years he went more than once. Mrs. Scott always accompanied him on his longer trips in the United States and to foreign countries. He depended upon her to supervise his personal traveling requirements, and when she died on 15 October 1939, he was left like a ship without a rudder so far as his home life was concerned. Hired help was inadequate to supply the void in his domestic life left by the death of his devoted wife.

The Law School of the University of Illinois opened in September 1897 with Dr. Andrew Sloan Draper, President of the University, as acting dean. Dr. Draper had been a Judge of the Court of Commissioners of Alabama Claims, established by Congress to hear and determine claims for damages inflicted on Northern commerce by Confederate cruises operating out of British ports, for which the Geneva Tribunal held the Government of Great Britain liable to the Government of the United States in the sum of $15,500,000. Association with Dr. Draper no doubt rekindled in Dr. Scott his earlier interest in international law. It was then that he edited and published his first casebook on international law.[11] The volume was dedicated to President Draper. One of his leading decisions, defining a bay at international law, was reproduced textually in the casebook.[12] On the title page is a quotation from Dr. Johnson: "War and Peace divide the business of the world". Originally planned as a revision of *Cases and Opinions on International Law* (1893) by Freeman Snow, Dr. Scott's former instructor in international law at Harvard University, the changes made in the new volume were such that it was decided to issue the revision as an independent work. The cases were selected from the decision of American and English courts with a syllabus and annotations. The syllabus was prepared by William C. Dennis, then Assistant Professor of Law at the University of Illinois, who subsequently rejoined Dr. Scott in the Department of State as Assistant Solicitor and culminated a brilliant international legal career as President of Earlham College at Richmond, Indiana.

---

[11] J. B. Scott, *Cases on International Law* (Boston, Boston Book Co., 1902). Reissued by West Publishing Company, St. Paul, Minnesota, in 1906.
[12] *The Alleganean*, in Scott, ibid., p. 143.

As this work sets out Dr. Scott's early ideas on the place of international law in the system of modern jurisprudence, we quote his own words from the preface:

> The idea underlying this volume is that international law is part of the English common law; that as such it passed with the English colonists to America; that when, in consequence of a successful rebellion, they were admitted to the family of nations, the new republic recognized international law as completely as international law recognized the new republic. Municipal law it was in England; municipal law it remained and is in the United States. No opinion is expressed on the vexed question whether it is law in the abstract; our courts, State and Federal, take judicial cognizance of its existence, and in appropriate cases enforce it, so that for the American student or practitioner it is domestic or municipal law.

The copy in Dr. Scott's personal library of his first edition is inscribed in his handwriting to his wife, "Adele C. Scott, in grateful recognition of gracious, generous and unstinted help in the labor of preparation".

A second edition was published in the American Casebook Series in 1922.[13] In his expanded preface to this edition Dr. Scott quoted with approval Sir Henry Maine's statement as to the binding force of international law, namely, that "the state which disclaims the authority of international law places itself outside the circle of civilized nations".[14] Writing after the First World War, Dr. Scott commented: "International law seems to have stood fairly well the strain of war. It is no doubt true that the belligerent practices of nations have not squared with their peaceful professions. Nevertheless the law of nations emerges from the World War as a system with foundations unimpaired, although the structure bears outward marks of violence and unsightly scars which only time can cover". But, he continued, "whether we admit it with open eyes, or ostrich-like bury our heads in the sand, there is such a thing as justice, independent of the state, above it and beyond it, although the formulation of its principles may change according to time, place, and

---

[13] J. B. Scott, *Cases on International Law* (St. Paul, West Publishing Co., 1922).
[14] H. S. Maine, *International Law* (London, John Murray, 1888), p. 38.

circumstances". From "this justice", he concluded, "nations must derive their rules of law".

He ended this preface with the wish that "members of the profession in foreign countries examine the decisions of their own courts, the awards of mixed commissions and sentences of arbitral tribunals in whose cases their respective governments have special interest, and produce collections of cases, not only for the benefit of the profession to which they belong, but also for the purpose of instruction in the law schools, universities, and other seats of learning in their respective states".

The last edition of the casebook appeared in 1937.[15] In editing it, Dr. Scott enlisted the aid of a former student whose name appears on the title page. In the preface Dr. Scott goes all the way in support of the legal nature of international law. "The legal nature of the law of nations", he says, "has now been sufficiently demonstrated both to justify and to require the teaching of international law as a branch of legal science in the law schools not merely of the United States but of every country in the international community". Accordingly, "in the present edition, international law is not developed merely by English and American decisions, but by those of some sixty sovereign nations of the world", as well as by cases of arbitration. This arrangement, he explained, is "grounded upon the belief that arbitral decisions are essentially judicial decisions" and that "municipal courts everywhere, upon assuming jurisdiction of a case involving international law, treat that law as the municipal law of the country in which the suit is brought, in the sense that international law forms a part of the municipal legal system of every sovereign member of the international community".

"Even a slight familiarity with foreign cases involving the law of nations", he continued, "will suffice to show that, although they are more or less conditioned in form by local procedure and in substance by local law, they are nevertheless ultimately decided in accordance with the rules and precepts of international law. The stream is indeed everywhere colored by the soil through which it reaches the sea, but the sea itself is international ... Slowly, almost imperceptibly throughout the centuries, the law of nations has won recognition and acceptance as the true law".

---

[15] J. B. Scott and Walter H. E. Jaeger, *Cases on International Law* (St. Paul, West Publishing Co., 1937).

The impress of Dr. Scott's four-year tenure as the first dean of the Law School of the University of Illinois was eulogized by one of the speakers at the dedication of the Law Building on 13 October 1927 in the following sentences:

> Surely if ever a great future was presaged for a new organization by the distinctive character of its first leader, the naming of the scholarly James Brown Scott as the first dean of the Law School was prophetic of the present occasion. To the thinking person who has paused to analyze the history of this law school, it is clear that Dean Scott's early ideals of scholarship and constructive thought which have been so eminently wrought out in his own subsequent career, left an indelible impression upon the new institution.[16]

Dr. Scott's valedictory at the University of Illinois took the form of a poem inscribed upon a memorial medallion of President Draper. The lines read as follows:

No epaulette or sword that reeks
With blood of man unjustly slain;
No politician's greed or craft
That smacks of contests low and vain.

No ermined judge, within whose hands
The scales of justice slip and fall,
Unmindful of his fellow man
Whose weaknesses surround us all.

A simple form in simple garb;
An eye that courts not shuns its kind;
A manly heart that beats for man
And man to man forever binds.

The youth that strays within these halls;
The graduates who may return;
Will find this lesson wrought in bronze
As long as hope and honor burn.

James Brown Scott
June 6, 1903

---

[16] Address of Judge Fred L. Wham, United States District Court, *University of Illinois Bulletin* (29 May 1928), p. 29.

Another of the guests and speakers at the dedication of the Law Building at Urbana in 1927 was the first Dean of the Law School himself. Reminiscing upon the intervening twenty-eight years, Dr. Scott recalled that when he entered upon the performance of his duties as Dean the Law School was assigned a modest suite of rooms in the main building. "A year later, the School was raised to the dignity of a college and, the chemists forsaking their laboratory, the College was installed in their deserted quarters". The elevation of the School to the rank of a College had an immediate effect upon the law students, who "developed an *esprit de corps*, taking their part in the life of the University – literary, social and athletic". To-day, the former Dean continued in his oration, "the College leaves its 'outgrown shell, by life's unresting sea' – installing itself in another deserted building, the Library, on its way upward and onward, to a building of its own".

Dr. Scott then expounded his conception of the relation of law to what he said are sometimes called the "polite arts", a relationship he consistently demonstrated in all of his writing and speaking on legal subjects. "Law", he said:

> is not a trade; it is not a craft; it is a profession; it is an art. It should therefore be conceived of as a profession and as an art. It should be included among the arts, and a knowledge of it and of the space which it occupies in the world's progress should form a part of the intellectual equipment of men and women of taste and refinement. Such a knowledge is not, I beg to assure you, inconsistent with artistic feeling and literary expression.

After reminding his hearers of the careers and accomplishments of a number of the great leaders of the British and American Bars and of the Bench – Blackstone, Kent, Stephen, Maitland, Erskine, Russell, Brougham, Curran, Coke, Bacon, Hale, Scott, Eldon, Mansfield, Kenyon, Ellenborough, Tindal, Parke, Campbell, Romilly – he told a parable to illustrate that the Law School in assuming "its place in the University, will necessarily yield to the subtle but all-pervading atmosphere of the immediate present, and of the ever-growing future". "Once upon a time", he said, adding "it happens every day – a young and progressive family left its outgrown quarters, exchanging the modest 'home' for an imposing 'residence'. The new carpets required new furnishings, the new furnishings, a new wardrobe for Madame, and more elegant manners on the part of the Lord and Master. Unconsciously, they were fitting themselves into the newer atmosphere. They were taking their place in society".

The application of the parable to Dr. Scott's visit to his old surroundings can be best told in his own words:

> My dear young friends, I had the very great honor to be connected with this Law School from its beginning, indeed, I was its first dean; and, had the privilege of addressing your predecessors on their migration from the older building, which was assigned to the Law School and dedicated under my deanship. I am, not unnaturally, anxious that your removal to more adequate quarters should be celebrated in a more elaborate way, becoming a profession and an art. And inasmuch as Mrs. Scott was a student at the University at that time – as I have already mentioned – we have both thought that we would like, in memory of a previous association, to leave with you something which, seen daily, may enter into your daily life. It seems to us, upon reflection, that the best way to convince you that law is an art and a profession would be to confront you with evidence of that art and of that profession. Therefore, we ask the Dean of the College of Law to accept, in our behalf and in our joint names, a collection of portraits, mezzotints, stipples, and line engravings, of some of the greatest judges of the profession, so that, strolling through the building in your leisure hours, you will feel yourselves in an atmosphere, not only of your own age, but of the centuries; and that as no one can be oblivious to his environment, and no person can fail, unconsciously and without effort, to be impressed by the atmosphere with which he is surrounded, you will leave the Law School of the University of Illinois in the fullness of knowledge, for the practice of your profession and of your art, with the assurance and the consciousness that, if you do not advance their traditions, they will neither be tarnished, nor suffer in your hands.
>
> Therefore, we offer you twenty-eight prints – a beautiful one, as we would like you to think, for every year from the date of my connection with the Law School, and one from each of us for you – as they say – to "grow on".

Dr. Scott ended his inspiring address with some verses of Austin Dobson so that "you, who are living in the present, and busied with the traditions of the past, may think somewhat of the future":

In after days, when grasses high
O'er-top the stone where I shall lie,
  Though ill or well the world adjust
  My slender claim to honored dust,
I shall not question nor reply.
I shall not see the morning sky,
I shall not hear the night-wind sigh,
  I shall not be mute, as all men must
      In after days!
But yet, now living, fain were I
That some one then should testify,
  Saying – *He held his pen in trust*
  To Art, not serving shame or lust.
Will none? ... Then let my memory die
      In after days!

The collection of fine pictures of men distinguished in the history of the law of the English-speaking peoples was a hobby of both Dr. Scott and Mrs. Scott. The walls of their home were completely covered with them. Mrs. Scott was commissioned by the University of Pennsylvania to go to London and purchase prints for its collection. When the home could accommodate no more, collections of previous purchases were presented to several educational institutions with which they had been associated. A collection of one hundred was presented to the Georgetown University Law School.

When Dr. Nicholas Murray Butler was installed as President of Columbia University on 19 April 1902, James B. Scott was present representing the School of Law of the University of Illinois. At the end of the next academic year he resigned to accept a professorship at the Law School of Columbia. He became an editor of the *Columbia University Quarterly* and a contributor to the *Educational Review* edited by Dr. Butler. Having founded one law school, having served four years as the first dean of another, and being now a professor at one of the leading law schools in the nation, he thought the time had come to look into the methods of the study and teaching of law. He reasoned that since law is a system, the result of organic development, "the conclusion is inevitable that law must be studied as a science". His indoctrination with the teaching methods at Harvard University was revealed by his reliance upon a colloquy between President Eliot and Professor Langdell repeated by the former as follows:

He told me that law was a science. I was quite prepared to believe it. He told me the way to study a science was to go to the original sources. I knew that was true, for I had been brought up in the science of chemistry myself; and one of the first rules of a conscientious student of science is never to take a fact or a principle out of secondhand treatises, but to go to the original memoir of the discoverer of that fact or principle. Out of these two fundamental propositions – that law is a science, and that science is to be studied in its sources – there gradually grew, first, a new method of teaching law; and, secondly, a reconstruction of the curriculum of the school.[17]

Addressing himself to the question – What is the purpose for which the science of law is to be taught? – he discussed in turn the several alternative answers which he said might be given, namely, (a) the teaching of law as a part of a liberal education, (b) as an introduction to general jurisprudence, or (c) as a means of livelihood. If law be taught as a means of general culture, "there is no doubt that lecture courses in a university curriculum, if given by a competent professor, will supply at least a superficial familiarity with its origin and history, essential and fundamental principles". If the purpose of studying law be "rather to inculcate a knowledge of jurisprudence as such, it may well be that lectures such as Blackstone's may be of importance, and lectures upon the origin and history of Roman law will be indispensable". But, he added, "it would seem to the writer that the maintenance of this system of instruction is only justified by the conservatism of seats of learning and by the proverbial conservatism of the English mind; for it is impossible adequately to appreciate the system of common law from a superficial statement of its general principles, and even a detailed study of Roman law must fail of its ultimate purpose without a sound and thorough training in the various branches of the common law before undertaking the system of private Roman law". Finally,

if the aim be to impart a knowledge of the law for the purpose of the practitioner, that could only be done by a detailed and careful study of the various subjects making up the body of law as it exists

[17] Quoted in J. B. Scott, "The Study and Teaching of Law", *Educational Review* (September 1904), p. 133.

> at present. And for that purpose, the various branches of law should be studied in their historical development.

As this last is the purpose of law students as a class, Dr. Scott then set forth the merits of "binding one's self to a lawyer, receiving his instruction in the office and following him and observing his methods in court". The drawing of papers, he elaborated, "is learned by drawing papers, just as writing is learned by pen and pencil". Skill in the trial and conduct of a case in court is "learned by trying and conducting cases in court, and the knack is found to consist in individual experience". Scott was fully cognizant of the fundamental contribution to the beginnings of the science by those who had no other recourse than to bind themselves to a lawyer:

> The sages of the common law, the great judges, lawyers, and text-writers of England have been trained in this practical way and are so trained today, for England does not have and does seem to desire an epidemic of the American law school. To condemn the system that has produced the common law, the source and body of the law we use every day in office or court, would manifestly be absurd. But can a busy and competent lawyer sacrifice clients to the student? If he does, he becomes a law teacher, and his office a law school ... The law school is therefore not only an advantage, but is a necessity, and the growth of the American law school is a consolidation rather than a surprise; for the establishment and continuous growth of law schools in the last fifty years clearly show the reading law in a lawyer's office has not been, and, indeed, could not be, in the very nature of things, accompanied by satisfactory results. Schools of law, it is confidently asserted, not only give a rounded and systematic preparation for the practice of law, but it is established that they give the most satisfying preparation.

The three methods of teaching and studying law – the lecture system, the use of text-books, and the use of selected cases – were then compared and a heavy balance found in favor of the last mentioned because it not only imparted a knowledge of the law, as did the first two methods, but it also disciplined the mind in legal reasoning and analysis.

Dr. Scott put into practice at Columbia Law School his ideas on the best method of teaching the law subjects he professed. He edited a volume on cases on quasi contracts[18] and two volumes of cases on equity jurisdiction.[19] In this work he was assisted throughout by J. Reuben Clark, Jr., then a member of the New York Bar.

After giving credit to previous collections of cases at his disposal, Dr. Scott, constant to his belief that the "spirit of Poesy" illumines law and equity, ended his preface to these two volumes with the following lines of Rudyard Kipling:

When 'Omer smote 'is bloomin' lyre,
He'd 'eard men sing by land an' sea;
An' what he thought 'e might require,
'E went an' took – the same as me!

The market-girls an' fishermen,
The shepherds an' the sailors, too,
They 'eard old songs turn up again,
But kep' it quiet – same as you!

They knew 'e stole; 'e knew they knowed.
They didn't tell, nor make a fuss,
But winked at 'Omar down the road,
An' 'e winked back – the same as us!

His attachment to the casebook method of teaching subjects in the legal curricula under his professorships expanded at Columbia University to the entire range of subjects taught in the law school. He urged that the lecture system be discarded "because in it the lecturer does the work and the student is either a willing receptacle or offers a passive resistance". He boldly predicted that the lecture system was doomed. In 1905 he and his intimate friend, George W. Kirchwey, then Dean of Columbia University Law School, interested the West Publishing Company, law publishers of St. Paul, Minnesota, in an American Casebook Series.

Before the arrangements were consummated Dr. Scott had resigned his professorship at Columbia and moved to Washington to become Solicitor of the Department of State. Nevertheless, the West Publishing Company closed a contract with him in March 1906 to become the "general editor, supervisor and promoter of the

---

[18] J. B. Scott, *Cases on Quasi Contracts* (New York, Baker, Voorhis & Co., 1905).
[19] J. B. Scott, *Cases on Equity Jurisdiction* (New York, Baker, Voorhis & Co., 1906). 2 vols.

Series". The prospectus for the series, printed over Dr. Scott's signature on 3 June 1906, enumerated thirty-one subjects to be included. They were selected because a knowledge of them "is universally required for admission to the bar".

With the assistance of the General Editor, the publishers within a few months made contracts with acceptable authors for twenty-seven out of the thirty-one titles named in the prospectus. The series was announced publicly in the *American Law School Review* for December 1907 with twenty-seven assigned subjects and authors. Several conferences were held in Washington, New York, and Chicago by the publishers and General Editor with the authors concerning the aims and purposes of the series and the selection and preparation of the cases. As a result of those conferences, the General Editor prepared and the publishers in June 1908 distributed to the authors a set of printed detailed Instructions to Editors, with an appendix of standard forms.

In his preface to the series which was reproduced in each casebook, the General Editor emphasized that Training and Knowledge are the keynote of the Series. The Series would consist, he said, of:

> scholarly casebooks, prepared with special reference to the needs and limitations of the class-room, on the fundamental subjects of legal education, which, through a judicious rearrangement of emphasis, shall provide adequate training combined with a thorough knowledge of the general principles of the subject. The collection will develop the law historically and scientifically; English cases will give the origin and development of the law in England; American cases will trace its expansion and modification in America; notes and annotations will suggest phases omitted in the printed case. Cumulative references will be avoided, for the footnote may not hope to rival the digest. The law will thus be presented as an organic growth, and the necessary connection between the past and the present will be obvious.

The only serious objections Dr. Scott saw to the case method "are that it takes too much time to give a student the requisite knowledge of the subject in this way and that the system loses sight of the difference between the preparation of the student and the lifelong training of the lawyer". To this objection he answered that "it would seem axiomatic that the size of the casebook should correspond in general to the amount of time at the disposal of the instructor and student". He argued that "if only a half to two-thirds of the cases in the present collections can be discussed in class, the present casebooks are a third to a half too long. From a purely practical and economic standpoint it is a mistake to ask students to pay for 1,200 pages when they can only use 600". Taking the hour-unit as the basis of calculation, Dr. Scott stated that his experience, supplemented by the experience of others in the classroom:

> Leads us to the belief that approximately a book of 400 pages may be covered by the average student in half a year of two hours a week; that a book of 600 pages may be discussed in class in three hours for half a year; that a book of 800 pages may be completed by the student in two hours a week throughout the year; and a class may reasonably hope to master a volume of 1,000 pages in a year of three hours a week. The general rule will be subject to some modifications in connection with particular topics on due consideration of their relative importance and difficulty, and the time ordinarily allotted to them in the law school curriculum.

His duties as principal legal adviser of the Department of State, lecturer at nearby universities, and representing the government in international conferences left little leisure to Dr. Scott to fulfill his functions as General Editor of the American Casebook Series. He gave what time he had at his disposal after office hours late in the evenings, on week-ends, and during vacation periods not otherwise occupied, but progress in the Series was too slow for the publishers. The contract contemplated completion and publication of twenty-five books within three years. Only four volumes were issued during that period and eight in the first four years. At the end of eight years, in 1914, eighteen books were published with eight more under contract. In the meantime Dr. Scott had left the Department of State and taken up his duties with the Carnegie Endowment for International Peace.

In his new position he had no more time than before to give to the American Casebook Series. The publishers accordingly wrote to him on 21 December 1914, suggesting that since he had become "involved in other respectable occupations, and also by reason of your itinerancy ceased to be available as a consulting or reviewing editor", they had come to the point where they felt the need of expert advice and assistance with authors in rounding up the enterprise. The publishers therefore suggested that they would like to engage a new General Editor in the person of Professor William R. Vance, then recently transferred from the Yale Law School to be Dean of the Law Department of the University of Minnesota, at Minneapolis, twin city of St. Paul, the home of the West Publishing Company.

Dr. Scott promptly concurred in the suggestion of the publishers with the best of good grace. In his reply to the President of the Company, dated 24 December 1914, he said:

> You never did a wiser thing than to dismiss me as general editor of the Series, unless to appoint me as its editor, and you could have taken no action more calculated to assure the success of the Series, in which I have taken a deep interest, even although I am not so closely connected as formerly with academic life, nor could you have found a better man as general editor than our dear friend Vance.

The new General Editor took over the Series on 1 January 1915. At that time the following nineteen casebooks had been published under the general editorship of Dr. Scott:

Administrative Law: Freund, Ernst (Professor of Law, University of Chicago)
Agency: Goddard, Edwin C. (Professor of Law, University of Michigan)
Bills and Notes: Smith, Howard L. (Professor of Law, University of Wisconsin) and Moore, William U. (Professor of Law, University of Chicago)
Carriers: Green, Frederick (Professor of Law, University of Illinois)
Conflict of Laws: Lorenson, Ernest G. (Professor of Law, University of Minnesota)
Constitutional Law: Hall, James Parker (Dean, University of Chi cago Law School)
Corporations: Richards, Harry S. (University of Wisconsin Law School)
Criminal Law: Mikell, William E. (Professor of Law, University of Pennsylvania)
Criminal Procedure: Mikell, William E. (Professor of Law, University of Pennsylvania)
Criminal Law and Criminal Procedure: Mikell, William E. (Professor of Law, University of Pennsylvania)

Damages: Mecham, Floyd R. (Professor of Law, University of Chicago) and Gilbert, Barry (Professor of Law, University of California)
Insurance: Vance, W. R. (Dean, University of Minnesota Law School)
Partnership: Gilmore, Eugene A. (Professor of Law, University of Wisconsin)
Persons (Including Marriage and Divorce): Kales, Albert M. (Pro fessor of Law, Northwestern University)
Pleading (Common Law): Whittier, Clarke B. (Professor of Law, University of Chicago)
Sales: Woodward, Frederic C. (Professor of Law, Stanford University Law School)
Suretyship: Hening, Crawford D. (Professor of Law, University of Pennsylvania)
Trusts: Kenneson, Thaddeus D. (Professor of Law, New York University)
Wills and Administration: Costigan, Jr., George P. (Professsor of Law, Northwestern University)

In number of pages the books varied from 421 to 1,452. The average size was 737 pages.

The publishers were not too greatly disappointed with the results accomplished under Dr. Scott's editorship. In their letter to him of 21 December, they added:

> When all this is said, and acknowledging all the disappointments and delays, I still feel that we have done a creditable piece of work, and have rendered a real service to the cause of sound legal education in the United States. In fine, we have realized to some extent the high ambitions with which we undertook this great task, and I do not now despair of carrying it through to a successful conclusion in a few years more, with Vance's assistance.

About that time Dr. Scott also had the satisfaction of reading in the Report on Legal Education published by the United States Bureau of Education in 1914 that "The case method is today the principal method of instruction in the great majority of the schools of his country".

2

SOLICITOR FOR THE DEPARTMENT OF STATE

Dr. Scott was appointed Solicitor for the Department of State on 23 January 1906 by Elihu Root, then Secretary of State. At that time the legal advisers of the various executive departments were nominally officers of the Department of Justice and Dr. Scott's commission was actually signed by the Attorney-General, the Honorable George W. Wickersham. The story of the appointment was told by Dr. Scott to the members of the American Society of International Law at its Thirty-First Annual Meeting in Washington D. C. on 29 April 1937 in the course of a warm appreciation of the services of Elihu Root, who had died a few months previously on 7 February:

> My acquaintance with Mr. Root was accidental, during the time when I was professor of law in Columbia University Law School. A cold which had settled in my larynx had both enlarged and stiffened the vocal cords, so that it was difficult for me to speak above a whisper—or at any rate to address a class. It so happened at that time the Solicitor—now termed the "Legal Adviser"—of the State Department had but recently resigned. I therefore wrote a letter to Mr. Root, then Secretary of State, to the effect that I would be glad to accept the position, if he cared to appoint me. In the letter I intimated that I did not need the position; that I had had no practical experience in international relations, although my hobby was international law, and that I would not care to have the position if it were reserved for political appointment. The two references which I gave were Dr. Butler, then and now President of Columbia University, and Chandler P. Anderson (now deceased), who was intimately associated with Mr. Root. I concluded my somewhat impertinent application—as I now look upon it—by expressing the hope that the letter would reach his eye before it (meaning the letter) was thrown into the waste-basket.

Why Mr. Root answered the letter, I do not know. His reply was a note of a few lines, acknowledging the receipt of the communication, assuring me that he would under no circumstances make a political appointment and asking me to come to Washington for an interview. I learned later from Mr. Bacon, then Assistant Secretary of State, that Mr. Root was so amused at the nonchalant tone of the letter that he took it to the next Cabinet meeting and read it aloud; whereupon President Roosevelt – the first of the line—thumped the table with his hand and said: "Elihu, we must appoint that man", the statement probably being due to the fact that the President himself, as well as the applicant, was a Harvard man.

Secretary Root had followed the strenuous T. R.'s advice, but before making the appointment summoned me to Washington, as has been said, apparently to look me over. Accordingly, I repaired to the capital of the nation, only to learn that the Secretary had been suddenly called to New York. Mr. Bacon (also a Harvard man, I may add) thereupon suggested that I should take the night train and wait upon the Secretary at his New York residence. This I did, carrying with me a somewhat overloaded valise, as I then had—and still have, as many of you probably know—the habit of carrying around a library. With trepidation I rang the doorbell, and in the course of time the door was opened by no less a person than the Secretary of State, who graciously asked me to enter. By this time my nonchalance had left me. I stumbled over the valise with its portable library and, to my horror if not to his, I fell into his arms. I would like to record what Mr. Root said on this occasion, but apparently the impact was so unexpected and so unusual, that, as I recollect it, he only smiled and ran his hand through his hair. I should add, however, that he asked me in and we sat down to an exchange of views. He explained to me what the duties of the office were and they seemed to be more than I had bargained for—Mr. Root was apparently very anxious to settle the outstanding claims against Venezuela involving injury to American interests caused by President Castro's Administration. He graciously explained them, saying that he wanted a Solicitor who would be able to relieve him of the burden. I said frankly that I had not had any experience in this line and that I would not feel justified in accepting a position which would require analysis of the cases and the preparation of a memorandum stating them, unless Mr. Root would himself allow me to have his advice from time to time on difficult points. Again he smiled and said that as he would have to sign the memorandum, it might be well to take counsel from time to time. And from that moment, during my tenure of office and, I am

> bound to say, throughout the entire thirty-one years of our association, Mr. Root's arms were stretched forth, as it were, in encouragement.

In a letter about Dr. Scott to Dr. Nicholas Murray Butler, dated 18 December 1909, Mr. Root told him, "I consider it one of the most fortunate events of my administration of the State Department that I was able to secure him for Solicitor". Concerning his appointment, Mr. Root added: "He came to the State Department without any influence or backing of any kind. I had never known him and nobody spoke for him. He was selected solely for what he had already done and from what I could learn about inquiries I made".[1]

The duties of the office of Solicitor for the State Department, which seemed to Dr. Scott "to be more than I had bargained for" were described in the *Congressional Directory* as follows:

> He drafts and interprets treaties, conventions and protocols, and other international agreements; deals with questions of municipal, foreign and international law, and handles diplomatic claims of American citizens against foreign governments; claims of foreigners against the government of the United States; questions of personal and private rights of aliens in the United States and of American citizens in foreign countries, such as acquisition, inheritance, and transfer of property; arrest, detention, fines, imprisonment, personal injury, acts of insurgents, taxation, breach or annulment of concessions or other contracts; failure to pay interest or principal on government obligations, sequestration or confiscation of property; complaints regarding action of executive, legislative, judicial, or military authorities; questions concerning the rights and privileges of American diplomatic and consular officers abroad and foreign diplomatic and consular officers in the United States, and concerning the rights and immunities of sovereigns and public property; questions relating to the jurisdiction over and control of public or private vessels; questions relating to citizenship, naturalization, expatriation, extradition and extraterritoriality; questions relating to the acts and rights of belligerents, neutrals and insurgents on land or sea; and a large number of miscellaneous legal questions not included in the above classification.

---

[1] P. C. Jessup, *Elihu Root* (New York, Dodd, Mead & Co., 1938), I, p. 456.

As indicated by Dr. Scott in his personal narrative above quoted, the first major question assigned to him as Solicitor was the settlement of some five pecuniary claims of large amounts of American citizens against the Government of Venezuela. Memoranda and opinions in the cases were prepared and submitted to the Secretary of State on 24 May 1906. They embody some 150 pages of a government document.[2]

After examining the memoranda and opinions, Secretary of State Root offered to arbitrate the five claims. Solicitor Scott recorded that "Secretary Root affixed his signature to the communication to the Venezuelan Government (some seventy-odd legal pages), after suggesting the change of a word, remarking as he changed it that his was what Mr. Boffin would call a 'tenderer word'". But the Venezuelan Government eventually preferred to settle four of them through diplomatic channels. The fifth was submitted to the Permanent Court of Arbitration at The Hague, which reached a decision in favor of the United States on 25 October 1910.[3]

Shortly after relating the Venezuelan episode, Dr. Scott continued his account as follows:

> Mr. Root requested an opinion about a difficult situation which had arisen in Cuba. I prepared the memorandum as requested and he looked it over with great care. I knew that the matter was one of importance and that it should be backed up by precedent. I succeeded in finding authorities, but it turned out that his authority was to prevail. He put his finger on a particular phrase and asked me if I believed this statement. I replied: 'It is the opinion of the Attorney General'. Whereupon he said to me: 'Do you believe it is right?' To which I replied that the Attorney General's opinion was binding upon me as a member of the Department of Justice (as was the Solicitor of the State Department in those days). Mr. Root asked me again if I believed it; if I thought it was right. To which I said: 'No, I do not, but I understand it was a precedent'. He went on reading and somewhat later he repeated the process. This time it was the statement of a former Secretary of State

---

[2] *Correspondence relating to Wrongs Done to American Citizens by the Government of Venezuela.* Senate Document No. 413, 60th Congress, 1st Session.
[3] For Dr. Scott's account of these cases and of the diplomatic negotiations which led to their settlement, see the *American Journal of International Law*, III (1909), pp. 436, 985. The award of the Hague tribunal is also printed there. Ibid., V (1911), p. 230.

which was apparently to be overruled. Mr. Root graciously asked my authority. To which I replied, having grown a bit wiser in the interval, that it was the prerogative of a Secretary of State to overrule his predecessor, the predecessor in this case being none other than Secretary Hay. Mr. Root removed his eyeglasses, laid them quietly on the table, reached with his free arm for the lowest drawer of his desk, opened it as well as a small box of cigars —for which he had a weakness—selected one, bit off the end, lighted it and then turning to me said: 'Overruled'. Then he picked up his eyeglasses, wheeled his chair around and added: 'We must always be careful, and especially so in our relations with the smaller states, that we never propose a settlement which we would not be willing to accept if the situation were reversed'. I mention this incident in some detail because it shows you Mr. Root as I knew him and as he was.

Some time later Mr. Root was keenly distressed by the so-called 'Wile' claim against Nicaragua, which he had inherited from his predecessors. From time to time one or other of the senators from Louisiana would drop in and ask the status of the claim and, after hearing what Wile's advocate had said, Mr. Root would have a note sent to the American Minister in Nicaragua asking to report on the condition of the claim. Finally Mr. Root came to the conclusion that something was wrong, and he suggested to Mr. Bacon and the then Solicitor that we should get the papers together and run them through. This was on a Saturday afternoon. We worked into the night and all day Sunday, Mr. Root reading, removing his glasses and reflecting upon the import of the papers which he had read. He did not ask our opinion; for when Mr. Root personally took up a project he made it his from the beginning and read it through. All day Sunday we spent together, at the end of which time he said that the Wile claim should never have been presented; that it was inequitable and that on the morrow he would ask the Nicaraguan Minister to repair to the Department of State.

When the Minister appeared, Mr. Root stated that he had been led to read personally the entire Wile *dossier* by the feeling that if the claim were valid it would have been settled long since. Thereupon he eyes the Minister—for Mr. Root always had the habit of looking his visitor in the eye—and said that in his considered opinion the claim should not have been presented; that the Government of the United States would therefore withdraw its support; and that he would merely suggest to the Nicaraguan Minister that whatever part of Wile's claim could be considered equitable should be admitted. After the Minister's withdrawal, greatly pleased by the conversation, Mr. Root turned to Mr. Bacon and then to the Solicitor and said that thereafter he would not authorize the continuance of a claim merely because of political pressure, but that in such case he would himself read the dossier and make a prompt answer to the senator or representative pressing a claim.

These illustrations are but two of the many which could be vouched. Whether a case was large or small and no matter what country was involved, it is proper to say that Mr. Root conducted the State Department not merely as a practitioner for his client, the United States, but as a judge on the bench.[4]

---

[4] J. B. Scott, "Elihu Root (February 15, 1845–February 7, 1937), An Appreciation", *Proceedings of the American Society of International Law* (1937), pp. 7–9.

3

THE SECOND HAGUE PEACE CONFERENCE

In the chronicle of events that occurred during Dr. Scott's tenure as Solicitor for the Department of State, the one that had the most important bearing upon his future career was the Peace Conference held at The Hague in 1907. That was the second of a series which began in 1899 upon the call of the Czar of Russia.

Background to the Second Hague Peace Conference

The calling of the First Conference was described by Dr. Scott in an article on the Second Conference, as follows:[1]

> On the twelfth day of August (24 August, new style) 1898 the staid and sedate diplomats accredited to the Court of St. Petersburg were astonished to receive from the hands of Count Mouravieff, Russian Minister for Foreign Affairs, a circular note proposing a conference to consider the question of the limitation of armaments, and the burdens which they had imposed, which, in the opinion of the Czar, were unendurable in themselves and fatal to economic and social progress.[2]

In a memorandum which accompanied the note Count Mouravieff expressed the sentiments which inspired the Russian Czar as follows:

> The maintenance of general peace and a possible reduction of the excessive armaments which weigh down upon all the nations present themselves, in the actual present situation of the world,

---

[1] *American Journal of International Law*, II (1908), pp. 8–9.
[2] The Hague Court Reports (New York, Oxford University Press, 1916), p. xii.

> as the ideal toward which should tend the efforts of all governments.
>
> The Czar expresses the hope that "This conference will be, with the help of God, a happy augury for the century which is about to open. It will gather together in a powerful unit the efforts of all the powers which are sincerely desirous of making triumphant the conception of a universal peace. It will, at the same time, strengthen their mutual harmony by a common consideration of the principle of equity and right, upon which rest the security of states and the well-being of nations.[3]

To continue with Dr. Scott's description:

> The circular astonished the diplomats; it was not favorably received in many quarters. Thereupon a new circular was prepared enlarging the scope, relegating disarmament to a less important position, but enlarging the scope of the program, or of the invitation, by including the consideration of various methods by which arbitration might be advanced and the peaceful solution of international difficulties made the rule. This second circular, dated 11 January 1899 (30 December 1898) was much better received, and on the 18 May 1899, the First Peace Conference of this modern world, without a war as its immediate cause, met at the House in the Wood at The Hague, for the purely academic consideration of very great and important questions.

The Conference opened on the birthday of the Czar, 18 May 1899, in the summer palace of the Dutch Royal family about a mile from the city of The Hague. Thus was inaugurated the modern era of international conferences in time of peace to avoid or regulate future wars. The significance of the occasion was not overlooked by the President of the First Commission of the Conference, M. Auguste Beernaert of Belgium, who remarked at its second meeting on 26 May 1899, "In the history of the world, it will be the first time, I think, that representatives of almost every civilized country are seen to meet peacefully, without a dispute to settle, without complaints to be redressed, without any thought of personal advantage, and this in the two-fold and liberal purpose of perpetuating

[3] The Hague Peace Conferences of 1899 and 1907.

harmony and softening the evils of war, or of regulating it for the day when it cannot be avoided".[4]

The work of the Conference, according to Dr. Scott, took shape in three conventions:

> The first was the convention for the peaceful settlement of international disputes, which convention established, first, the right of nations to offer their good offices and mediation without having the offer or mediation considered as an unfriendly act by either or any of the contending parties; second, a commission of inquiry to ascertain the facts of an international difficulty of great and serious importance, so that the facts involved might be found impartially by a commission composed of neutrals as well as nationals. Third, the convention for the pacific solution of international conflicts provided a court of arbitration ... Each nation was to select and appoint, and notify to a board created at The Hague, not more than four persons of good moral character and competent in international law. In case of a conflict each party was to select two from this list of judges. The judges were to elect their umpire, their presiding officer, or the nations were to provide otherwise for the selection of the umpire. In order that the tribunal thus constituted might be of service and in order that litigants might know the exact procedure to be followed before it, an elaborate system of procedure was drawn up and approved.[5]

The Hague Conference of 1899, contrary to uninformed criticism, was not completely lacking in effectiveness. The peaceful settlement of a grave incident, which occurred during the Russo-Japanese War of 1904–1905, and which might have brought on World War I ten years before it actually occurred, is thus described by Dr. Scott:

> We all recall the Dogger Bank incident in Admiral Rojesvensky's remarkable tour of the world. Japanese vessels were supposed to be lying in wait in the North Sea. The Russian squadron opened fire. It is not related that any Japanese vessels were sunk, but certain English fishing smacks were injured and lives were lost. It is difficult to appreciate the state of mind of the Russian

---

[4] Proceedings of the Hague Peace Conference, Conference of 1899 (New York: Oxford University Press for the Carnegie Endowment for International Peace, 1920), pp. 272–273.

[5] *American Journal of International Law* (January 1908), pp. 9, 10–11.

> admiral, because one would not expect to find Japanese cruisers in the North Sea, or if one did find such cruisers, the fact of their presence would be well known. However, the Russian authorities maintained that they felt the presence of the enemy, whether through a mistake of signaling or not; fire was opened and lives were lost. Were it not well established, this would be unbelievable; but it happened. And the next step was not an unbelievable one – the next step was war. Wars have arisen for less cause than that. The national honor of both countries was involved. Great Britain could not allow its subjects to be shot with impunity; Russia could not well consent to discipline its naval authorities without an investigation. Now, an investigation to be valuable must be impartial, must be conducted more or less by neutrals, and for the first time the provisions of the convention for the peaceful solution of international conflicts in the matter of commissions of inquiry were used. A report was made by this board finding the attack unjustified, and Russia settled the damages. Rulers of nations and their responsible governments often seek to avoid war but are frequently unable to do so. Therefore, this machinery was a God-send by which a bitter dispute between two countries concerning a matter of fact might be referred to an impartial board for examination and report.[6]

So much for the Commission of Inquiry established at The Hague in 1899. The Arbitration Tribunal likewise was not barren of effective results. As Dr. Scott pointed out, "four great and important cases have been submitted to the Hague Tribunal, have been adjudicated and the judgments cheerfully and promptly accepted by the litigating nations. Nations appeared before the bar as suitors and resorted to law instead of force".

The four cases were the *Pious Fund Case* between Mexico and the United States; the *Venezuelan Preferential Case* between Germany, Great Britain and Italy, on the one hand, and Venezuela on the other; the *Japanese House Tax Case* between France, Germany, and Great Britain, on the one hand, and Japan, on the other; and the *Muscat Dhows Case* between France and Great Britain.[7] To a volume which he edited, giving the facts and decisions in these and other cases decided by the Hague Court, Dr. Scott contributed an

---

[6] AJIL, ibid., pp. 9–10.

[7] *The Hague Court Reports* (New York: Oxford University Press for the Carnegie Endowment for International Peace, 1916).

introduction showing the development of international arbitration as a part of the foreign policy of the United States and the influence of its example upon the nations at large. The opening paragraphs of his introduction serve likewise as an introduction to the work of the Hague Peace Conferences. They are therefore quoted as follows:

> Arbitration, the gift of the Grecian world, was frequently resorted to in the Middle Ages, but was passing out of the minds of men and the practice of nations in the eighteenth century, when it was brought again to honor by the Republic of the New World. The statesman to whom the renascence of arbitration is due was John Jay, who was Secretary of State for Foreign Affairs during the Confederation from 1764 to the institution of the Government under the Constitution, and who continued to act as Secretary of State in Washington's administration until Jefferson's assumption of the office on 22 March 1790, upon his return from France, in which country he had represented the United States as its Minister. It is important to bear this is mind, because it was John Jay who, as Secretary of State under the Confederation, proposed the arbitration of the outstanding difficulties with Great Britain and sent a report to Congress of 21 April 1785, advocating this form of settlement. The report was sent to Congress recommending that 'effectual measures should be immediately taken to settle all disputes with the Crown of Great Britain' with respect to the northeastern boundary of the United States, and Secretary Jay suggested that the papers in the case 'should be transmitted to the Minister Plenipotentiary of the United States at that Court, with instructions to make a proper representation of the case, and to propose that commissioners be appointed to hear and finally decide those disputes'.[8]

It was likewise John Jay, as Acting Secretary of State in Washington's Cabinet, who urged President Washington to secure by arbitration the settlement of the outstanding difficulties which unfortunately had not been settled as Jay had proposed. Washington, acting upon Jay's suggestion, sent a copy of Jay's original report to the first Congress under the Constitution, stating in his letter of transmission, dated 9 February 1790, that "it is desirable that all

---

[8] *American State Papers*, I, p. 94.

questions between this and the other nations be speedily and amicably settled".[9]

Congress took no action, and the disputes between Great Britain and the United States remained unsettled, a constant source of irritation and a pretext for war if either country should be disposed to resort to force. The outbreak of the French Revolution and the war between Great Britain and France in 1793 further embittered the relations of Great Britain and the United States, because France claimed and exercised the right, over the protest alike of Great Britain and the United States, to fit out and to arm privateers within the jurisdiction of the United States; to cruise upon British commerce, taking the prizes when captured either within or without our territorial waters into American ports, and to condemn them in prize courts organized within our jurisdiction. The actions of Great Britain were not wholly beyond criticism, and the two nations found themselves slowly drifting into war, when Washington proposed to Great Britain to negotiate directly in order to settle all their outstanding difficulties, and selected John Jay, then Chief Justice of the Supreme Court of the United States, to repair to England as the representative of the United States in such negotiations.

It was in a way poetic justice that Jay, who had originally proposed, in the days of the Confederation, to settle the outstanding disputes with Great Britain by arbitration, and who had influenced Washington to espouse that method of settling controversies with the mother country, should have been chosen to carry into effect his own recommendations. Some of the outstanding difficulties he was able to settle by direct negotiation; others, particularly the claims which he had previously proposed to arbitrate and the difficulties which had arisen since the outbreak of the wars of the French Revolution, he was unable to settle by direct negotiation, but he succeeded in prevailing upon Great Britain to submit these disputes to arbitration. He preserved the peace of his country, and by the treaty which bears his name, he introduced to the favorable notice of the modern world arbitration for the settlement of disputes which diplomacy had failed to adjust. But in so doing, he sacrificed every hope he might have cherished for political preferment, for his treaty, which was very unpopular with the partisans of a stiff foreign policy, was advised and consented to by a narrow margin in

---

[9] Ibid., I, p. 90.

the Senate; the appropriations for carrying it into effect was passed in the House by yeas 51, nays 48,[10] and Jay himself shared the unpopularity of his treaty. He had, however, no illusion as to the outcome of his mission, saying, 'If Washington shall think fit to call me to perform this service, I will go and perform it to the best of my abilities, foreseeing as I do that consequences to my personal popularity. The good of my country I believe demands the sacrifice, and I am ready to make it'. To Mrs. Jay he confided his views without reserve. 'This is not of my seeking', he said in a letter to her; 'on the contrary, I regard it as a measure not to be desired, but to be submitted to'. And in another letter, a little late, after Jay had been appointed special envoy to Great Britain, he wrote: 'No appointment ever operated more unpleasantly upon me; but the public considerations which were urged, and the manner in which it was pressed, strongly impressed me with a conviction that to refuse it would be to desert my duty for the sake of my ease and domestic concerns and comforts'.[11]

Jay's treaty provided in its 5th, 6th, and 7th articles for the arbitration of the boundary dispute between the two countries; the settlement of disputes concerning debts claimed by British merchants, to be due and unpaid, but which could not be collected because of legal impediments interposed by the States of the Union; and, finally, the complaints of citizens of the United States, on the one hand, and of British subjects, on the other, for losses since the outbreak of the war between Great Britain and the United States. The success of the commission organized under the 7th article to settle this last category of claims, and the admirable opinions of the commission showing that model judgments could be rendered between nations, as well as within nations, convinced the world that arbitration could be safely resorted to. The result was that during the nineteenth century arbitration became the favorite method of settling disputes between nations after the breakdown of diplomacy, and the submission by Great Britain and the United States of the so-called *Alabama* claims to the arbitration of the Geneva tribunal in 1872, showed the nations that arbitration had no limits which good-will and mutual desire might not overcome. It thus happened that in the course of the nineteenth century the nations

---

[10] *Annals of Congress*, V (4th Cong., 1st sess.), p. 1291.
[11] George Pellew, *John Jay* (1898), pp. 267–268.

generally had had sufficient experience in arbitration to suggest that the new remedy had come to stay; that it was in their interest to device machinery in order to facilitate a recourse to arbitration and a method of procedure in order to bring the issue to a decision.

"The Institute of International Law, founded in 1873, upon the initiative of the American Publicist, Francis Lieber, and through the efforts of the Belgian publicist, Rolin-Jaequemyns, foresaw the need and the advantages of a code of arbitral procedure, and within a year after its organization drafted a code which served as the basis of discussion at the First Hague Conference, and which with sundry amendments, not always for the better, was adopted by that august assembly. It was not only the jurists who foresaw the necessity of facilitating a recourse to arbitration and provided the means therefor; men in public life felt the need and took appropriate steps to meet it. Thus through the happy cooperation of Mr. William Randal Cremer, a labor Member of Parliament, and Frederic Passy, then a Member of the French Chamber of Deputies, the Interparliamentary Union was formed in 1888, and held its first meeting in Paris the next year, on the centenary of the French Revolution. At the meeting of the Union at The Hague in 1894, five years before the great and fertile idea of the Czar took visible form and shape in the capital of the Netherlands, the following resolution was voted:

1. National sovereignty remains inalienable and inviolate;
2. Adherence by any government to the creation of a permanent international court must be entirely voluntary;
3. All adhering States must be on a footing of perfect equality before the permanent international court;
4. The decision of the permanent court must have the force of decisions, subject to execution.[12]

These enlightened and practical men of affairs foresaw that arbitration should have its machinery just as the jurists of the Institute of International Law foresaw the need and provided a code of procedure for international tribunals. A year later, that is to say, in 1895, at the Brussels session, a project based upon these resolutions was adopted by the Interparliamentary Union, and this draft of a

---

[12] Lange, *Union Interparlementaire. Resolutions des Conférences et Décisions principales du Conseil* (2d ed.; 1911), p. 50.

Permanent Court of Arbitration,[13] like the draft of arbitral procedure of the Institute of International Law, served as the basis of discussion at the Czar's Conference held at The Hague in 1899, where it was accepted in principle, adopted with many modifications and put into effect.

Efforts were made at the First Hague Peace Conference to conclude a general treaty of obligatory arbitration but they were unsuccessful. Germany declined to go further than to agree to the establishment of the so-called Permanent Court of Arbitration, consisting of a large panel of previously designated arbitrators from which nations in dispute might select a limited number to whom controversies might be voluntarily submitted for solution. The best that advocates of a wider use of arbitration could obtain from the Conference was a declaration that "in questions of a legal nature, and especially in the interpretation or application of international conventions, arbitration is recognized by the signatory powers as the most effective, and at the same time the most equitable, means of settling disputes which diplomacy has failed to settle (Article 16 of the Convention for the Pacific Settlement of International Disputes). As if to rebuff those powers which had blocked a general treaty, the signatories of the convention reserved to themselves a right, which they had without claiming it, of concluding, either before the ratification of the Hague Convention or later, new agreements, general or particular, with a view to extending obligatory arbitration to all cases which they may consider it possible to submit to it (Article 19 of the same convention).

Dr. Scott's description of the results of the First Peace Conference at The Hague was concluded in the following paragraphs from his article in the *American Journal of International Law* previously quoted:

> The second great convention of the First Conference was the convention for the adaptation of the Red Cross to maritime warfare. That, of course, is a technical subject, but even the layman can see what a great advance it was to have the humane principles of the Geneva Convention of 1864 and the additional articles of 1868 applied to maritime warfare as well as land warfare.
>
> The third great convention was the codification of the laws and customs of land warfare, which, composed by experts, assumed

---

[13] Ibid., p. 53.

the proportions of an elaborate code. While based upon the Laws and Customs of War, adopted by the Conference of Brussels (27 August 1874), the declaration of Brussels drew its life and spirit from Dr. Francis Lieber's Instruction for the Government of Armies in the Field, known in army circles as General Order No. 100 of 1863. The United States may therefore claim not a little proprietary interest in this great convention of 1899.

The First Peace Conference at The Hague was not the happy augury for peace among nations that the Czar hoped for. The sequel to the Conference was recorded by Dr. Scott as follows in a series of lectures which he delivered at Johns Hopkins University in 1908:[14]

> The small wits have busied themselves with the fact that the adjournment of the First Conference was followed by the prolonged and questionable war in South Africa, and that the august initiator of the Conference, unwilling to reduce his armaments by land or sea, or to resort to the convention for the settlement of international disputes, which his conference adopted, rushed headlong and madly into a war of conquest with Japan. Nor was the fact unnoted that Japan absorbed the hermit kingdom of Korea shortly before the meeting of the Second Conference, and that during the very sessions of this august assembly, France was employing influences somewhat stronger than moral suasion in Morocco. The question was often asked in familiar conversation at The Hague, which of the States will be the first to resort to war? And inasmuch as Russia, the initiator of the First Conference, was plunged into warfare within a few years after its adjournment, it was suggested that the United States, the real initiator of the Second Conference, might succumb to the same fatality and in practice disavow its peaceful professions. Those who will may find humor in the situation.
>
> It is an unfortunate fact that these wars were not prevented by good offices, mediation, or the system of arbitration created by the First Conference; but we must never forget that each nation must determine for itself its political policy, and that, while it may yield to good offices and mediation, arbitration is primarily for the solution of legal questions, that is to say, questions susceptible of judicial interpretation or decision. Questions of foreign policy, based solely upon political hopes and aspirations, do not lend themselves easily to arbitration, and the desire of Great

---

[14] Revised, enlarged, and published in *The Hague Peace Conferences of 1899 and 1907* (Baltimore: The Johns Hopkins Press, 1909). 2 vols.

Britain to control the future of South Africa, as well as the ambition of Russia to possess an ice-free ort to the south of Vladivostok, even at the expense of Korea, involve moral as well as political considerations.

There was, on the other hand, a public reaction which demanded a continuance of the work at The Hague, which Dr. Scott also recorded in the same lectures:

> The First Conference had in mind a successor, but the years were slipping by and the friends of progress and therefore of peace, became anxious lest the Conference of 1899 might stand as an isolated experiment, and the hopes created by its meeting be defeated, or their realization indefinitely postponed. Private discontent took public form and expression, and slowly but surely public opinion began to influence those whom we are accustomed to call in our country 'the servants of the people'. In 1903, the American Peace Society presented to the Massachusetts legislature a petition for a stated international congress, and this body in 1903, true to its traditions of 1837 and 1838, "unanimously passed resolutions calling upon the Congress of the United States to authorize the President "to invite the governments of the world to join in establishing, in whatever way they may judge expedient, a regular international congress to meet at stated periods to deliberate upon the various questions of common interest to the nations and to make recommendations thereon to the governments.
>
> In support of the petition of the American Peace Society, a memorial was presented to the Senate and House of Representatives of the United States, relative to the establishment of an international congress, signed by the Attorney-General and all the justices of the Supreme Court of Pennsylvania, and endorsed by the Governor of the State. In the year 1904, the United States celebrated the peaceful acquisition of the territory embraced in the Louisiana Purchase, and at the meeting of the Interparliamentary Union held in St. Louis, 13 September 1904, "resolutions were adopted requesting the President of the United States to invite all nations to send representatives to an international conference to deliberate upon: (a) The subjects postponed by the Hague Conference; (b) The negotiation of arbitration treaties between the nations which shall be represented in this conference; (c) The establishment of an international congress which shall meet at stated periods to discuss international questions.

The resolutions were presented formally by a delegation of the Interparliamentary Union to President Roosevelt, "who immediately and without reserve pledged himself to the furtherance of the great cause".

Convocation of Second Hague Peace Conference

In fulfillment of the Presidential promise, Secretary of State John Hay on 21 October 1904 addressed a circular note to the governments signatory to the acts of The Hague Conference of 1899 inquiring to what extent they were disposed to join in a second conference at The Hague to continue the work of the First. The responses to the note were favorable, but Russia and Japan made reservations because of the war then existing between them in the Far East. Through the good offices of President Roosevelt, the Russo-Japanese War was concluded by the Treaty of Portsmouth signed 5 September 1905, whereupon the Russian Ambassador waited upon President Roosevelt and stated that his Government was ready to assume the responsibility of summoning the Second Conference. Dr. Scott records that "with the chivalry characteristic of our President, he gladly renounced to Russia the honor".[15]

The Second Peace Conference met at The Hague on 15 June 1907 in the Hall of the Knights. The delegation of the United States was headed by Joseph H. Choate, former American Ambassador to Great Britain, with two additional commissioners plenipotentiary with the rank of ambassador – Horace Porter, former American Ambassador to France, and Uriah M. Rose; three commissioners plenipotentiary with the rank of minister – David Jayne Hill, American Minister at The Hague; William J. Buchanan, former United States Minister to Argentina and Panama; Brigadier General George B. Davis, Judge Advocate General of the United States Army; and Rear Admiral Charles S. Sperry, former President of the United States Naval War College. Dr. Scott was accredited as a technical delegate and expert in international law. In that capacity he was authorized to take part in the work of the commissions, subcommissions, and committees and in the deliberations of the plenary meetings at the Conference. Charles Henry Butler, Re-

---

[15] Ibid., I, p. 93.

porter of the decisions of the Supreme Court of the United States, was accredited as a technical delegate and expert attaché of the delegation. There were also a secretary and two assistant secretaries.

The subjects on the agenda of the Conference were divided between four commissions, the first dealing with arbitration and international commissions of inquiry, and the other three with military and naval questions. The official roster shows that Dr. Scott was registered as a member of the two subcommissions of the First Commission, as well as of the subcommissions of the other commissions, but his activities were centered mainly on arbitration and an international court of justice. He was also a member of the general Drafting Committee of the Conference and of its subcommittee consisting of a single delegate from each of the Great Powers and the Netherlands. In addition, he served on three editing committees known as committees of examination appointed by the Commissions, and several smaller special committees.

It is believed that his committee assignments were more numerous than those of any other member of the American delegation. His knowledge of history and international law and his facility in the French language made his services very valuable at a European conference.

Towards an International Court of Justice

The establishment of an international court of justice was a major objective of the United States in participating in the First Hague Conference of 1899. Secretary of State John Hay, in his instructions to the American delegates to that conference, expressed the view that "The duty of sovereign States to promote international justice by all wise and effective means is only secondary to the fundamental necessity of preserving their own existence. Next in importance to their independence is the great fact of their interdependence. Nothing can secure for human government for the authority of law which it represents so deep a respect and so firm a loyalty as the spectacle of sovereign and independent States, whose duty it is to prescribe the rules of justice and impose penalties upon the lawless, bowing with reverence before the august supremacy of those principles of right which give to law its eternal foundation".

"The establishment of an international court", he said, "would express the desires and aspirations of this nation" as shown by "the long-continued and widespread interest among the people of the United States". He attached to his instructions an historical resumé demonstrating that interest as shown in resolutions of state legislatures and the Congress of the United States from the early days of the nation. The proposed Conference at The Hague, Secretary Hay thought, "promises an opportunity thus far unequalled in the history of the world for initiating a series of negotiations that may lead to important practical results". He accordingly handed them a Plan for an International Tribunal, enjoining them to propose it at an opportune moment and to use their influence in the Conference in the most effective manner possible to promote the adoption of its substance or of resolutions directed to the same purpose.[16]

The efforts of the American Delegation in 1899 culminated in the establishment of the so-called Permanent Court of Arbitration under the Convention for the Pacific Settlement of International Disputes. Upon their return from the Conference, the American Delegates reported to Secretary of State Hay:

"On the assembling of the Conference the feeling regarding the establishment of an actual permanent tribunal was evidently chaotic, with little or no apparent tendency to crystallize into any satisfactory institution. The very elaborate and in the main excellent proposals relating to procedure before special and temporary tribunals, which were presented by the Russian delegation, did not at first contemplate the establishment of any such permanent institution. The American plan contained a carefully devised project for such a tribunal, which differed from that adopted mainly in contemplating a tribunal capable of meeting in full bench and permanent in the exercise of its functions, like the Supreme Court of the United States, instead of a court like the supreme court of the State of New York, which never sits as a whole, but whose members sit from time to time singly or in groups, as occasion may demand".

When Mr. Hay's successor as Secretary of State, Mr. Elihu Root, came to the writing of his instructions to the American Delegates to the Second Peace Conference at The Hague, he took up the

---

[16] *Instructions to the American Delegates to the Hague Peace Conferences and Their Official Reports*, edited with an introduction by James Brown Scott (New York: Oxford University Press, for the Carnegie Endowment, 1916), pp. 6–16.

effort in behalf of a permanent tribunal where it had been left by the First Conference. In his letter to them of 31 May 1907, Secretary Root said that it should be their effort "to bring about in the Second Conference a development of the Hague tribunal into a permanent tribunal composed of judges who are judicial officers and nothing else, who are paid adequate salaries, who have no other occupation, and who will devote their entire time to the trial and decision of international causes by judicial methods and under a sense of judicial responsibility". If and when the court were established, Secretary Root thought the "judges should be so selected from the different countries that the different systems of law and procedure and the principal languages shall be fairly represented". Moreover, he thought "the court should be made of such dignity, consideration, and rank that the best and ablest jurists will accept appointment to it, and that the whole world will have absolute confidence in its judgments".[17]

In urging the need for such a permanent court, Secretary Root directed attention to the distinction between arbitration and the judicial settlement of international disputes: "The two methods are radically different, proceed from different standards of honorable obligation, and frequently lead to widely differing results". The "principal objection to arbitration", he explained, "rests not upon the unwillingness of nations to submit their controversies to impartial arbitration, but upon an apprehension that the arbitrations to which they submit may not be impartial. It has been a very general practice for arbitrators to act, not as judges deciding questions of fact and law upon the record before them under a sense of judicial responsibility, but as negotiators effecting settlements of the questions brought before them in accordance with the traditions of usages and subject to all the considerations and influences which affect diplomatic agents . . . It frequently happens", he continued, "that a nation which would be very willing to submit its differences to an impartial judicial determination is unwilling to submit them to this kind of diplomatic process". From all of which he concluded "If there could be a tribunal which would pass upon questions between nations with the same impartial and impersonal judgment that the Supreme Court of the United States gives to questions arising between citizens of the different States, or between foreign

---

[17] Ibid., pp. 79–80.

citizens and the citizens of the United States, there can be no doubt that nations would be much more ready to submit their controversies to its decision than they are now to take the chances of arbitration".[18]

Unlike Secretary of State Hay in 1899, Secretary of State Elihu Root did not attach a plan for an international tribunal to his instructions to the American delegation to the Second Hague Conference. He left that plan to be drawn at the Conference. The work of drafting the project was assigned by the American delegation to its technical members, Messrs. Charles Henry Butler and James Brown Scott.[19]

The draft of six articles was presented and urged for adoption by the head of the American delegation, Mr. Choate, on 1 August 1907.[20] In presenting it, Mr. Choate quoted from a Letter written by President Theodore Roosevelt to Andrew Carnegie on 5 April 1907, on the occasion of the National Arbitration and Peace Conference which opened in New York on 15 April of that year. The President expressed the hope "to see the Hague Court greatly increased in power and permanency and the judges in particular made permanent and given adequate salaries so as to make it increasingly probable that in each case that may come before them they will decide between the nations, great and small, exactly as a judge within our own limits decides between the individuals, great or small, who come before him". After alluding to the limited use made of the Permanent Court of Arbitration established at The Hague in 1899, Mr. Choate suggested improving it along the lines indicated in Secretary's Root's instructions, as follows:

---

[18] Ibid., p. 79.

[19] See Scott, *American Addresses at the Second Hague Peace Conference*, pp. 206-209. Mr. Butler was the author of a standard work on *The Treaty-Making Power of the United States*, and was for many years corresponding secretary of the American Society of International Law.

[20] Ninth Meeting, First Subcommission of the First Commission, to which had been committed proposals for improvements to be made in the Convention of 1899 relative to the Pacific Settlement of International Disputes. The American draft came up in regular order when the Subcommission reached the provisions of the 1899 Convention relating to the Permanent Court of Arbitration. *The Proceedings of the Hague Peace Conferences*, transl. of Official Texts by the Carnegie Endowment for International Peace, II, p. 312 (hereinafter: Translation of the Hague Proceedings).

> The fact that there was nothing permanent or continuous or connected in the sessions of the court, or in the adjudication of the cases submitted to it, has been an obvious source of weakness and want of prestige in the tribunal. Each trial it had before it has been wholly independent of every other, and its occasional utterances widely distant in point of time and disconnected in subject-matter, have not gone far towards constituting a consistent body of international law or of valuable contributions to international law, which ought to emanate from an international tribunal representing the power and might of all the nations. In fact it has thus far been a court only in name – a framework for the selection of referees for each particular case, never consisting of the same judges. It has done great good as far as it has been permitted to work at all, but our efforts should be to try and make a tribunal which shall be the medium of vastly greater and constantly increasing benefit to the nations and to mankind at large.
>
> Let us then seek to develop out of it a permanent court, which shall hold regular and continuous sessions, which shall consist of the same judges, which shall pay due heed to its own decisions, which shall speak with the authority of the united voice of the nations, and gradually build up a system of international law, definite and precise, which shall command the approval and regulate the conduct of the nations. By such a step in advance we shall justify the confidence which has been placed in us and shall make the work of this Second Conference worthy of comparison with that of the Conference of 1899.[21]

The American project did not go into the details of the constitutions, powers, and character of the proposed court. These, Mr. Choate suggested, should be the result of consultation and conference among all the nations represented in a suitable committee to be appointed by the President of the Commission.

Mr. Choate spoke in English. For the benefit of the delegates who did not fully understand him, a translation in French was immediately read by Baron d'Estournelles de Constant, of the French Delegation. This became routine throughout the conference whenever Mr. Choate spoke. Dr. Scott followed in French, explaining at length the views of the American delegation.

The American proposal met with general approval. There was considerable feeling, however, that the existing Court of Arbitra-

---

[21] Ibid., II, p. 314.

tion, from which nations voluntarily selected their own arbitrators as each case arose, should not be supplanted by a permanent court of the same judges to whom all disputes would have to be submitted. Mr. Choate gave assurance that the American plan "does not in the least depart from the voluntary character of the Court already established" and that "no nation can be compelled or constrained" to go before the proposed new court. From the discussion which followed, it seemed likely that no plan for establishing a new court would have been accepted as a complete substitute for the old court. The American plan was kept alive only as an alternative tribunal with freedom of choice between the old and the new courts by the prospective litigants. Other plans were introduced but were later withdrawn.

Some of the smaller powers reserved their approval until an acceptable method of electing the judges of the proposed new court had been devised. The American plan provided for a court of fifteen judges to be "appointed in the manner to be determined by this Conference". Under the theory of sovereign equality among States, each nation would be entitled to membership on the court, and as there were forty-four[22] nations represented at the Second Hague Conference, equal representation would have results in a court of as many judges, obviously too unwieldy for a judicial body.

Following two days of general discussion, it was decided on 3 August to proceed with a detailed consideration of the American plan and to appoint a committee for that purpose as suggested by Mr. Choate. He also suggested that all other plans for a permanent tribunal be referred to the same committee, which was done.[23]

Dr. Scott was selected to be the reporter of the committee, which became known as the Committee of Examination B.[24] It held eight meetings, from 13 August to 18 September.[25] During the last ten days from the date of its appointment of 3 August and the start of the meetings of the Committee on 13 August, a new project was elaborated by Germany, the United States, and Great Britain. A

---

[22] Forty-six nations were invited to the Conference, but two—Costa Rica and Honduras—did not attend.

[23] Tenth Meeting of the First Subcommission, Translation of the Hague Proceedings, p. 354.

[24] For the full membership of Committee of Examination B, see Translation of the Hague Proceedings, p. 595.

[25] The proceedings of those meetings are recorded in ibid., pp. 595–706.

writer on "The Origin of the Hague Arbitral Courts" stated, "I believe I am not far from the truth in suggesting that Herr Kriege, Dr. Scott, and Eyre Crowe, technical delegates of these respective powers, were jointly responsible for the resultant project of convention, in full harmony with the other members of their delegations. This project was a new and much more elaborate thing than the American proposal, and it may be said that the idea of the projected court took definite form only in its twenty-six articles".[26]

The joint project was deposited at the first session of the Committee of Examination B on 13 August by Mr. Choate, who made a speech urging its adoption on behalf of the three sponsoring governments. He said, "Ever since the appointment of the committee of examination this project has been the object of serious study by the three Governments of Germany, the United States, and Great Britain. We shall be much disappointed if it be not accepted".

The discussion of the articles was so thorough, beginning with the title of the proposed court, that a drafting committee was immediately named to revise the articles as they passed through the debate. Dr. Scott represented his government on this six-member drafting committee.[27] The title given to the proposed permanent court in the joint project was "International High Court of Justice". This was objected to because it "would somewhat correspond to the idea of 'United States of the World', an idea which would be very harmful to the development of arbitration". It was argued further that "it is essential that we should leave to arbitration the dominating place which belongs to it in the organization of international justice. Without it we would gradually slip into the Utopia of the United States of the World". To all of which Mr. Choate replied, "We shall leave it to the committee to baptize the child ... After the child shall have been baptized it is not its name, but its acts, that will make it succeed in life".

The crucial question of electing the judges to constitute the court came up for discussion at the second session of the Committee of Examination on 17 August. Dr. Scott, speaking in French, developed the basis of the German-American-British plan and introduced tables,[28] which the committee had prepared providing that

---

[26] Denys P. Myers, "The Origin of the Hague Arbitral Courts", *American Journal of International Law*, X (1916), p. 301. See Dr. Scott's Statement, p. 84.
[27] Translation of the Hague Proceedings, p. 601.
[28] See Translation of the Hague Proceedings, pp. 609–613.

each of the eight great powers should be permanently represented on the court by a judge, and making provision for nine additional members to be elected by the signatories to serve in rotation for staggered periods of varying lengths of time according to the relative statistics of population, industry, and commerce of the respective signatories. The ingenious manner in which Dr. Scott presented that difficult proposition can only be appreciated by reproducing his remarks *in extenso*:

> The project for the organization and jurisdiction of a permanent court, which the three delegations have had the honor to lay before the committee, necessarily presupposes the presence of judges, for without their presence the court exists, if at all, in name, not in fact. The selection of the judges, therefore, is of fundamental importance, and it may be said that the creation of the court depends in a large measure upon a method of selection which shall satisfy the legitimate desires of the countries represented at the Conference.
>
> If each country were to appoint one judge, and if these judges so appointed should be entitled to sit at one and the same time, the problem would be simple. Forty-six judges, however, form a judicial assembly, not a court. We wish, however, a court, not a judicial assembly. It would seem that a court of the kind we propose could not consist of more than fifteen or seventeen members without becoming unwieldy, and on that theory it is necessary that some means be devised for the selection of that or of a smaller number. The difficulty of the problem is at once apparent, but difficult as it is, the problem must be solved. It is evident that no plan can be satisfactory which does not give to every state the right to representation, for in international law the equality of right is axiomatic.
>
> Each State—be it large or small, an empire of one hundred million or a republic of a few hundred thousand—should possess the right to appoint, and should actually appoint, a judge of its own choice for the full period contemplated by the Convention, namely, twelve years. The exclusion of a single State from the proposed court, or the denial of the right of a single State to appoint, would proclaim the principle of juridical inequality and vitiate in advance a project, however carefully it be drawn and however acceptable it might otherwise be.

Having paid homage to the principle of the sovereign equality of all nations, Dr. Scott proceeded in an attempt to convince his hearers that the acceptance of the principle of rotation for some of the judges would not be in derogation of that axiomatic principle of international law.

> It may be admitted, however, that the exercise of the right might be regulated without in any way questioning the existence of the right. If every nation has the right to appoint, and does appoint, a judge, it is no derogation from the principle of sovereignty and equality that the judges so selected may sit at various times and in rotation. . .
>
> Animated by the desire to establish the court and to contribute effectively to its creation, we submit, with great diffidence, to your careful consideration a plan, frankly admitting its imperfections, but feeling that it may be acceptable unless a better plan should be proposed. The plan which we lay before you is based, in general, upon the principle of population, for we believe it self-evident that large aggregations of people have large interests, and that there is, in general, a relation between population on one hand and industry and commerce on the others.
>
> We also believe that industry and commerce give rise to conflicts, and that it may well be that a nation with a very numerous population, and with large commercial and industrial interests, feels it necessary to have a constant representation in the court, in order that its interests may be protected and safeguarded by a judge of its own choice.
>
> We admit, however, that the interest of the smaller nation is just as keen, although their conflicts may be less frequent or less serious; and it would seem just, therefore, that no nation, however small it may be, should be deprived of the same right to watch over and protect its interests by a judge of its own choice.
>
> We do not believe that any one principle should be pushed to its logical extreme without due regard to other interests. The theorist and logician might be content to rise or fall in the defense of a principle adopted by him. The practical man – the man of affairs, the statesman – must many a time modify, indeed sacrifice, a principle, however just, to meet a present and pressing need.
>
> While, therefore, we have adopted population in general as a satisfactory principle, we have at one and the same time consciously departed from the principle in order to do justice to various other material interests.
>
> We have also felt that the systems of law at present existing in the civilized world should be considered, and we have not hesitated to depart from the principle of population, or to give less attention to industry and commerce, when different systems of jurisprudence demanded recognition. Nor have we been unmind-

> ful of the traditions of the past, and we confess that in apportioning representation in the court we have not overlooked the fact that great traditions have a pressing claim upon us, and that they may well of themselves modify the results that would spring from the rigid application of an abstract principle. Questions of political geography have influenced us, and we have taken into consideration the geographical situation as affecting the liability to international conflict.
>
> Should we apply exclusively the principle of population without taking into consideration other elements which complicate the problem, we feel that injustice might be done to less populous States. But whatever these elements may be, we must insist that no distinction be made between the States of Europe and of America possessing approximately the same qualifications, whether those qualifications be population, industry, or commerce.
>
> It seems to us, therefore, possible to assign to certain States a permanent representation in the court, and, with due regard to population, industry, system of law, and language, to permit each State representation for a longer or shorter period by a system of rotation.

The tables which he laid before the Conference gave the terms of judges of the nine powers, other than the permanent members of the eight Great Powers, for each of the twelve-year terms for which all of the judges would be elected. Judges from three countries were to serve for ten years, judges from thirteen countries for four years, from four countries for two years, and from eighteen countries for one year. The terms of judges to serve more than one year were not to be for consecutive years, but divided into staggered periods. For example, the ten years' service of the Spanish judge during the full term of twelve years for which he would be elected, was to be accomplished by rotating him off the bench in the fourth and tenth years of the court's calendar.

The following analysis of the tables was then made by Dr. Scott:

> A careful analysis of the table which we have the honor to lay before you shows that in each year the various languages, the various systems of law, will be represented, and that the Spanish-American law will be represented every year by two or more judges out of the seventeen.
>
> It should be stated further that each country entitled to appoint a judge is entitled to appoint a deputy judge for a like period, and that in the absence of the principal judge the deputy may sit.

> Should the State prefer to appoint one judge for a term and the same judge as a deputy for a like period, it would follow that it could in this way acquire an additional representation, as will appear from the table before you.
>
> The method suggested leaves to each State the right to be represented, and regulates, it is hoped, in a fair and equitable manner the exercise of this right. Should, however, nations prefer to combine, thus forming groups, and elect judges and deputy judges for the sum total of their terms, the system proposed is flexible enough to permit this. Each State is thus left entire liberty, either to be represented directly by a judge of its own nation or to combine with others to select a common judge for a longer period.

Suppose it should have happened in a given case that a government plaintiff or defendant before the court was not represented upon the bench by a judge of its own choice. In such event, Dr. Scott replied that his committees are

> Prepared to submit a plan which will permit the appointment of a judge of each of the litigant parties when such judge is not already upon the bench. In this way each nation before the court may be represented by agent, advocate, and counsel in order to see that its case is properly presented to the consideration of the court, and will have, in addition, a judge upon the bench itself in order to see that the case, as presented, receives the careful consideration of the court. The rights of the litigants will thus be protected and safeguarded in the council chamber as well as in the court room.

He concluded his address by the following general observations:

> We are conscious, however, that the plan we present to you, however correct or acceptable it may be in principle, and however satisfactory it may be in practice, is nevertheless open to criticism. We assure you, however, that the plan presented is not the result of a sudden inspiration, but is the product of careful, indeed painstaking, examination of the problem and the means by which it may be met and solved.
>
> We feel that each State will consider itself entitled to greater consideration than is assigned to it, but we hope the system we propose is so reasonable as to prove acceptable – at least in theory.
>
> It will be noted that the table presented is based upon the juridical equality of all the States represented in or invited to the Conference, and that each State, therefore, has and must have the

> right to appoint a judge for the proposed court, even though the judges may serve in rotation and for shorter periods. In proposing that the judges appointed by Germany, the United States, Austria-Hungary, France, Great Britain, Italy, Japan and Russia serve for the full period of the Convention, we do not lose sight of the juridical equality, but recognize the fact that the greater population, industry and commerce of these States entitle them to a correspondingly greater, that is larger, participation in the court. It should be noted, however, that although the judges of these populous States would form a permanent nucleus, they do not constitute the quorum of the court.
>
> It may well be that other and different combinations will be more satisfactory to the members of the committee. We present this plan for the composition of the court in the hope that it may at least serve as a basis for discussion and suggestion, even though it should not be acceptable in all its details.

The method of electing the judges by a system of rotation, and all other methods proposed, turned out to be unacceptable to the Powers not accorded continuous representation on the court. The discussion of this question provided the opportunity for several fervid orations on the equality of nations by opponents who refused to accept Dr. Scott's explanation that the plan was in conformance with that principle. The joint project passed through three readings and to save it from defeat on the question of the composition of the court, articles relating thereto had to be withdrawn. At the final session of the Committee of Examination on 18 September, the project was approved by a close vote, on a motion of Sir Edward Fry, the chief British delegate, as amended by Mr. Choate, which read, "The Conference recommends to the signatory Powers the adoption of the project, hereunto annexed, of a Convention for the Establishment of a Court of Arbitral Justice, and putting it in force as soon as an agreement has been reached upon the selection of judges and the constitution of the Court".[29]

Delegates of eight countries voted for the Fry-Choate motion, five voted against, and two abstained.

The project as thus approved by the Committee of Examination was made the order of business at the session of the First Commission held 9 October. The report of Dr. Scott, as Reporter of the Committee of Examination, was presented first. Delegates of a

---

[29] Translation of the Hague Proceedings, pp. 701–705.

dozen other governments made speeches or critical comments. On the following day, 10 October, when the reading of the articles began, they were approved by overwhelming votes of 37 for to 3 against, with 4 abstentions. When the Fry-Choate motion was reached in the course of Dr. Scott's report, it was held to be technically a declaration and passed along to the Plenary Session of the Conference subject to the unanimity rule prevailing there. It was brought up at the Ninth Plenary Session of the Conference on 16 October. Before recognizing Dr. Scott as the reporter on the project, the President of the Conference, M. Nelidov of Russia, referred to the work of the First Commission for the institution of a Permanent Court of Arbitral Justice as a "conscientious and learned study, the details of which ... will furnish very valuable material for those who will consider the question later on, and will be an honor to this Conference. Nevertheless", he continued, "we have had to take into consideration that the understanding necessary for the establishment and the operation of the projected institution has not been reached, and we have been obliged to confine ourselves to declaring the principles unanimously admitted and to turn over to our Governments the task of completing our work and reaching an agreement upon the means to put it into practice".[30]

Dr. Scott then made a formal statement requesting the Conference to adopt the recommendation approved in Committee of Examination B. He did not discuss the basis of the constitution of the court as, he explained, "the draft does not contain precise provisions upon the method of organization of the Court nor upon the choice of judges". These questions, he said, "were long discussed in the committee without any solution being reached which was acceptable to all the States represented. It is to be hoped that a basis for agreement may soon be found on this subject, and it is in this hope that the committee pronounces itself in favor of the adoption of the recommendation".[31]

The vote upon the recommendation was then taken, and it was adopted by 38 votes in favor, none against, with 6 abstentions. It appears as one of the *voeux* in the Final Act of the Conference. Writing upon the result after the close of the conference, Dr. Scott commented, "The fact of the Court was long in suspense. The op-

---

[30] Translation of the Hague Proceedings, I, p. 325.
[31] Ibid., I, pp. 326–327.

position to it was bitter at times. The existence of the Permanent Court of Arbitration made it more difficult to establish the new one, and it was not until the last day but one of the Conference that the project was adopted and referred to the Powers".[32]

In the report of the American Delegation to the Secretary of State, which was written by Dr. Scott, after describing the proposed court and its operation, he wrote this hopeful conclusion:

> It is evident that the foundations of a Permanent Court have been broadly and firmly laid; that the organization, jurisdiction, and procedure have been drafted and recommended in the form of a code which the Powers or any number of them may accept and, by agreement upon the appointment of the judges, call into being a Court at once permanent and international. A little time, a little patience, and the great work is accomplished.

Towards Compulsory Arbitration

Following the Hague Convention of 1899, a great many nations concluded separate treaties of arbitration. The treaties followed the general pattern of stipulating to refer to the Permanent Court of Arbitration established at The Hague by the Convention of 1899 "differences which may arise of a legal nature, or relating to the interpretation of treaties existing between the two contracting parties, ... which it may not have been possible to settle by diplomacy ... provided, nevertheless, that they do not affect the vital interests, the independence, or the honor of the contracting states, and do not concern the interests of third parties" (Article I).

Great Britain concluded a series of ten such treaties, beginning with France, on 14 October 1903. President Theodore Roosevelt, in his message to Congress on 7 December of that year, stated:

> There seems ground for the belief that there has been a real growth among the civilized nations of a sentiment which will permit a gradual substitution of other methods than the method of war in the settlement of disputes. It is not pretended that as yet we are near a position in which it will be possible wholly to pre-

[32] Scott, "Work of the Second Hague Peace Conference", *American Journal of International Law*, II (1908), p. 26.

> vent war, or that a just regard for national interest and honor will in all cases permit of the settlement of international disputes by arbitration; but by a mixture of prudence and firmness with wisdom we think it is possible to do away with much of the provocation and excuse for war, and at least in many cases to substitute some other and more rational method for the settlement of disputes. The Hague court offers too good an example of what can be done in the direction of such settlement that it should be encouraged in every way.[33]

In the following year, on 20 October, Secretary of State John Hay sent instructions to American diplomatic officers accredited to the signatories of the Hague Convention directing them to inquire whether the governments to which they were accredited would be willing to sign similar treaties with the Government of the United States. As a result of these inquiries, Secretary Hay, in December 1904 and June 1905, concluded separate arbitration treaties with ten other countries.

Article II of the treaties was in the standard form providing that "In each individual case the high contracting parties, before appealing to the Permanent Court of Arbitration, shall conclude a special agreement defining clearly the matter in dispute, the scope of the powers of the arbitrators, and the periods to be fixed for the formation of the Arbitral Tribunal and the several stages of the procedure".

The Senate advised and consented to the ratification of the Hay treaties, but with an amendment providing that the special agreement required by Article II should be subject to submission to and approval by the Senate. Secretary Hay declined to accept the Senate's amendment and refused to proceed with the exchange of ratifications of the treaties.

In his instructions to the American delegates to the Second Hague Peace Conference, Secretary of State Elihu Root expressed the view that so many separate treaties of arbitration had been made between individual countries since the First Conference as to bring the subject of a general treaty of obligatory arbitration into the field of practical discussion. To secure such a treaty, he instructed the delegates to use their best and most earnest efforts. At the same time, he informed them of the Senate's attitude concerning the Hay arbitration treaties and cautioned them to avoid having the same

---

[33] John B. Moore, *Digest of International Law*, VII, p. 102.

question arise regarding any general arbitration treaty they might sign at The Hague by accompanying their signatures with an explanation of the necessity of submitting each special agreement to the Senate.

Proposals for a general treaty of obligatory arbitration came up for consideration at the Conference before the Commission which dealt with improvements to be made in the provisions of the 1899 Convention relative to the Pacific Settlement of International Disputes. Dr. Scott was made a member of that Commission. At its first meeting on 22 June 1907, its president, M. Leon Bourgeois of France, inquired whether "it would not be of a considerable moral importance to consolidate by a common engagement the stipulations already concluded separately between the various nations". When the Commission met on 25 June, the subject of arbitration was referred to the First Subcommission. All of the civilian members of the American delegation, including Dr. Scott, were made members of the subcommission. In addition, Dr. Scott was designated to assist in the work of the secretariat of the subcommission headed by Baron d'Estournelles de Constant of France. It was decided to take the Convention of 1899 as the basis of discussion and to proceed with the reading of the text article by article against the projects for revision that had been submitted by various governments. General discussion of the articles continued until the fourth meeting of 9 July, when a Committee of Examination was appointed. Dr. Scott was designated by Mr. Choate to represent the United States on that committee.

At the sixth meeting of the Subcommission on 18 July, Mr. Choate, speaking in English and followed by a summarized translation in French read by Baron d'Estournelles de Constant, presented the position of the United States on the principle of obligatory arbitration, and submitted a project pursuant to Secretary Root's instructions. It included an article providing that the special agreement (*compromis*) in each particular case shall be concluded "conformably to the constitution or laws of the high contracting parties". Mr. Choate explained that "the form of this article is rendered necessary by the constitutional needs of securing for every such agreement or protocol, before it can become effective, the approval of some other branch of the government besides the one which signs the agreement as part of the treaty-making power; for instance, in the United States, the Senate of the United States, and, as is believed, other departments of government in many other states".

At the next meeting of the Subcommission, 23 July, the chief delegate of Germany, Baron Marschall von Bieberstein, referred to the long series of treaties of obligatory arbitration concluded between various states since the First Hague Conference as constituting general progress, but, he added, "it would be an error to believe that a general *compromis* clause agreed upon between two States can serve purely and simply as a model, or, so to speak, as a formula for a world treaty". He states the difference between the two cases as follows:

> Between two States which conclude a general treaty of obligatory arbitration, the field of possible differences is more or less under the eyes of the treaty makers. It is circumscribed by a series of concrete and familiar factors, such as the geographical situation of the two countries, their financial and economic relations, and the historic traditions which have grown up between them. In a treaty including all the countries of the world, these concrete factors are wanting, and hence, even in the restricted list of juristic questions, the possibility of differences of every kind is illimitable. It follows from this that a general *compromis* clause which, between two States, defines with sufficient clearness the rights and duties which flow from it, might be in a world treaty too vague and elastic and hence inapplicable.[34]

However, he argued, the reservations embodied in existing arbitration treaties and proposals submitted to the Conference did not conform with the idea of obligatory arbitration. Without mentioning the United States, he added: "Even the appearance of a bilateral obligation disappears in the dealing with countries where, in virtue of their constitutions, the decision with regard to the application of a *compromis* clause does not eventually belong to the signatory government, but to a legislative element". Therefore, Germany favored only retaining the general principle of arbitration stated in Article 16 of the 1899 Convention. Its chief delegate was not convinced that the new phraseology proposed was more compulsory than the existing one. He referred to the conflict in Roman law between *obligatio* and *mera facultas*, and observed: "You will

---

[34] Translation of the Hague Proceedings, II, p. 286.

forgive an old jurist for being skeptical with regard to an attempt to reconcile these enemies".

Sir Edward Fry, chief delegate of Great Britain, at the following meeting, 27 July, supported the American project. He referred to the series of ten obligatory arbitration treaties concluded by his country since 1903 for the settlement of questions of law and of the interpretation of diplomatic documents. The experience of Great Britain led that country to believe that the time had come to take a forward step by concluding a general agreement for the settlement by arbitration of any questions susceptible of such solution. He did not agree that such an agreement would be weak and indefinite from the juridical point of view. He answered that "nations are not solely governed by juridical conceptions, nor are they only inter-united by the *vincula juris*". He believed that "the treaty which we have in mind will be of great importance in history as being a collective expression of the consensus of the civilized world".

The Subcommmission concluded on that day its general examination of the articles on International Arbitration of the Convention of 1899 and referred them to the Committee of Examination to which Dr. Scott had already been appointed.[35]

The Committee of Examination had already held its first meeting on 13 July to begin the consideration of the revision of the Convention of 1899 for the Pacific Settlement of International Disputes. The articles covering Good Offices and Mediation and International Commissions of Inquiry were first taken up. At the fifth meeting, held 3 August, the various projects on obligatory arbitration reached the Committee. It will be recalled that the American formula, based upon the separate arbitration treaties already concluded, called for the reference of disputes to the Permanent Court of Arbitration at The Hague. A general objection was at once raised in the Committee to the consideration of proposals which would oblige the signatories to submit their disputes to that court. Upon the motion of M. Ruy Barbosa, chief delegate of Brazil, the Committee decided that the term "obligatory arbitration" referred to the principle only and not to the character of the arbitral tribunal. This led Dr. Scott at the next meeting of the Committee of 6 August to declare that the American proposition had in view only obligatory

---

[35] The complete membership of the Committee may be found in Translation of the Hague Proceedings, II, p. 375.

arbitration and was not intended to establish one single competent court. The American project was accordingly amended to eliminate reference to the Permanent Court of Arbitration at The Hague and to substitute instead merely the word "arbitration".

Dr. Kriege, the second delegate of Germany, repeated in the Committee Baron von Bieberstein's objections to a general treaty of obligatory arbitration, and added others. He disagreed with the argument in the subcommission of the chief delegate of Great Britain. He said that the acceptance of any of the projects would be obligatory in form only and not in essence, and thus run the danger of compromising the great idea of obligatory arbitration. Therefore, the German delegation intended to vote against all propositions.[36] Commenting later on Dr. Kriege's speech, Dr. Scott wrote: "Dr. Drago, sitting next to me, wrote on a slip of paper: "This is the death of arbitration", and it was. Weeks of discussion failed to overcome the opposition of Germany and its slender following".[37]

In subsequent meetings of the Committee, which continued until 4 September, the delegate of Austria-Hungary joined with the German delegates in criticizing the American article providing for the submission of the *compromis* to the Senate. These criticisms became so pointed that at the fourteenth meeting of the Committee, on 31 August, Dr. Scott made a detailed reply, as follows:

> In considering the *compromis*, we must be careful not to exaggerate its importance and make it the matter of supreme moment, to the detriment or exclusion of the treaty, for the *compromis* depends upon the treaty and has no independent existence. If there is no treaty, there can be no *compromis*. If we consider the nature of the treaty as an international act, we shall be better able to appreciate the nature and importance of the *compromis*.
>
> A treaty is an agreement between two or more nations both willing and able to agree. A contract is the solemn expression in legal form of the realized intention of the parties. If concluded between individuals, it is a contract of private law; if concluded between States, it is a public contract to which we give the name of treaty. The act of the parties expressed in terms of law carries with it the obligation to do or not to do a particular act, and pledges their good faith to the performance of the act in all its

---

[36] Translation of the Hague Conference Proceedings, II, p. 420.

[37] *The Hague Peace Conferences of 1899 and 1907* (Baltimore: The Johns Hopkins Press, 1909), p. 128.

parts. There are two kinds of treaties. The first creates a status complete in itself without further action on the part of the contracting parties. There is, however, a second class which creates mutual rights and duties and binds each party to the strict observance of its terms. It is only necessary to cite the instance of the treaty providing for the payment of a sum of money. Such a treaty obligates the contracting party to raise the sum required in accordance with the rules of its internal organization, and to pay the debt in order to extinguish its obligation. It is the treaty that creates the international obligation, but its execution depends upon the cooperation of a branch or department of the internal administration. Whether this internal organ be composed of one or many persons is a matter of indifference to international law, for international law has nothing to do with the domestic machinery by which or through which the international duty is performed.

But to return to the *compromis*. We shall suppose that the contracting parties foresee that the interpretation of the treaty and consequently its execution may give rise to a divergence of views, perhaps to serious disagreement. They therefore agree in advance to adjust their differences peaceably and provide by arbitration an impartial and final settlement. But in order to submit the controversy to arbitration it is necessary that the parties agree upon the issue or the question to be submitted. This is the substance and essence of the *compromis* as prescribed by Article 31 of the Convention for the Pacific Settlement of International Disputes, and by Article 4 of the American project.

The formulation of the issue is the result of negotiation and is only reached when the parties in conflict are agreed upon the points in controversy. If the claims of State A are unreasonable, it cannot be expected that State B will accept them, nor can we hope for an agreement if the counterclaims of State B are unacceptable. It is only when negotiation has succeeded in eliminating all questions foreign to the controversy, and in ascertaining the exact question in dispute, that we have the basis of a settlement, and it is only when the formulation of the object and the exact determination of the issue are accepted by both parties that an agreement exists. To become binding it is necessary that the projected agreement be ratified in each of the States by the department or body charged with the conduct of foreign affairs. This may be a single individual, the responsible head of a State, or the chief executive acting in cooperation with an internal body or branch of the Government. For example, in the United States this power is lodged with the President by and with the advice and consent of the Senate. In any case the proposed accord is not binding until ratified by the competent power, and this competent power or branch of the Government is determined by the constitutions and the laws of the contracting parties. It is no doubt true that a single body or person will act more rapidly than a numerous body or complex organ, but it is not the domestic organ; it is the accord which interests us, for the organ, as previously stated, is indifferent to the eyes of international law. Thc moment that an obligation exist the channel through which it is executed has only an academic interest.

In order that this point may be clearly grasped (says Dr. Scott), and that there may be no misunderstanding as to the delay which might be necessary for bringing about the collaboration of the national organ, the United States has endeavored to express in clear and explicit terms the fact that the elaboration of the *compromis* depends upon the authority which is competent to conclude treaties. In America, for instance, it is the Executive and the Senate.

It may not always be necessary to submit the *compromis* to the Senate, and in practice this is not ordinarily done. The recent agreement to arbitrate the controversy arising out of the question of the Pious Funds and the *compromis* submitting the Venezuelan difficulties to arbitration were not submitted to the Senate. But we desire to reserve the right to submit the *compromis* to the Senate and we notify the contracting Powers of the reservation.

The refusal to accept an unreasonable *compromis* is not and cannot be a violation of a treaty. On the contrary, it is unreasonable to suppose than an unreasonable claim or pretension will be accepted as presented. The rejection of an unreasonable claim or pretension is not a breach of the contract, for the parties only bound themselves to accept a reasonable claim or pretension arising out of and connected with the contract. The refusal to accept simply means that the claim is unacceptable because it is unreasonable, and it is only when the claims and counterclaims are acceptable to the contracting parties that we can expect a *compromis* to be ratified. It is not to be supposed that a Government will reject an acceptable proposition. No single case of this kind has arisen in our history, and the question is and must remain purely academic. It is doubtless true that a treaty creates an obligation, a *juris vinculum*, but the refusal to agree to a *compromis* containing an unreasonable demand is no breach of a treaty imposing the acceptance of a reasonable contention. It is simply the rejection of an unacceptable *compromis*, not the breach of the treaty creating the duty to negotiate a *compromis*. The *compromis* is the result of the negotiation between two States upon the footing of absolute equality, from which it fol-

> lows necessarily that each State is the sole judge whether the proposed *compromis* is or is not acceptable.
>
> To sum up, if it is intended that the right to submit the elaboration of the *compromis* to national constitutional and legislative provisions must be reversed, *expressis verbis*, we fully admit the legality of this requirement. As far as we are concerned, the reservation goes without saying, imposes itself automatically; but, in order to avoid possible misunderstanding, which might lead to recriminations and cause our good faith to be suspected, we have deemed it necessary to state the situation fairly and squarely, such as it appears in the constitutional theory and practice of our country.[38]

All of the articles of the American project were approved in the Committee by substantial majorities. The Committee was proceeding on the understanding that its votes were provisional and subject to later reconsideration after all projects had been examined. It accordingly proceeded to discuss an Austro-Hungarian proposal intended as a substitute for all other proposals. It was limited to the addition of a short paragraph to Article 16 of the Convention of 1899 expressing the desirability of submitting to arbitration questions of a legal nature or involving the interpretation or application of treaties in so far as circumstances permit. This proposal received less than a majority of the votes of the Committee.

Since no project had received a sufficient number of votes to be approved in Committee under the rule of unanimity, the Reporter of the Committee, Baron Guillaume, of Belgium, was given the task of presenting the record before the First Commission for final action. His report on the revision of the entire Convention of 1899 was started in the meeting of the Commission on 4 October. Article 16 to which the subject of obligatory arbitration appertained was reached on the following day and several successive days, with sessions in the mornings and afternoons being devoted to it. The chief delegates of leading countries took part in the debate. When the articles in the American project were reached requiring the *compromis* in each case of arbitration to be concluded "conformably to the respective constitutions or laws of the signatory Powers", the chief delegate of Austria-Hungary returned to his attack upon the requirement of the United States Senate that every *compromis*

---

[38] Translation of the Hague Proceedings, II, pp. 522–524.

be approved by it. He argued that the refusal of the Government of the United States to ratify its arbitration treaty with Austria-Hungary after the Senate amended it showed that the Washington Cabinet itself considered the attitude of the Senate an obstacle to the enforcement of an arbitration treaty. This led Dr. Scott to deliver another speech on that subject in the meeting of the Commission on 7 October:

> . . . the American delegation is always happy to receive enlightenment and to learn something new about American constitutional law; for the objection to the *compromis*, that is, to the framing of the issue, is really an objection of a constitutional nature. The formulation of the *compromis*, to which so much importance is attached, is in our view merely a question of internal law, and we understand neither the reason nor the desire to make it a question of international law. From an international standpoint but one thing is important, namely, that the special agreement to arbitrate be concluded; but it is a matter of indifference by which branch of the Government this is done. Whether it is the act of the President or of the Secretary of State, his delegate, or the work of the Senate, or whether it requires the happy cooperation of the Senate and the President, matters little, for each of these organs acts in the name of the Government. The agreement to arbitrate is a governmental act, and international law applies only to a nation, and not to its organs, which have no personality in the law of nations.
>
> We are told that there is a marked difference between the manner in which the agreement to arbitration is concluded in a monarchy and the system which prevails in a republic, and much distrust is expressed regarding the latter. We cannot share this view. What does it matter whether the agreement to arbitrate is the act of an emperor or of his delegate, or whether it is the act of a limited body or even of the whole legislature? The main thing is that it be concluded, and the manner of concluding it is indifferent, as is also the organ of the government charged with this duty by the laws and constitutions of the various countries.
>
> It seems to us, moreover, that in attacking the *compromis* the existence of the treaty of arbitration is lost sight of. The *compromis* is in reality nothing without the treaty, for it is the treaty which creates an obligation to conclude it. Before concluding a *compromis*, there must be a treaty of arbitration which has been ratified by the proper authority (in the United States, the Senate) after having been negotiated by the executive. It is only then that there exists a *juris vinculum*, the famous legal obligation so often

mentioned by the irreconcilable and undaunted enemies of every stipulation for arbitration. When a particular case arises there exists, by virtue of a treaty, an obligation to conclude the *compromis*, but it is a general obligation; the legal obligation in such a case only comes into existence when the two nations bind themselves, or rather have bound themselves, by concluding the special agreement to arbitrate. If one of the two parties refuses to conclude this, it is clear that the other will not be obligated. How can it be asserted that one of the two nations can be bound if the other is not. The *compromis* is a special compact between two contracting parties, and as such it necessitates diplomatic negotiation, terminating in an understanding upon the form and the purport. Then only is the *juris vinculum* formed. If, for instance, a European nation is ready to conclude a *compromis* and presents a formula, it is not bound until its partner, for instance, the United States, has accepted the terms of the formula. But, on the contrary, if we suppose that, as is not at all improbable, the United States proposes the formula, there will be no obligation until the European nation, the empire of Austria-Hungary, has declared its acceptance of it. Before this there is nothing but a tentative proposal, there is no obligation contracted regarding the special subject of the controversy, and there is only a general obligation arising from the treaty of arbitration binding alike the two signatory Powers.

The opponents of arbitration reproach us with not furnishing them the *juris vinculum* necessary for their protection. More generous than even they desire, we are willing and ready to offer them not one *vinculum*, as they ask, but two, namely, one arising in the general treaty, and another resulting from the special *compromis*.

The fears of monarchical nations are therefore wholly unfounded. The *compromis* does not arise automatically. The two parties can only be obligated concurrently by their mutual consent, and no inequality can therefore exist between them. There is in reality no actual obligation upon which a material execution can be based, until the question, regarding which the *compromis* has been concluded, is submitted to the arbitrator and an award has rendered the *compromis* executory. If the *compromis* is not concluded, there is no foundation for the arbitral award and no one is bound by a non-existent judgment. Therefore, when a monarchical nation sees a danger to itself in its readiness to conclude a *compromis*, it is frightened by an imaginary peril.

Moreover, instead of discussing the way in which the *compromis* should be concluded, which is irrelevant to the present purpose, it would be much more appropriate to point out the cases in which the United States has refused to conclude a *compromis* after binding itself to do so by a general treaty of arbitration. Not a single instance of such a refusal has been cited. It is therefore to be inferred that none such exist, for otherwise, with the profound knowledge of the constitutional and diplomatic history of the United States possessed by our learned adversaries, they would not have failed to point them out. It is common knowledge that the United States has always been willing to conclude treaties of arbitration. Recourse to arbitration is our favorite method of settling international disputes, and our marked success whenever we have submitted them to arbitration furnishes the best demonstration of the fact that our country is in an excellent position to conclude the *compromis*. There is surely no need at The Hague, in the very city where the United States has successfully resorted to the august tribunal here established, to dwell longer upon this point.

We do not pretend that the conclusion of the agreement to arbitrate never presents a difficulty, but we do maintain that this difficulty is technical, not legal. It may well be that a monarchical country can overcome this difficulty more easily if the conclusion of the *compromis* depends in its case solely upon the will of one individual. Nevertheless it cannot elude it, for even a monarch or a minister must, as well as a collective body or a parliament, weigh the pros and cons and consider whether the *compromis* is or is not acceptable. The treaty of arbitration does not make it obligatory to conclude any but an acceptable *compromis*, and any other will be rejected by an individual will as well as by the will of a collective body. It may frequently happen that the preparation of the agreement by the latter requires more time, because the complex organ moves more slowly than the individual body. The difficulty, however, is not one of an international legal nature.

In its final analysis, whatever be the form of government, the question of the formulation of the *compromis* resolves itself, from the standpoint of international law, into a question of good faith. Every power which signs a clause of arbitration can obviously evade it, but there is no reason to suppose that the legislative body is less mindful of obligations assumed than are executive organs, or that a country which a parliamentary form of government is more inclined to violate its engagements than a country whose constitutional form of government is of an autocratic character. Whenever and wherever good faith exists, the settlement of the *compromis* can only be a question of time. Complications of an internal character will by no means prevent a nation careful of its honor from fulfilling its engagements. On

> the basis of international law the nation with which it has contracted can ask nothing more. The means of action furnished by the law of nations stops at the frontiers, and the foreign State may not concern itself about the manner in which the obligation, whose fulfillment it seeks, shall be executed. It is for the contracting State alone to determine the means of meeting its international duties.
>
> These truths are so self-evident that the article of the American project which has given rise to this discussion may well seem superfluous, but we have thought it advisable and necessary to dwell on this point in order that no misunderstanding shall arise regarding the delay which may sometimes be necessary in order to secure the cooperation of an internal body, for instance, in the United States, the Senate, which is alone competent to approve treaties negotiated by the executive.
>
> It may be, however, that it will not be necessary in every instance to submit the *compromis* to the Senate. This does not always happen in actual practice, and it has been observed that in the recent arbitration of the Pious Funds case and in the Venezuelan controversy the *compromis* was not submitted to the Senate. We have, however, felt obliged to reserve the right to submit the *compromis* to the Senate, and loyalty has compelled us to inform the Powers of this reservation. The reservation, however, merely means that the conclusion of the *compromis* is subject to the provisions of the Constitution and the internal laws, which would seem to follow as a matter of course. Therefore, in reserving the right in express terms we are actuated solely by a desire to avoid any possible misunderstanding, which might result in incriminations or recriminations likely to engender a suspicion of bad faith. For this reason we have thought it necessary to explain the situation frankly and fully, as it appears in the constitutional theory and practice of our country.[39]

The vote was taken immediately following this colloquy and the United States proposal was approved by a vote of 26 for, 7 against, and 9 abstentions.[40]

Objection was immediately raised by several delegates, including those of Austria-Hungary and Germany, to the inclusion of the American proposal on obligatory arbitration in the revision of the 1899 Convention under the threat that such action might compel

---

[39] Translation of the Hague Proceedings, II, pp. 110–113.
[40] Translation of the Hague Proceedings, II, p. 113.

those powers which voted against it to withhold their signature to the convention. The President of the Commission, Mr. Nelidov, who was also President of the Conference, expressed the opinion that the American project, not having obtained the approval of all the delegations, could not be inserted in a Convention adopted unanimously. Mr. Choate, on behalf of the American delegation, concurred in this view and suggested that the American proposal be incorporated in a separate convention.[41]

In the following session, 9 October, the delegate of Russia, Mr. Martens, proposed that the American project be annexed to the revised Convention of 1899 as a separate act to be binding only on such powers as sign or adhere to it. The delegates of Austria-Hungary and Germany immediately objected that the Russian proposal was out of order and not acceptable to them. The President refused to sustain the point of order and postponed discussion of the Russian compromise until the following day. At that time, Dr. Scott, speaking for the American delegation, states that the United States could not accept the Russian proposal. A vote was then taken, with 31 voting for, 5 against, and 8 abstentions; whereupon Mr. Martens withdrew the Russian proposal.

The Austro-Hungarian delegate requested a vote on his proposal which had been rejected in the Committee of Examination. He made an extended speech in support of it. Mr. Choate replied with vigor. He denounced the Austro-Hungarian proposal as absolutely contrary to the clearly manifested will of the overwhelming majority of the Commission. The feeble minority, he said, now proposes to annul everything that had been done in favor of obligatory arbitration during the last three months. He urged that "it is for the Conference alone to determine whether it will accept it with unanimity or with that approximate unanimity which we claim to be sufficient, and whether it shall find a place in the Final Act". He pleaded: "Let us hold on to that advanced ground which we have attained thus far". When the vote was taken, the Commission defeated the Austro-Hungarian proposition by 24 against, 14 for, and 6 abstentions. [42]

The President of the Commission at once proposed the appointment of a small committee of members representing the dif-

---

[41] Ibid., II, p. 118.
[42] Ibid., II, p. 176.

ferent opinions to draft a formula acceptable to everyone. His proposal was approved, and Dr. Scott was made a member of the small committee. This committee submitted a draft on the following day, reading as follows:

> The Commission,
>
> Actuated by the spirit of mutual agreement and concession characterizing the Peace Conference,
>
> Has resolved to present to the Conference the following declaration, which, while reserving to each of the States represented full liberty of action as regards voting, enables them to affirm the principles which they regard as unanimously admitted:
>
> The Committee is unanimous,
>
> 1. In admitting the principle of obligatory arbitration;
>
> 2. In declaring that certain disputes, in particular those relating to the interpretation and application of the provisions of international agreements, may be submitted to obligatory arbitration without any restriction.
>
> Finally, it is unanimous in proclaiming that, although it has not yet been found feasible to conclude a Convention in this sense, nevertheless, the divergences of opinion which have come to light have not exceeded the bounds of judicial controversy, and that, by working together here during the past four months, the collected States not only have learned to understand one another and to draw closer together, but have succeeded in the course of this long collaboration in evolving a very lofty conception of the common welfare of humanity.[43]

Mr. Choate expressed the keen disappointment of the American delegation at the failure to include the American project in the Final Act of the Conference, and announced that the delegation could not vote for the resolution without abandoning the principles for which it had so long contended; but in response to an appeal from the President for unanimity, the American delegation, with three others, abstained from voting. There being no vote against it, the resolution was declared unanimously adopted by the Commission. It came before the plenary session of the Conference on 16 October in the form of a declaration, where it was again unanimously adopted

---

[43] Ibid., II, p. 191.

by 41 votes, with 3 abstentions, including the United States.[44] It is so recorded in the Final act of the Conference.

Prize Jurisdiction

The circular note of the Czar of Russia proposing the First Peace Conference at The Hague was issued on the very day, 12 August 1898, that the United States and Spain signed the armistice ending hostilities in the Spanish-American War. By the terms of the armistice, confirmed in the Treaty of Peace signed at Paris on 10 December 1898, the United States ended its exclusive status as a North American continental Power, then and still erroneously and derogatively described as one of isolation from the rest of the world. Up to that time, its defense periphery was embodied in the Monroe Doctrine. As the result of its victory in the Spanish-American War, the United States took over the sovereignty and became responsible as a world power for the ceded Spanish Islands in the Caribbean Sea and the Pacific Ocean. Simultaneously, the unsettled political conditions in the Hawaiian Islands were brought to an end by the joint resolution adopted by Congress on 7 July 1898, providing for the annexation of the islands to the United States. The transfer of sovereignty actually took place on the same day, 12 August, as the armistice was signed with Spain.

The domestic political issue involved in the expansion of our foreign policy, labeled Imperialism v. Anti-Imperialism, was fought out in the campaign of 1899 between President William McKinley and William Jennings Bryan, and decided in favor of the former. However, the concept of a Monroe Doctrine for the world did not become part of our political thinking until it was introduced by President Woodrow Wilson in defense of his proposal for United States membership in the League of Nations following World War I. The advice and practice of Washington and Jefferson of abstention from entangling alliances with Europe and neutrality in its political quarrels were still regarded at the turn of the century as inviolable cardinal principles of American foreign policy. Accordingly, the delegates of the United States, when signing the Convention for the Pacific Settlement of International Disputes at

---

44 Ibid., I, p. 332.

The Hague on 29 July 1899 put on record a declaration that nothing contained in the convention "shall be so construed as to require the United States of America to depart from its traditional policy of not intruding upon, interfering with, or entangling itself in the political questions or policy of internal administration of any foreign State; nor shall anything contained in the said Convention be construed to imply a relinquishment by the United States of America of its traditional attitude toward purely American questions".[45] Secretary of State Root reminded the American delegates to the Second Hague Conference of that declaration as "illustrating the caution which you are to exercise in preventing our participation in matters of general and world-wide concern from drawing us into the political affairs of Europe".[46]

It fell to Dr. Scott as the American member of the First Commission of the Second Hague Conference to renew the reservation of 1899 to the revised convention of 1907.[47] The reservation was repeated in the plenary meeting of the Conference on 16 October by Dr. David Jayne Hill.[48]

The attempt of the Czar of Russia at the dawn of the twentieth century to lessen the burden of armaments by international agreement not only did not succeed, but seems to have increased the growing tensions in the European arms race. Within a few years would arrive "Der Tag" toward which Imperial Germany looked to begin her conquest of a place in the sun. British Imperialism was equally determined to retain her empire upon which the sun never set. France and other European Powers were maneuvering for territory and preferred position in Africa. The Chinese made a bloody but futile effort to expel the white man and his ways from their ancient land, an effort which might have been more disastrous to China had not Secretary of State John Hay successfully interposed the American "Open Door" policy.

It was in that atmosphere of international tension that the Powers approached the Second Hague Peace Conference in 1907. Some of them obviously were not interested in substituting arbitration or

---

[45] Translation of the Hague Proceedings, Conference of 1899, p. 99.
[46] *Instructions to the American Delegates to the Hague Peace Conference and Their Official Reports*, edited with an Introduction by James Brown Scott (New York: Oxford University Press, 1916), p. 74.
[47] Translation of the Hague Proceedings, Conference of 1907, II, p. 123.
[48] Ibid., I, p. 329.

judicial settlement for the sword as means of pursuing their national objective; some were greatly interested in the rules under which the next great naval war would be fought.

Prize jurisdiction is an ancient one founded in the customary law of nations and sanctioned by the national laws and judicial decisions of belligerents. Prize law covers the rules and conditions under which a belligerent may capture and confiscate neutral ships and cargoes on the high seas when engaged in contraband trade with the enemy, or when running a blockade, or when carrying out a great variety of other activities considered to amount to unneutral service. According to international law, a belligerent Power must establish, and submit to the jurisdiction of, a prize court to which any person aggrieved by its belligerent acts has access. The court itself is established by the municipal law of the belligerent but in theory at least it administers international law: Now different governments have different views as to what are the rules of international law governing belligerent and neutral activities. The same governments have been known to take conflicting views of the same principles at different times, according to whether they happened to be belligerent or neutral.

Great naval powers did not and do not see eye to eye on a number of important questions of prize law. They look with concern to the rules that the courts of any potential enemy might apply to their ships and cargoes in a future naval war. A possible accommodation of the conflicting decisions of national prize courts might be found if appeals from them could be taken to an international court, which has never existed.

The two leading naval powers of the time, Germany and Great Britain, announced at the second plenary meeting of the Hague Conference of 1907 their intention to introduce propositions for the establishment of an International Prize Court. The American Delegation had no instructions on the subject. Our government relied upon its traditional policy of neutrality to keep the country out of war in Europe. Since the propositions for the establishment of an International Court of Prize related to the pacific settlement of international disputes, they were referred to the First Commission of the Conference. The Commission in turn referred the projects to a subcommission. In the meeting of the subcommission on 4 July, Mr. Choate suggested that the best service the American Delegation could render "is not to urge strongly our strong and fixed opinion, but to suggest, if possible, some middle way by which the opposing views entertained by different nations may be harmonized and reconciled so as to create the court. "Better any court", he argued, "than no International Court at all".[49]

The preliminary discussion showed general agreement on the creation of an International Prize Court. Pursuant to Mr. Choate's suggestion, the German and British projects were referred to a committee of examination. During the work of this committee on 12, 17, and 22 August,[50] a joint proposition was formulated by the delegations of Germany, Great Britain, France, and the United States, and adopted by the Commission on 10 September. It was approved in plenary meeting on 21 September by 37 votes to 1, with 6 abstentions, and made the subject of a special convention of the Conference.

The International Prize Court was to be composed of fifteen judges, with an equal number of deputy judges, to serve for a period of six years. The judges appointed by the eight Great Powers – Germany, the United States, Austria-Hungary, France, Great Britain, Italy, Japan, and Russia – were to sit continuously, while seven others appointed by the other signatories of the convention were to serve by rota as shown in a table of distribution annexed to the Convention.[51] The convention provided that in certain enumerated cases an appeal against the judgments of national security might be brought before the International Prize Court on the ground that the judgment was wrong either in fact or in law.

Writing in the *American Journal of International Law* in January 1908, a few months after the close of the Hague Peace Conference of 1907, Dr. Scott wrote hopefully that there remained only the ratification of the International Prize Court Convention by the contracting powers "in order to call into being this great and beneficent institution. For years", he commented, "enlightened opinion has protested against the right of belligerents to pass final judgment upon the lawfulness of the capture of neutral property". Under the proposed convention, he continued, "the interests of neutrals were to be placed in the hands of neutral judges with a representation of the belligerents, in order that the rights of all con-

---

[49] Translation of the Hague Proceedings, Conference of 1907, II, p. 800.
[50] Ibid., II, pp. 813–848.
[51] Ibid., II, pp. 847–848.

cerned may be carefully weighed and considered". He restated the salient features of the convention as follows:

> In the first place, national prize courts are to officiate as in times past. One appeal is allowed from a national court to a higher court of the captor's country. Thereupon, at the expiration of two years an appeal may be taken directly from the national court and the case transferred to the international prize court at The Hague. This court thereupon becomes seized of the law and the facts involved in the case and the decision pronounced becomes final and binding upon the litigant parties.[52]

In his annual message to Congress of 3 December 1907, President Theodore Roosevelt recommended the court as an indication of "the great advance which the world is making towards the substitution of the rule of reason and justice in place of simple force. Not only will the international prize court be the means of protecting the interests of neutrals, but it is in itself a step towards the creation of the more general court for the hearing of international controversies ... The organization and action of such a prize court cannot fail to accustom the different countries to the subcommission of international questions to the decision of an international tribunal, and we may confidently expect the results of such submission to bring about a general agreement upon the enlargement of the practice".

President Roosevelt undoubtedly expressed the general, if not the universal, sentiment in the United States in favor of the court; but the proposal raised a serious constitutional question which became the subject of much discussion in the highest legal circles, including members of the Supreme Court and the Senate of the United States. It was argued that the judicial power of the United States is vested by the Constitution exclusively in the Supreme Court and such inferior courts as the Congress may from time to time establish (Article III, Section 1), and that the Federal Government cannot by treaty or act of Congress provide for the exercise of judicial power by a court located in a foreign country, not established by the Congress of the United States, and superior in authority to the Supreme Court of the nation. Dr. Scott's position was

---

[52] J. B. Scott, "Work of the Second Hague Peace Conference", *American Journal of International Law*, II (1908), pp. 1–28.

"that the court to be established at The Hague is not a court of the United States, and, therefore, is not contemplated by the Constitution". The Hague Court, he maintained, "is a diplomatic tribunal for the settlement of questions which would otherwise be adjusted by diplomacy or referred to a mixed commission specially constituted for their determination, or which, if not determined by either of these methods, might result in war".[53]

The International Prize Court Convention was transmitted to the Senate with the other Hague Conventions on 27 February 1908 with the favorable recommendation for their approval by the President and Secretary of State. Action upon it, however, was deferred by the Committee on Foreign Relations because of the constitutional question involved.

The United States was not the only country in which objections were raised to the establishment of the court. British naval authorities called attention to the lack of uniformity in certain important principles of prize law the court would be called upon to interpret and apply. The British Government attempted to meet this situation by calling a conference of the leading maritime nations for the purpose of agreeing upon a uniform code of prize law to be applied by the proposed international prize court. This conference, known as the International Naval Conference, was held in London from 4 December 1908 to 26 February 1909. An agreement, called the Declaration of London, was signed on the last day of the Conference by the representatives of all the participating governments, namely, Germany, the United States, Austria-Hungary, France, Great Britain, Italy, Japan, the Netherlands, Russia, and Spain.

To obviate the constitutional difficulty to the ratification of the convention by the United States, Secretary of State Root took advantage of the meeting of the London Naval Conference to propose an amendment to the Prize Court Convention which would permit the United States to ratify it without submitting the decisions of its Supreme Court for confirmation or reversal to the proposed International Prize Court. He instructed the American delegation to the London Conference to propose "an additional article or protocol for the consideration of and eventual acceptance by the conference by which each signatory of the convention of 18 October 1907 shall

---

[53] J. B. Scott, "The International Court of Prize", *American Journal of International Law*, V (1911), p. 302.

possess the option, in accordance with local legislation, either to submit the general question of the rightfulness of any capture to the determination of the International Prize Court, or to permit an appeal from the judgment of a national court in a specific case direct to the International Prize Court as contemplated by the convention of 18 October 1907".

A proposal was offered at the London Naval Conference by the American delegation in accordance with Secretary Root's instructions but the other delegates deemed it to be beyond the scope of their instructions to amend the Hague Convention. However, the London Conference adopted a recommendation that the American proposal be otherwise adopted by their respective governments.

To take his place in the United States Senate to which he had been elected by the legislature of the State of New York, Elihu Root resigned the Secretaryship of State on 26 January 1909, a few weeks before the expiration of President Theodore Roosevelt's term of office on 4 March 1909. Mr. Robert Bacon, Assistant Secretary, was appointed Secretary during the few weeks remaining of the term. President Taft appointed Philander C. Knox as Secretary of State. Both President Taft and Secretary Knox were in complete sympathy with the views of their predecessors on the importance of continuing the work initiated at the Hague Peace Conferences. Secretary Knox asked Dr. Scott to remain as Solicitor for the Department of State, and it became the latter's most agreeable function to bring his new chief up to date on the steps that had been taken to bring an international court into existence in accordance with the recommendations of the Hague Conference of 1907.

From then until he resigned from the Department to enter the service of the Carnegie Endowment for International Peace early in 1911, Dr. Scott's Departmental duties became more and more concentrated on the establishment of an international court. On 28 June 1910, his official title was changed to Solicitor in International Arbitrations, effective 1 July. Commenting upon the approval by the Senate on 15 February 1911 of the International Prize Court Convention and Additional Protocol, he wrote to Dr. Nicholas Murray Butler:

> I hope you will be pleased to observe that I had the honor to sign for the United States on this occasion. The truth is, but it cannot be made known, I prepared all the documents concerning the Prize Court since the adjournment of the Conference, and I

> have advised every step taken for the Court of Arbitral Justice and framed its provisions at the Conference, piloted it through the stormy sessions, and have, I believe, launched it upon a successful career. But this is between ourselves, and it matters little who gets the credit, provided the institutions be established. However, I thought you might like to know this, because it is the justification for my forty-odd years of existence.[54]

On 18 October 1909 Secretary Knox sent an identical circular note to the signatories of the International Prize Court Convention of 1907, proposing that they make provision for the alternative procedure recommended by the London Naval Conference. As the result of diplomatic negotiations thus initiated, an agreement called an Additional Protocol was signed at The Hague on 19 September 1910, with Dr. Scott representing the United States. The protocol stipulated that any signatory prevented by difficulties of a constitutional nature from accepting the International Prize Court Convention of 1907 should have the right to declare in its instrument of ratification or adherence that in prize cases whereof their national courts have jurisdiction, recourse to the International Prize Court can only be exercised against them in the form of an action for damages for the injury caused by the capture. Signed originally by thirteen Powers, the Additional Protocol was later approved by all the signatories or adherents of the International Prize Court Convention. The approval of the convention and additional protocol was advised and consented to by the United States Senate on 15 February 1911. That body later, on 24 April 1912, approved the ratification by the United States of the Declaration of London.

The favorable action of the Great Powers assembled at the London Naval Conference upon the proposal of the United States to make possible the establishment of an International Prize Court, raised Dr. Scott's hopes that something might also be accomplished through the same channels for the establishment of the Court of Arbitral Justice, the convention for the creation of which the Hague Peace Conference of 1907 also recommended be brought into force as soon as an agreement could be reached respecting the selection of the judges and the constitution of the court. During the brief interval when his friend Robert Bacon was Secretary of State, the

---

[54] Letter of 27 April 1911, written after he had left the Government service.

latter, on 6 February 1909, sent a second instruction to the American delegation to the London Naval Conference stating that;

> The Department of State considers the adoption of the alternative method of procedure for the International Prize Court renders possible the composition of the Court of Arbitral Justice by the addition to the draft protocol concerning the Prize Court of another paragraph to provide that any signatory of the convention for the establishment of the Prize Court may provide further in the act of ratification that the said court should be competent to accept jurisdiction of and to decide any case submitted to it for arbitration arising between signatories of the proposed new paragraphs, and the International Prize Court should thereupon accept jurisdiction and adopt for its consideration and decision of the case the project of Convention for the establishment of the Court of Arbitral Justice recommended for adoption through diplomatic channels by the Second Hague Conference.

The London Naval Conference considered this second American proposal to be beyond the scope of the Conference and took no action upon it. Shortly after the adjournment of the conference, Secretary of State Bacon on 5 March 1909 sent a cable to the American Ambassador in London stating that it was the intention of the United States to send a note on the subject to each of the Powers represented at the London Naval Conference. The note was actually sent on 18 October 1909 by Mr. Bacon's successor, Philander C. Knox. The proposal was embodied in the same identical circular note proposing alternative procedures for the ratification of the International Prize Court Convention. In their replies to this note, Great Britain, Germany, and France proposed a meeting at Paris to consider its contents. A commission of the four Powers met at Paris in March 1910, composed of Mr. Kriege representing Germany, Mr. Renault representing France, Mr. Crowe representing Great Britain, and Dr. Scott representing the United States. The alternative method of procedure for the International Prize Court was quickly agreed upon, and the four Powers further agreed to take steps, after the establishment of the Prize Court, to constitute the Court of Arbitral Justice using the Prize Court system of electing the judges, provided eighteen Powers should agree to it.

A draft convention was formulated modifying the original Hague Convention in certain particulars so that the Court of Arbitral Justice could be created by a limited number of Powers. Further modifications were contained in a revised draft convention formulated at The Hague by the same representatives in July 1910. An Additional Protocol on the modified procedure for the International Prize Court was signed at The Hague on 19 September 1910, with Dr. Scott again representing the United States.

Unlike the United States where many treaties become the supreme law of the land without the action of Congress, in England it is necessary for Parliament to enact legislation to implement treaties before they can be enforced in the British courts. Consequently, before either the Declaration of London or the International Prize Court Convention could be ratified by the British Government, it became necessary for Parliament to enact legislation amending the English law relating to naval prize. From the very start the Declaration met with the most violent opposition from those who envisaged a future war with Germany in which the island might be reduced to starvation because of foodstuffs being placed on the list of prohibited contraband trade. The greater part of the press denounced the Declaration, a petition to the King against its ratification by the Imperial Maritime League was signed by a long list of commercial associations, mayors, members of the House of Lords, general officers, and other public officials. Flag rank officers to the number of 138 addressed to the Prime Minister a public letter of protest against the Declaration. It is not surprising, therefore, that when the Naval Prize Bill came before the House of Lords on 15 December 1911, it was rejected.[55]

The unfavorable action of Great Britain upon the Declaration of London sealed the fate not only of the International Prize Court Convention, but of the American proposal to invest it with the functions of the Court of Arbitral Justice. From then on, Dr. Scott turned his attention to the possibility of establishing that court separately from the Prize Court, by using the method of electing the judges of the latter as the solution of the unsolved problem of electing the judges of the former.

[55] See Editorial Comment, *American Journal of International Law*, VI (1912), p. 180.

American Society for Judicial Settlement of International Disputes

To promote public opinion in the United States in favor of a Permanent Court of International Justice, Dr. Scott resorted to a familiar medium of propaganda in this country, namely, the formation of a society for that purpose. In association with Theodore Marburg, of Baltimore, former United States Minister to Belgium, they founded in February 1910 the American Society for Judicial Settlement of International Disputes.

Dr. Scott was the first President and he later served as Secretary. Many prominent people became identified with the Society. William H. Taft became Honorary President after the expiration of his term of office as President of the United States. The Society held six national conferences between the years 1910 and 1916 and issued a quarterly bulletin. The Society's publications were widely distributed in the United States and abroad and it received many letters of encouragement. For example, after the outbreak of war in Europe in 1914, a barrister in London wrote under date of 17 February 1915: "Notwithstanding the fearful struggle into which dynastic ambition and the lack of popular control over foreign policy and an unwise license to private trade in armaments have cast Europe, there are many of us who sincerely look to American thought, as represented by your society, for converting the European peoples to the establishment of some permanent tribunal".

Although only a small portion of disputes between nations are justiciable, Dr. Scott did not concede that the services of an international court of justice would be limited to that extent.

"We do not today", he argued, "fight a duel because we are at odds with our neighbor about a question of policy excluded from the jurisdiction of a court, because the influence of judicial procedure has so pervaded the public that it has driven out the last vestige of self-redress". In elaboration of the analogy, he continued: "By the creation of a habit of mind to settle disputes without a resort to force, the people everywhere discuss their disputes and decide them without disturbing the peace of the community, because of the fact that the influence of the court has pervaded all classes of society and has formed the habit stronger than law of settling their differences by rational means".[56]

The society discontinued its activities upon the entry of the United States into World War I in 1917. At the close of that war, other societies or groups, such as the World Court League and the League to Enforce Peace, took up the advocacy of an international court of justice. The American Society for Judicial Settlement of International Disputes, Dr. Scott then reported, "should regard itself as a pioneer and as having completed its work. The mission which it imposed upon itself will be carried out by other societies and by other organizations".[57]

Court of Arbitral Justice

Dr. Scott did not confine his efforts in behalf of the establishment of an international court of justice to the promotion of popular sentiment for it. He turned also to his professional associates in international law. He was a member of the Institute of International Law, a select group of distinguished scholars, many of them statesmen or high government officials, from most of the nations of the world, but predominantly European. With the assistance of a number of his influential European friends who had served with him at the Hague Conference, he brought the subject before the meeting of the Institute at Christiana in August 1912. On the 28th of that month, the Institute unanimously adopted a resolution stating it to be highly desirable that satisfaction be given to the *voeu* adopted by the Second Peace Conference in favor of the establishment of a Court of Arbitral Justice.

The question was thoroughly discussed before the resolution was adopted. The principal doubt raised in the minds of some of the members who took part in the discussion was the same as had been raised at The Hague, namely, whether the proposed new permanent court was intended to take the place of the so-called Permanent Court of Arbitration already established at The Hague. After other members of the Institute had explained that this was not to be the case, Dr. Scott took the floor and gave a detailed exposition of the

---

[56] Carnegie Endowment for International Peace Year Book, 1916, p. 148.
[57] Ibid. 1918, p. 158.

functions of the proposed new court and contrasted them with the old court of 1899 and other methods for the peaceful settlement of international disputes. As usual in international conferences, Dr. Scott spoke in French. He later translated the proceedings into English, from which the following quotation states his views in his own language:

> Mr. J. B. Scott calls attention to the fact that in questions of a political nature, which governments have not been able to settle through diplomatic channels, a compromise may be reached by the existing court. But, if the governments wish to settle their differences by the impartial application of principles of law, they must appeal to a court composed of jurists, that is to say, of men accustomed to apply principles of law to concrete problems. It may well be that the compromise of an international dispute is to be preferred to its judicial determination, but governments should know in advance and by the very nature of the institution to which resort is had, whether to expect a judgment based upon principles of justice also known in advance. Thus, within the last two years, Chile and the United States submitted a dispute – the so-called Alsop case – which diplomacy had failed to adjust and which the parties would not agree to arbitrate, to the King of Great Britain as amicable compositor. It may also be the desire of the disputants that a controversy shall be settled in general reliance upon principles of law or, as the convention for the peaceful settlement of international disputes puts it, "on the basis of respect for law," but not necessarily determined by the mere application of those principles to the exclusion of those larger and broader views, which we usually identify with equity. But the governments should clearly know whether they are to expect a judicial or an equitable adjustment. In the present method of arbitration, it is impossible to forecast the probable result, because it cannot be known in what proportion the judges of the parties' choice may apply law or lean to equity, and it is to be feared that governments hesitate to resort to the present permanent court by reason of the doubt and uncertainty which must exist from its composition and from the tendency of persons appointed under such conditions to compromise. If, however, a court existed with a permanent body of judges, who had had either judicial experience or the training of lawyers and jurists, nations in litigation might well be inclined to submit the case to the judgment of such a tribunal, because the principles of law to be applied or rejected can be divined in advance and the members of the court, judges by profession or lawyers by training, cold be relied upon to apply

those principles of law, which either are or can be known by the parties before the submission of the case. In this way nations would be free to choose the method of adjustment appropriate to the dispute or to the principle involved, and instead of one method for the peaceable settlement of international disputes, we would have three – namely, amicable composition, arbitral adjustment, judicial decision.

We may readily admit that peaceful settlement is in and of itself the goal toward which we strain our eyes, or in other words, that peaceful settlement is the substance; the method of settlement is a matter of form. A little reflection, however, will convince us that this is not really so, and that the manner of settling a controversy is not a matter of indifference to believers in peaceful, especially judicial settlement. The opinion of an amicable compositor can neither be forecast nor serve as a precedent. Arbiters of the parties' choice are supposed to be free to exercise their discretion in reaching a settlement, and, if this be so, it is clear that their holding need not influence a future body as free to exercise its judgment and discretion as they. In the case of a tribunal composed of permanent judges, it is at once evident that they must of necessity consider carefully before rendering a judgment , as, when once rendered, they cannot very well question, overthrow or otherwise refuse to follow it, for by so doing they discredit themselves as well as their judgment. A permanent court is therefore from its very nature calculated to develop international law by a series of precedents, just as, for example, the development of the common law of England is due almost wholly to judicial decisions. The proposers of the Court of Arbitral Justice had in mind this inherent and inevitable tendency of a court of justice, when they recommended the Court of Arbitral Justice as capable of assuring the continuity of arbitral jurisprudence. Mr. Scott is therefore a declared and outspoken partisan of the proposed Court of Arbitral Justice, which must, in his opinion, of necessity inspire a greater confidence among the states than the existing court, and which would be capable of developing international law as a system of law for the peaceful settlement of international controversies. While fully aware of the difficulties involved in the composition of such a permanent tribunal, he nevertheless believes that they will be overcome if the nations really want the court, and devote themselves seriously and with singleness of purpose to its creation.[58]

President Taft had strongly supported the efforts of his Secretary of State to bring about the establishment of the Court of Arbitral Justice in conjunction with the International Prize Court. In an address delivered in autumn 1912 he stated:

> I am strongly convinced that the best method of ultimately securing disarmament is the establishment of an international court and the development of a code of international equity which nations will recognize as affording a better method of settling international controversies than war. We must have some method of settling issues between nations, and if we do not have arbitration, we shall have war. Of course, the awful results of war with its modern armaments and frightful cost of life and treasure, and its inevitable shaking of dynasties and governments, have made nations more chary of resort to the sword than ever before; and the present, therefore, because of this, would seem to be an excellent time for pressing the substitution of courts for force. I am glad to come here and to give my voice in favor of the establishment of a permanent international court. I sincerely hope that the negotiations which Secretary Knox has initiated in favor of an International Prize Court—after the establishment of that court—will involve the enlargement of that court into a general arbitral court for international matters.

After Mr. Taft failed of reelection in November 1912, he and Secretary of State Knox became desirous that the Court of Arbitral Justice be established before their administration terminated on 4 March 1913. Although Dr. Scott had left the service of the Government nearly two years before and was then busy with the work of the Carnegie Endowment for International Peace, they again turned to him for help. He prepared for the Secretary of State a detailed memorandum showing how the Court of Arbitral Justice might be established by and for a limited number of Powers. After recounting the efforts to establish the Court at the Second Hague Conference and to bring it into being with the International Prize

---

[58] Extract from the proces-verbal of the Institute of International Law, 28 August 1912, translated for the Year Book of the Carnegie Endowment for International Peace 1912, pp. 124–125.

Court in collaboration with Germany, France and Great Britain, the memorandum states that "these circumstances raise a presumption amounting to a conviction, that the time has come to confer with the Governments of Germany, France and Great Britain, in order to see if steps cannot be taken in the immediate future, either to put into effect the Court of Arbitral Justice, as modified by the draft convention adopted at the Paris Conference of 1910, as amended by the subsequent conference at The Hague on 25 July 1910, or to consider whether they and the other Powers which may be favorable to the institution of the proposed court would be willing to compose the court by a smaller number of judges than that contemplated by the draft convention of 25 July 1910". Dr. Scott qualified his proposal "with the distinct understanding that the court", when thus constituted, "would be temporary in its nature, in the sense that the establishment of a larger and more general tribunal might be considered at the next Peace Conference". He believed and confidently asserted "that the establishment of the court for a limited number of powers, that is to say, by the powers that may wish it, would advance, not retard, the creation of a more general court, and would at once and the same time advance the cause of judicial settlement, and that the experience acquired by its creation and operation would be useful in any subsequent negotiations for the establishment of a larger court of Arbitral Justice". [59]

What happened at that time was told by Dr. Scott in confidential correspondence with Dr. Nicholas Murray Butler, to whom he applied to get permission to leave the work of the Endowment for several months to make a trip to Europe. In a letter of 25 November 1912, he wrote to Dr. Butler: "A couple of days ago I was thunderstruck by the request of the Secretary of State that I take up the negotiations for the establishment of the Court of Arbitral Justice, and you will be thunderstruck when you learn that the President and Secretary have asked me to go at once to Europe in an official capacity, in order to endeavor to persuade Germany, France and Great Britain to agree to establish the Court, provided Russia, Austria-Hungary, Italy and Japan will come in, thus making it a Court of eight, leaving it open to the other Powers to adhere upon terms

[59] Text of Memorandum, approved by Secretary of State Knox, 25 November 1912, in a private and confidential print entitled "The Proposed Court of Arbitral Justice", 1 August 1915, pp. 6–18.

and conditions to be subsequently agreed upon, or to modify the Court, when created, at a future Hague Conference". Dr. Butler promptly telegraphed in reply that the "public importance of the President's request takes precedence over everything else" and he congratulated Dr. Scott on this "splendid opportunity for new service". He wrote Dr. Scott the same day, 26 November, that "The opportunity is so great that you have no right to refuse it".

There were difficulties in the way of the success of the mission which Dr. Scott knew as well, if not better, than anyone else. Three months prior to the request to him, President Taft had, on 24 August, approved the Act of Congress to provide for the opening and operation of the Panama Canal containing the provision that "no tolls shall be levied upon vessels engaged in the coastwise trade of the United States". The British Government had protested against that provision as a violation of the terms of the Hay-Pauncefote Treaty of 1901 under which the United States had obtained the exclusive right to build the canal. It provided that the canal should be free and open to vessels of all nations "on terms of entire equality". The British Government had proposed that the United States either repeal the law or submit the difference of interpretation to international arbitration in accordance with the arbitration treaty of 1908 in force between the two countries.

The controversy had aroused bitter feelings in both countries, and the Government of Great Britain was on the point of presenting a formal demand upon the Government of the United States. In his confidential letter of 25 November to Dr. Butler, Dr. Scott expressed the hope that something might be done about the Court of Arbitral Justice "if Great Britain will co-operate. The trouble is that the Mother Country feels itself tricked by the arbitration treaty and is 'sore' on the Panama tolls. If Mr. Taft would authorize me to state that the legal question would be arbitrated, as it should be, upon Great Britain' request, in accordance with the arbitration treaty of 1908, I would have a lever with France as well, as France nowadays follows the lead of England. Germany has always been in favor of the court and might prefer to associate solely with the great Powers in getting it started. In this case, the Triple Alliance and the Triple Entente would join us and Japan would for obvious reasons come in. There would be no difficulty about representation, as under this plan each of the eight nations would have a judge as of right during the life of the convention". In his letter of reply of 26 November, Dr. Butler agreed with Dr. Scott by stating: "I am perfectly certain that you will be rebuffed in England, France and Germany unless you carry the President's personal promise that he will support and recommend arbitration of the Panama Canal Tolls matter. Of course", Dr. Butler continued, the President "cannot pledge the Senate, but his own attitude must be made clear and then we must bring public opinion to bear in his support to convince the Senate of its high duty".

The next day, 27 November, Dr. Scott wrote another letter to Dr. Butler bringing him up to date. "If I can get the right kind of instructions, the chances are favorable to the institution of the court, and", he added, "I have strong hopes of a specific instruction on the part of the administration to agree to submit the question of Panama tolls to the judicial determination of the proposed court, if established. For your very confidential information, I may say that Mr. Knox informed me yesterday that he would urge the President so to do, that he believed the President would follow his advice, and that within twenty-four hours he could assure me that I would be given the necessary authorization".

After having received these assurances, Dr. Scott proceeded with his usual thoroughness, to prepare the way for his mission in Europe. He asked Dr. Butler to write personal letters to some of his warm friends in England, France and Germany, such as Lord Morley, Mr. Winston Churchill, Mr. Asquith, Lord Haldane, M. Poincaré, and some influential friends in Germany. He wished "to establish friendly relations with these gentlemen to show them that the present proposition is not merely official, but supported by the recognized leaders of public opinion in our country, and that, in addition to possessing the confidence of the administration, I am supported in my present endeavor by the class of men among whom you are a leading spirit".[60]

Dr. Butler replied that "so soon as your instructions are in sufficiently definite shape to enable me to write letters with some point to them, I shall be most happy to give you letters to the people whom you name". He expressed his opinion that "If the President and Mr. Knox are now thoroughly in unison on this matter of arbitrating the Panama Canal Tolls, much may be accomplished, not only abroad, but at home before 4 March. I am advised confidentially from London that the British case has been put in the

---

[60] Letter of 27 November 1912.

mails, and it probably reached Washington on Monday or Tuesday last. The tactical stroke now for us to make would be for us to use our acceptance of Great Britain's proposition to arbitrate as a reason for the immediate institution of the Court of Arbitral Justice as you outlined it, with a view to making this Panama Canal Case the first on the Calendar of the new Court".[61]

A silence then ensued on the part of the Department of State which seemed long to Dr. Scott in view of the immediacy with which he had been requested to go to Europe. The silence was broken on 16 December when he was informed by Secretary of State Knox that the plan was impossible to carry out as contemplated, although it had not been given up. Dr. Butler was informed at once of this development by telegram and letter. In his letter Dr. Scott said: "Mr. Knox feels the importance of having me assure the Powers that the Panama toll question will be arbitrated, as without this assurance it is doubtful whether they would consider the project to establish a court to try our cases among others, when we were unwilling to submit the Panama question to arbitration under the treaty of 1908. He, of course, understands that the administration could only express its willingness to prepare the *compromis* under the Treaty of 1908, leaving it to the Senate to approve or reject it. He had hoped to reach an agreement shortly after the arrival of the British note, but the President is to go to Panama and directs that no answer shall be sent until his return. This will mean that nothing can be done before the first of January. The delay is, I understand, caused by the express direction of the President and is not favored by Mr. Knox".[62]

In acknowledging this letter on 17 December, Dr. Butler expressed disappointment but not surprise. "There is something going on in Washington", he said, "in relation to this whole Panama matter that I do not understand and have been unable to get track of. The delay is practically fatal". On the same day Dr. Butler wrote a letter to the *New York World* urging Congress either to repeal the objectionable law or submit the dispute "to an international court of arbitral justice for judicial determination, in accordance with principles of law and equity".[63]

---

[61] Letter of 29 November 1912.
[62] Letter of 16 December 1912.
[63] *New York World*, 18 December 1912.

Dr. Scott agreed with Dr. Butler that the delay in the settlement of the Panama Canal tolls dispute was fatal to the establishment of the Court of Arbitral Justice at that time. He wrote to Dr. Butler: "We are missing a great opportunity. . . Those of us who have recently been in Europe or are in touch with European thought know the criticism to which we justly expose ourselves when we refuse to submit questions arising squarely under a treaty of arbitration. Our prestige has been, I fear, badly shattered, and two or three occurrences of this kind will question the leadership in the peace movement, which was ours until but yesterday".[64]

It remained for Mr. Taft's successor in office, President Woodrow Wilson, to ask and obtain the repeal of the Act of Congress exempting American coastwise vessels from the payment of tolls in the Panama Canal.

The Board of Trustees of the then newly-founded Carnegie Endowment for International Peace met in regular annual meetings in Washington on 12 December 1912, the day following the formal protest of Great Britain against the Panama Canal tolls law. A small committee was appointed to prepare a brief statement concerning the issues between the two governments to be signed individually by the members of the Board and published. The drafting committee was under the chairmanship of Dr. Charles W. Eliot, then President of Harvard University.

The statement, bearing the signatures of 22 of the 28 Trustees, was made public under date of 15 March 1913. Dr. Scott's name was included among the signers. They urged "on our fellow citizens the expediency of promptly repealing that action of Congress which gave rise to the difficulty".[65] The name of the President of the Endowment, Elihu Root, was not appended to the statement. He was then a United States Senator from the State of New York. He delivered a speech in the Senate on 21 January 1914, while President Taft was still in office, in which he forcibly argued that the United States Government should either "arbitrate the interpretation of that treaty" or "retire from the position we have taken".[66]

---

[64] Letter of 19 December 1912.

[65] The Statement was printed in full in the Endowment's Year Book for 1913–1914, pp. 79–81.

[66] *Addresses on International Subjects*, by Elihu Root (Cambridge, Mass.: Harvard University Press, 1916), pp. 207–240. This and seven other volumes of collected addressed and State papers of Mr. Root were edited and prepared under the super-

The controversy remained unsettled during the first year of President Wilson's administration, but at the beginning of the second year, on 5 March 1914, the President delivered a message to Congress in person in which he asked for the repeal of the protested law. He expressed his mature judgment "that exemption constitutes a mistaken economic policy from every point of view, and is, moreover, in plain contravention of the treaty with Great Britain concerning the canal". A bill to carry out the President's recommendation was introduced and hotly debated in Congress until June of that year. It finally passed the Senate on 11 June and was approved by President Wilson on 15 June. Senator Root delivered a lengthy and carefully considered second speech "in reply" on 21 May 1914. For both his Senate speeches Senator Root received much assistance, particularly in the historical material upon which he founded his powerful legal arguments, from the staff of the Carnegie Endowment's Division of International Law in Washington, under the direction of Dr. Scott.

A week after President Wilson requested Congress to repeal the Panama tolls law, Dr. Scott was served, as Secretary of the Carnegie Endowment, with a subpoena by the Sergeant-at-Arms of the Senate directing him to appear the following morning before a subcommittee of the Senate Committee on the Judiciary, which was investigating a charge that "a lobby is maintained to influence legislation pending in the Senate". Dr. Scott was directed to bring with him a statement of all receipts and disbursements of the Endowment from its organization.

Accompanied by the writer of this biography, Dr. Scott appeared the following morning, 13 March 1914, as directed. The interrogation was directed chiefly by Senators James A. Reed, of Missouri, and Thomas J. Walsh, of Montana. They were primarily concerned to discover whether the Endowment had printed and distributed material on the Panama tolls question at government expense or had abused the franking privilege of a Senator. When the Endowment's representatives produced receipts for the payment of all expenses from private printers, the Government Printing Office, and the post offices covering all printing and mailing of both the Trustees' statement and Senator Root's speech, the Senators

---

vision of Dr. Scott. The cost of publication was met by Robert Bacon, who appears on the title pages as joint editor with Dr. Scott.

lost interest and the hearing was brought to a close at 12:30 p.m. the same day.[67]

When hearings were being held in 1914 on President Wilson's bill to repeal the exemption provision of the Panama Canal Act of 1912, Dr. Scott was again summoned to appear before the Senate Committee on Interoceanic Canals. He testified on 18 April 1914, from mid-afternoon until 6:30 p.m. Senator Joseph L. Bristow, of Kansas, covered by his questions much of the same ground as in the previous hearing, and then he, and most of the other Senators left the hearing, except the Chairman, Senator James A. O'Gorman, of Maryland. He and Dr. Scott engaged, until the shadows of evening were falling, in a very courteous and highly intellectual discussion of the proper methods of teaching history in schools and colleges in a way that would promote friendly international relations.[68]

At both Senate hearings, Dr. Scott's mastery of the subject under inquiry, his personal conviction that the position of the United States was untenable in international law, the sincerity of his belief in the purposes of the Endowment, his patience, and his adeptness with the polite response, coupled with his high regard for the dignity of the Senate, all impressed his interrogators very favorably. Several Senators asked to be placed upon the Endowment's mailing list to receive its free publications and other literature. So far as the Endowment was involved in these hearings, it never heard of any report to the Senate on them. However, in the final stages of the debate in the Senate on the repeal bill, the Endowment and its founder were severely criticized by the opponents of repeal. The harder they became pressed on the merits of the question by the arguments of Senator Root and President Wilson's supporters in his own party, the more they were inclined to appeal for votes by stirring up prejudice against Mr. Carnegie and the use of his funds for philanthropy.

In his plan submitted to Secretary of State Knox for constituting the Court of Arbitral Justice with a limited number of powers, Dr. Scott had in mind a court of nine judges. A judge was to be appointed by each of the constituting Powers, thus avoiding any difficulty over the method of appointment, the unsolved problem

---

[67] Printed Hearings on Maintenance of a Lobby to Influence Legislation, Part 62, 13 March 1914, pp. 4770–4808.

[68] Printed Hearings on Panama Canal Tolls, Nos. 8 and 9, 18 April 1914, pp. 421–457.

which had prevented the establishment of the court at the Hague Conference. Besides the United States, he thought that the seven great Powers of Europe and Asia would agree to come in, plus the Netherlands as the host country. The court was to have its seat at The Hague in the Peace Palace. For sentimental reasons, Dr. Scott was happy to envisage an International Court of Justice at The Hague composed of nine judges like the Supreme Court of the United States sitting in Washington with the same number of justices.

Following the breakdown of negotiations by the United States to establish the Court and the settlement of the Panama Canal tolls dispute without need to resort to arbitration, Dr. Scott conceived the idea of asking the Government of the Netherlands as the proposed host country to reopen the subject through diplomatic channels with the other eight Powers prospective parties to the proposed court of nine judges. On 12 January 1914, while at The Hague, he wrote a letter to Jonkheer J. Loudon, Minister for Foreign Affairs of The Netherlands, whom he had met in Washington as Dutch minister, suggesting such action to him. Dr. Scott furnished the Minister for Foreign Affairs with a copy of his memorandum to Mr. Knox and an additional memorandum elaborating upon the reasons for the establishment of the court at that time. He also supplied copies of the documents and information regarding the previous efforts to establish the court for a limited number of Powers, and the draft of a convention adapted for signature by the nine powers he was then suggesting as members of the proposed court. Mr. Loudon promised to give the subject his careful consideration but other matters intervened to delay action until the outbreak of war on 1 August of that year ended all hope of establishing any kind of an international court until World War I was over.[69]

The unsettled differences between the United States and Canada when Elihu Root took office as Secretary of State were so numerous that he needed the services of special counsel to relieve him of some of the burdens involved in their examination and settlement. For this important work he engaged Mr. Chandler P. Anderson, of the New York Bar. Mr. Anderson was exceptionally well qualified to assist Mr. Root in his desire to clean the slate of out-

---

[69] The full text of Dr. Scott's letter to Mr. Loudon of 12 January 1914, with memorandum and other accompanying documents, was published in *The Proposed Court of Arbitral Justice*, ibid., pp. 1–109.

standing differences with our neighbor to the North as well as those south of the Rio Grande. He had been American Secretary of the Joint High Commission constituted in 1898 to adjust a number of unsolved questions then existing between Canada and the United States. The work of that commission was suspended after a few months of unsuccessful effort. Mr. Anderson had also been counsel for the United States before the Alaskan Boundary Tribunal and secretary of the Bering Sea Claims Commission, problems left over from the Joint High Commission. He was later appointed Agent of the United States in the arbitration of the North Atlantic fisheries question and became counselor of the Department of State under Mr. Root's successor, Secretary Knox. It was the good fortune of the writer of this biography to serve for a time as Mr. Anderson's assistant in his last-mentioned office.

The Solicitor for the Department of State was from time to time called upon in due course for expert legal assistance in connection with the negotiations with Canada. Dr. Scott described in his inimitable literary legal style the fisheries question "as perennial and inexhaustible as the fish which the skippers of Gloucester would fain catch off the shores of Newfoundland. Could the fish be persuaded to haunt our coasts instead of throwing themselves away against the shores and bays of an inhospitable, if not wholly unappreciative, island; or could our fishermen be forced to read the fable – for it must surely be only a fable – of the fox and the grapes, and then be persuaded to follow the wise moral of the tale, or if Newfoundland could be annexed to this country; of, finally, if this country could be annexed in some way to or absorbed by Newfoundland, then and not till then can we hope to obtain a fair and satisfactory solution of the fisheries".

As to the origins of the dispute, to continue Dr. Scott's description, "Canada and Newfoundland were won jointly by British and Colonial bravery and devotion; the fisheries were enjoyed in common until the outbreak of the Revolution, and in the Treaty of Peace of 3 September 1783, by which the mother country recognized the independence of the headstrong if not erring colonies, the fisheries were partitioned as an empire would be divided. So matters stood", Dr. Scott explained, "until the unfortunate and decisive war of 1812, by which fishing was interrupted, and was put an end to, by a treaty in which the rights of American fishermen found no place. Henry Clay had been rash enough in a burst of unprophetic enthusiasm to talk of dictating peace from the heights of Halifax, but on sober second thought and after two years of not over-successful war on land, despite some glorious victories on sea, he wisely sheathed the sword he never drew, and signed as negotiator the Treaty of Ghent (24 December 1814): a treaty in which the cause of the war—impressments of American seamen—was not mentioned and which left the fisheries unsettled and unmentioned.

"The question", Dr. Scott commented, was "complicated by patriotism and a strong and manly local sentiment" which made "New England unwilling to yield a tittle of its just rights". He added that "it was not to be supposed that the sailors of New England would forego the rights of fishing in the waters of Newfoundland merely because the Treaty of Ghent was silent on the subject. The war put an end to the danger and the skipper put out to the island as in the times past. The Old Englander, however, was as set in his ways as the New Englander, and contended that, as the right to fish was gained by the treaty, it was lost by the termination of the treaty which gave rather than acknowledged the right. Indeed, the ink had scarcely dried on the treaty before an incident occurred which drew forth in sharp contrast the opposing and irreconcilable views of the two countries ... Fish was, however, a local if not a national necessity, and what could not be got as a right must be got as a favor. Accordingly, the convention of 1818 was negotiated, by which the American fishermen were accorded certain privileges and a modified participation of the rights claimed and exercised under the Treaty of 1783".

Differences of interpretation of the Treaty of 1813 involving legislation and regulation of the fisheries which American fishermen protested as discriminatory and refused to accept caused annual incidents during the fishing seasons which irritated the relations between the two governments for nearly a century. Subsequent commercial treaties and diplomatic negotiations failed to settle the dispute until the two nations agreed to its arbitration by a special agreement of 27 January 1909, pursuant to the general arbitration treaty concluded on 4 April 1908 by Mr. Root for the United States with Great Britain. The tribunal of arbitration was chosen from the Permanent Court of Arbitration at The Hague. Mr. Root was chief counsel for the United States and Dr. Scott was of counsel.

Part of the argument of the United States before the Arbitral Tribunal was that by the Treaty of 1818 Great Britain had transferred to the United States a portion of her sovereign rights over the coastal waters defined in the treaty. This contention required a full discussion of the doctrine of international servitudes. Research upon it was assigned to Dr. Scott, and he compiled a collection of English translations of extracts from the works of Argentinian, Austrian, Belgian, French, German, Italian, Russian, Spanish, and Swiss publicists, together with extracts from the works of British and American publicists. These extracts were printed in a volume of 331 pages by the Government in a series of volumes which made up the United States Case, Countercase, Appendix, and Arguments.

The Tribunal met at The Hague on 1 June 1910, the hearings lasted until 12 August, and the award was rendered on 7 September. The Tribunal was asked to answer seven questions on disputed interpretations of the Treaty of 1818. In addition to answer the questions, the Tribunal made recommendations which were accepted by both governments, and as the result of subsequent negotiations they concluded a final agreement on 20 July 1912 which ended the dispute.

The result has been proclaimed as Mr. Root's "greatest diplomatic triumph as Secretary of State".[70] His argument before the tribunal lasted six days. Due to Dr. Scott's initiative, it was twice printed separately, first by the World Peace Foundation in 1912, and then in the collected addresses and state papers of Elihu Root published by the Harvard University Press in 1917. To the former Dr. Scott affixed a preface and introduction and to the latter a foreword and introductory note, with an appendix of historical and current texts. In the former, he states that the case bears "the impress of a single mind", that of Mr. Root. In the latter he said that Mr. Root in his argument before the Tribunal "spoke the final word" in the case—"a rare if not the only instance of a statesman appearing as chief counsel in an international arbitration, which, as Secretary of State, he had prepared and submitted". Dr. Scott's familiarity with the problems involved in the establishment of an international court of justice, obtained as a member of the American delegation at the Hague Peace Conference of 1907, was thus supplemented by practical experience gained in the conduct of an arbitration as counsel before the Permanent Court of Arbitration in 1910.

In the various forms of introduction to Mr. Root's argument published in these two volumes Dr. Scott supplied a detailed his-

---

[70] P. C. Jessup, *Elihu Root* (1938), II, p. 83.

torical narrative of the dispute from the beginning, with quotations from and references to treaties, diplomatic correspondence, and court decisions; and he analyzed the decision of the arbitral tribunal in the light of the historical background of each question submitted, of the contentions of both governments, and of the evidence. He took occasion also to explain some of the intricacies of procedure and evidence before an international tribunal as compared with the conduct of a suit in a national court. For example, in every international arbitration each contending government appoints an agent. What is the function of the agent as compared with an arbitrator, on the one hand, and with counsel, on the other. Dr. Scott informs the reader that

> the agent is ... a political officer and the counsel or advocates are legal functionaries, or lawyers ... The agent is entrusted by his government with the preparation of the case, for which purpose he is assisted by counsel, appointed by each of the nations in controversy. The agent, however, is the representative of his country in matters concerning the case. He confers with the agent of the other country, who has a like representative capacity, and between them, with the concurrence of their governments, they arrange the details for the trial of the case, and pass upon the many questions which are bound to arise from time to time. The agent is, on the other hand, the representative of his country before the tribunal, and, as a political agent or diplomatic person, his word binds his country, which the word of the advocate or counsel does not. The agent may or may not argue the case. In the Fisheries dispute, neither did.[71]

On the question of the production of evidence, Dr. Scott explains:

> In an ordinary lawsuit in a national court, evidence in the possession of the opponent can be produced by an order of the court, because the court is an agent of the sovereign will in the trial of the case and orders the litigants before it to conduct themselves according to law and directs them to produce the evidence which the law requires. The relation is that of sovereign and subject. In the society of nations

---

[71] E. Root, *North Atlantic Coast Fisheries Arbitration at The Hague. Argument on Behalf of the United States*. Edited by Robert Bacon and James Brown Scott (Cambridge, Harvard University Press, 1917), pp. xxxi–xxxii.

there is, as has been stated, no sovereign and no subject, as the nations are sovereign, independent, and equal States. Therefore, it is necessary for the nations in controversy to consent to produce the evidence which they may have bearing upon the case. It is not to be supposed, however, that the defendant in an ordinary case offers of his own free will the evidence which the plaintiff may need, but upon the demand of the plaintiff in appropriate cases the evidence requested should be forthcoming. Likewise, it is not to be expected that a nation would by its own motion open its archives to the country with which it was in controversy. But the submission of the case to arbitration pledges the good faith of the nation implicitly as well as expressly, and it is the custom of nations upon the request of the country with which they are in litigation to produce evidence necessary to the trial and disposition of the case . . . . Good faith, of course, requires that a document referred to by either nation must be forthcoming upon the request of the other, because it should not have the benefit of evidence which it does not disclose.[72]

---

[72] Ibid., pp. xxxii–xxxiii.

4

Carnegie Endowment for International Peace

The founding by Andrew Carnegie in December 1910 of what he called the Carnegie Peace Fund, when he was 75 years old, was the culmination of influences, some inherited and absorbed from his forebears and environment as a boy in Scotland, others due to enthusiasm for the work of the Peace Conference at The Hague in 1899 in establishing the Permanent Court of Arbitration for which Mr. Carnegie provided a Library and Court House, named the Peace Palace by its Dutch administrators, and to his admiration for President Taft's efforts to negotiate arbitration treaties without reservations as to questions of national honor or vital interests. According to Mr. Carnegie's biographer:

> For the last ten years of Carnegie's life, peace absorbed the greater part of his time. The lessons he had imbibed as a boy in Scotland, when Cobden and John Bright were the teachers of the family hearth, when hatred of war figured as a question in every parliamentary election, and peace meetings, with Uncle Tam Morrison as the leading speaker, were frequently held in the Anne Street Church—these ideas, implanted in the plastic Andrew's mind, became the reigning thoughts of his latest phase.[1]

During the Crimean War, after the Carnegies had migrated to the United States, Andrew at the age of eighteen took part in what he called a "campaign against war" by sending a letter to a Sabbath school paper in his home town of Allegheny City, Pennsylvania. Following the American Civil War, in which he served as a telegrapher in the Northern Army, the demand by the United States that Great Britain make monetary amends for the damages to

---

[1] B. J. Hendrick, *The Life of Andrew Carnegie* (1932), II, p. 332.

Northern commerce by the depredations of the Southern cruiser *Alabama* and other warships built or equipped in British ports, brought the two nations to the brink of war. In 1869 Great Britain launched what was then the largest and most formidable warship afloat—the steam-propelled ironclad *Monarch*. During the bitter discussions in the two countries about the *Alabama* claims, it was suggested in London how the *Monarch* could levy tribute from successive American cities. Upon reading these threats, Carnegie sent an anonymous message by the newly-opened Atlantic cable to John Bright, then in the British Cabinet, advising him that the first and best service possible for the *Monarch* was to bring home the body of a prominent American merchant who had died in London. In his Autobiography Mr. Carnegie comments: "Strange to say, this was done and thus the *Monarch* became the messenger of peace, not of destruction".[2]

In 1871 the British Government agreed to arbitrate the hotly-contested *Alabama* Claims by signing the Treaty of Washington. William E. Gladstone, whose Government signed the treaty, was later called upon in Parliament to explain the award rendered against Great Britain by the Geneva Arbitral Tribunal on account of the claims. He replied in the House of Commons on 15 June 1880: "I regard the fine imposed on this country as dust in the balance compared with the moral value of the example set when these two great nations. . . went in peace and concord before a judicial tribunal rather than resort to the arbitrement of the sword".[3]

When Gladstone was celebrating the fiftieth year of his service in Parliament, Mr. Carnegie met him at a dinner in London in July 1882. As a child, Carnegie had attended Gladstone meetings in his native town. At the London dinner, Carnegie undertook to point out weaknesses in the British constitutional system to the statesman who four years previously had stated that the "American Constitution was the most wonderful work ever struck off at a given time by the brain and purpose of man".[4]

When Gladstone asked Carnegie how to remedy the weakness in the British Constitution, he replied that Great Britain should abandon her monarchical system and reorganize the country on

---

[2] Andrew Carnegie, *Autobiography of Andrew Carnegie* (1920), p. 270.
[3] John Morley, *Life of Gladstone* (1921), p. 393.
[4] "Kin Beyond the Sea", *North American Review* (September 1878).

American lines. Three years later, Carnegie invited Gladstone to visit the United States. Such a visit, Carnegie thought, would render the two nations a great political service. England and America, he said, "have taught the world arbitration",[5] and he hoped to have Gladstone stand at a farewell banquet in New York "and proclaim to mankind that hereafter that nation is morally in the wrong who draws the sword without first offering to submit to arbitration".[6]

As the result of his discussions with Gladstone, in 1886 Carnegie published his book entitled *Triumphant Democracy*. He dedicated the volume "To the beloved Republic . . . with an intensity of gratitude and admiration which the native-born citizen can neither feel nor understand". In the Republic, he wrote "war can be declared only by the two Houses of Congress, approved by the President. Before the sword can be drawn, both branches of the legislature must be wrought up to the pitch of this extreme and momentous act . . . Surely", he added, "the Democracies of Europe have no question to consider more vitally important than the war power. How many useless wars in the past would have been avoided had the republican method prevailed! How many in the future would be prevented by its prompt adoption". Recalling the repeated declarations in Congress and in party platforms in favor of the peaceful arbitration of international differences, Mr. Carnegie felt convinced that "before America can have recourse to arms, no matter what party be in power, her adversary must first be offered arbitration and decline it". Consequently, he argued "that every civilized nation should be pledged, as the Republic is, to offer peaceful arbitration to its opponent before the senseless, inhuman work of human slaughter begins . . . We envy not", he concluded, "the nation which shocks the moral sense of mankind by refusing this olive branch of peace when presented".[7]

---

[5] This was obviously a reference to the arbitration of the *Alabama* Claims. Gladstone was the British Prime Minister whose government signed the Treaty of Washington in 1871, agreeing to arbitrate this dangerous dispute which the British Government for a time insisted involved its national honor and could not be arbitrated for that reason.

[6] Letter of 14 July 1885. Hendrick, note 1 above, I, p. 281.

[7] Carnegie, *Triumphant Democracy* (1893), pp. 379–384.

The Influence of William R. Cremer

Mr. Carnegie became a close friend and supporter of William Randal Cremer, a carpenter's apprentice in London, who was later knighted by the British Government and won the Nobel Peace Prize in 1903. During the Franco-German War of 1870, Cremer organized the Workmen's Peace Committee in London, which later became the International Arbitration League.[8] Cremer was elected to Parliament in 1885 and was one of the founders of the Interparliamentary Union at the World's Fair in Paris in 1889. The Union was organized to work through national parliaments for the reduction of armaments; it later included in its program the promotion of arbitration for the settlement of international disputes.

During the last decades of the nineteenth century, several longstanding disputes between the United States and Great Britain reached critical stages and threatened seriously to disturb their diplomatic relations. The *Alabama* Claims had been peacefully settled by arbitration in 1872 by a special agreement; but there was no general arbitration treaty between the two countries. In the summer of 1887 Cremer discussed with Carnegie in London the best means of promoting such a treaty. Shortly thereafter, Cremer obtained the signatures of 232 members of Parliament to a memorial addressed to the President and Congress of the United States urging the conclusion of a general arbitration treaty. Later the same year a group from Parliament headed by Cremer went to Washington and was presented to President Cleveland by Mr. Carnegie. The deputation also visited the House of Representatives and the Senate. As a result of their visit, Congress adopted a concurrent resolution on 3 April 1890 requesting the President to open negotiations with other governments for the peaceful settlement by arbitration of any differences or disputes which cannot be adjusted by diplomacy.[9] On 16 June 1893 Cremer succeeded in having the British Parliament adopt a resolution which urged the British Government to cooper-

---

[8] Cremer gave all but a small portion of the Nobel prize money to a trust fund for the benefit of the League. Mr. Carnegie added £1,000 to Cremer's gift and also gave the League an annual subvention. The League published in London for many years a periodical entitled *The Arbitrator*.
[9] *Congressional Record*, 51st Cong., 1st sess., vol. 105, p. 2986.

ate with the Government of the United States in the arbitration of international disputes.[10]

During the session of Parliament in the following year, 1894, Cremer drew up a second memorial to the President and Congress of the United States urging them to follow up the resolution of 1890 by inviting the British Government to join in negotiating an arbitration treaty with the United States. Cremer obtained the signatures of 354 members of the House of Commons to that memorial. He brought it to the United States and presented it personally to President Cleveland at the White House on 18 January 1895 and sent a copy to each member of Congress.

The diplomatic crisis between the United States and Great Britain growing out of the latter's refusal to arbitrate the Venezuela boundary dispute postponed negotiations for a general arbitration treaty between them. Mr. Carnegie had become familiar with that dispute at the First Pan American Conference held in Washington in 1889, to which he was an official delegate of the United States. He became an active partisan of President Cleveland's policy of insisting that Great Britain arbitrate the dispute. When President Cleveland, in a special message to Congress on 17 December 1895, threatened to use force unless Great Britain agreed to arbitrate the dispute, Mr. Carnegie actively supported the President's policy. He wrote a letter on 26 December 1895 to the Duke of Devonshire, Lord President of the British Cabinet, in which, in the interest of peace and goodwill between his native and adopted lands, Carnegie informed his lordship that in refusing to arbitrate the Venezuela dispute Great Britain was playing with fire. He also wrote to John Morley denouncing Lord Salisbury's refusal to arbitrate and urging Morley to assume the leadership of the Liberal Party in Parliament. "Here is a moral question worth all your other questions put together", he urged. In later correspondence with his London friend, William T. Stead, Carnegie informed him: "I took the ground that, man of peace though I was, it would be my duty to fight Great Britain if she refused to arbitrate. I am not a 'peace at any price' man, much as I should like to be. I believe it was my duty to be on the field at Bull Run. In the present state of civilization (barbarism)

[10] Howard Evans, *Sir Randal Cremer, His Life and Work* (London, 1909), p. 150.

wicked powers will wage war, which it is the duty of righteous powers to repel".[11]

In August of the following year the Czar of Russia issued his rescript inviting the Powers to the First Peace Conference at The Hague. After its receipt, the British Ambassador at Washington, Sir Julian Pauncefote, who had signed the ungratified arbitration treaty with Secretary of State Olney, called upon his successor, Secretary of State John Hay, in November of that year, to discuss the answer to be given to the Czar. Lord Pauncefote thought "it quite impossible that anything should be done at that conference in the direction of disarmament or of arresting armaments", but, he queried, "isn't it possible that there should be a movement in the direction of a court of arbitration". This diplomatic call laid the groundwork of the instructions of Secretary Hay to the American delegation to propose the establishment of an international tribunal. Similar instructions were given by the British Government to the British delegation, which was headed by Lord Pauncefote.[12]

The action of the Peace Conference at The Hague in 1899 in providing for a Permanent Court of Arbitration was regarded by Mr. Carnegie as "the greatest step toward peace that humanity had ever taken". He provided funds "to build for it and maintain in perpetuity at The Hague a Court House and Library (Temple of Peace).[13]

He thought that "The day that International Court is established will become one of the most memorable days in the world's history".[14] However, no general arbitration treaty was agreed upon at the Conference, and the nations which favored that procedure for

---

[11] Letter dated 4 October 1900. Hendrick, note 1 above, I, p. 426.

[12] Proceedings of the Fourth National Conference of the American Society for Judicial Settlement of International Disputes 1913, pp. 383–384.

[13] The Peace Palace, as it was subsequently called, was completed at The Hague in 1913 and Mr. Carnegie took part in its dedication in August of that year. In a speech on that occasion on 29 August he concluded his remarks by again alluding to the further step needed to be taken for the maintenance of world peace, namely, "an agreement between three or four of the leading civilized powers (and as many more as desire to joint—the more the better) pledged to cooperate against disturbers of world peace, should such arise". See *Manual of Public Benefactions of Andrew Carnegie*, p. 276.

[14] Autobiography, pp. 271–272.

the settlement of their disputes were forced to have recourse to bilateral treaties. Such agreements followed the common pattern of reserving from the obligation to arbitrate differences affecting their vital interests, independence, or national honor.

In 1902 Mr. Carnegie was elected Lord Rector of St. Andrews University in Scotland. In his rectorial address he urged a United States of Europe upon the model of the United States of America. He praised the Czar of Russia for calling the Peace Conference at The Hague which established a permanent arbitration tribunal, and he sought to prod "the other mighty Emperor"—Kaiser Wilhelm II of Germany—into action to save the peace of Europe. This speech produced an invitation to Mr. Carnegie to visit the Kaiser. Before accepting the invitation, he sent the Kaiser a memorandum urging him at the forthcoming Second Peace Conference at The Hague to take the lead in the formation of a League of Nations in which the member would "be pledged to arbitrate differences and also to contribute upon a fair basis men, ships, or money to enforce peace if broken".[15] Mr. Carnegie was the Kaiser's guest at Kiel during the early weeks of the Hague Peace Conference of 1907, and personally appealed to him to follow the course of action suggested in the memorandum, but Germany could not be steered from her fateful course.

A suggestion similar to that sent to the Kaiser was also sent by Mr. Carnegie in a letter to President Theodore Roosevelt when preparations were being made in Washington for the Second Peace Conference at The Hague: "One cannot think over the subject of war without coming to the 'League of Peace' idea as the easiest and best solution", he wrote. He at that time proposed to President Roosevelt precisely the formula adopted eighteen years later by the Assembly of the League of Nations in the Geneva Protocol of 1924 by which a nation which rejected arbitration and went to war would be considered and treated as a disturber of the peace.[16]

As President of the National Peace Congress held in New York in 1907 prior to the Second Peace Congress, at The Hague, later that year, Mr. Carnegie declared that "Honor is the most dishon-

---

[15] For the text of this unique communication, see Hendrick, note 1 above, II, pp. 311–313.

[16] Mr. Carnegie's Letter to President Roosevelt, 27 August 1906. Hendrick, ibid., II, p. 306.

ored word in our language. No man ever touched another man's honor; no nation ever dishonored another nation; all honor's wounds are self-inflicted". The inability of that Hague Conference to agree upon a general treaty of compulsory arbitration was followed by renewed activity in the conclusion of bilateral treaties containing the usual reservations.

President Taft and the Peace Fund

When William H. Taft became President of the United States in 1909, he became an outspoken advocate of unlimited arbitration for the settlement of international disputes. The President's efforts were thus described by Dr. Scott: "It is remarkable that the chief executive of a country, even an American president, should seek to raise international peace to the rank of a public issue and should devote not merely a large portion of his scant leisure to the elaboration of plans for peaceful settlement of international disputes, but should on public occasions, at banquets, before peace societies, in commemorative addresses, addresses on national holidays, such as Decoration Day, and before veterans of the Civil War, proclaim the advantages of international peace, and call upon his immediate audience and the general public to aid him in rendering the resort to force as impossible as it is from the larger aspect unreasonable".[17]

The President's statements did not pass unnoticed in England. In a speech delivered in the House of Commons on 13 March 1910, Sir Edward Grey, speaking for the Government and as Secretary of State for Foreign Affairs, said:

> Arbitration has been increasing. I should perhaps have thought it unprofitable to mention arbitration had it not been for the fact that twice within the last twelve months the President of the United States has sketched out a step in advance more momentous than any one thing that any statesman in his position has ventured to say before. His words are pregnant with very far-reaching consequences.
>
> Mr. Taft recently made the statement that he does not see personally any reason why matters of national honor should not be

---

[17] *American Journal of International Law*, V (1911), p. 719.

> referred to a court of arbitration. He has also expressed the opinion that if the United States could negotiate a positive agreement with some other nation to abide by the adjudication of an international arbitral court on every question that could not be settled by negotiation, no matter what they involve, a long step forward would be taken.
>
> These are bold and courageous words. We have no proposal before us, and unless public opinion rises to the height of discussing a proposal of that kind, it may not be carried out. But supposing two of the greatest nations of the world were to make it clear to the whole world by such an agreement that in no circumstances were they going to war again, I venture to say that it would have a beneficent effect . . . I should be delighted to receive such a proposal. I should consider it something so far-reaching in its consequences that it would require not only the signature of both governments but the deliberately decided sanction of Parliament. That, I believe, would be obtained.
>
> The general adoption of such a system might leave some armies and navies still in existence, but they would remain not in rivalry, but as the world's police. Nations are in bondage to army and navy expenditure. May the time soon come when they shall realize that the law is a better remedy than force.[18]

President Taft promptly reacted to Sir Edward Grey's challenge in a speech before the American Peace and Arbitration League on 22 March in which he said:

> I have noticed exceptions in our arbitration treaties, as to reference of questions of honor, of national honor, to courts of arbitration. Personally, I do not see any more reason why matters of national honor should not be referred to a court of arbitration any more than matters of property or matters of national proprietorship.
>
> I know that is going further than most men are willing to go, but as among men, we have to submit differences even if they involve honor, how, if we obey the law, to the court, or let them go undecided. It is true that our courts can enforce the law, and as between nations there is no court with a sheriff or a marshal that can enforce the law. But I do not see why questions of honor may not be submitted to a tribunal supposed to be composed of

[18] Quoted from J. B. Scott, "A New General Arbitration Treaty with Great Britain", *American Journal of International Law*, V (1911), p. 458.

> men of honor who understand questions of national honor, to abide by their decision, as well as any other question of difference arising between nations.[19]

The foregoing statement of President Taft was reported in a newspaper which Mr. Carnegie read while on a visit to the Grand Canyon of the Colorado. Upon reading it, he said to himself: "President Taft has really bridged the chasm between peace and war", whereupon he wrote an enthusiastic letter to the President and afterwards developed its contents in an article published in the Century Magazine for June 1910. On 14 December of that year Mr. Carnegie turned over to twenty-eight trustees ten million dollars in first mortgage 5% bonds of the United States Steel Corporation, the income of which they were to administer "to hasten the abolition of international war, the foulest blot upon our civilization". In his letter of gift, Mr. Carnegie expressed his belief that the shortest and easiest path to peace lies in the adoption of President Taft's platform.

Among the twenty-eight trustees selected by Mr. Carnegie to administer his Peace Fund of 1910 were a number of men who were associated with or participants in the two Hague Peace Conferences: David Jayne Hill, who as Assistant Secretary of State had drawn the instructions to the American Delegation to the Conference of 1899, and Andrew D. White, Chairman of that delegation; Elihu Root, who as Secretary of State had prepared the instructions to the American Delegation to the Conference of 1907, and Joseph H. Choate, the Chairman of that delegation; James Brown Scott, Solicitor for the Department of State under Mr. Root who had helped in the preparations for and was a technical delegate to the Conference of 1907; Charlemagne Tower, the American Ambassador at Berlin through whom Mr. Carnegie had conducted his correspondence with Kaiser Wilhelm II; and John H. Foster, a member of the Chinese delegation to the Conference of 1907.

By chance, the writer of this biography happened to be conferring with Dr. Scott in his office in the Department of State when his personal mail was delivered to him one morning in November 1910. After opening and reading one of the letters just arrived, Dr. Scott handed it to the writer and suggested that he read it. It was a

---

[19] Ibid., p. 720.

letter from Andrew Carnegie dated 14 November inviting Dr. Scott to become a trustee with a number of other prominent gentlemen whose names were given, of a fund to be set aside by Mr. Carnegie to promote international peace. When I handed the letter back to Dr. Scott, he commented that Mr. Carnegie would not include him in such a group of trustees unless it were expected that he would become actively engaged with the administration of the Peace Fund. On that assumption, Dr. Scott asked the undersigned to promise to resign from the Department of State and become associated with him in the organization and operation of the new venture, a promise which was given and fulfilled on 1 April 1911, following the adoption of by-laws and election of officers.

Formation of the Peace Fund

Mr. Carnegie had asked Mr. Elihu Root to become the President of the Peace Fund. He was then a United States Senator from the State of New York. He and Mr. Carnegie had been close friends for many years and had been in correspondence on matters of public international interest during Mr. Root's distinguished service in the Cabinets of Presidents McKinley and Theodore Roosevelt. Mr. Carnegie had made it a *sine qua non* of the founding of the Endowment that Mr. Root should be its President. Mr. Root agreed "on condition that Mr. Scott should be made the Secretary and executive head".[20] At the first meeting of the Trustees which was held in Washington on 14 December 1910, when Mr. Carnegie presented his gift, Mr. Root was elected temporary President and Dr. Scott temporary Secretary. They were made permanent officers at the second organization meeting also held in Washington on 9 March 1911. The name chosen for the Peace Fund was Carnegie Endowment for International Peace. The by-laws provided that the Secretary should be the chief administrative officer of the Endowment and, subject to the authority of the Board of Trustees, of the Executive Committee and of the President, should have immediate

---

[20] Statement of Mr. Root at the 25th anniversary of the founding of the Endowment, at the residence of Mrs. Carnegie in New York, 14 December 1936. Endowment Year Book for 1936, pp. 23–26.

charge of the administration of its affairs and of the work undertaken by it or with its funds.

Headquarters were established in Washington in accordance with Mr. Carnegie's wishes. Mr. Carnegie's original trustees adopted a proposed federal charter, which, however, Congress failed to enact into law. The Endowment operated for many years as an unincorporated association. A few months later, the activities of the Endowment were divided into three divisions with a separate Director to supervise each. A Division of International Law, located in Washington under the directorship of Dr. Scott, who thus held two positions, that of Secretary and Director;[21] a Division of Intercourse and Education, with Dr. Nicholas Murray Butler, as acting Director, with a temporary office in New York near Columbia University, of which he was President, and a Division of Economics and History, with Dr. John Bates Clark as Director. This Division was located in the headquarters buildings in Washington, but at Dr. Clark's request he was permitted to remain in New York because of his academic connections with Columbia University. Eventually, the divisions in New York became autonomous in their operations except for disbursements and accounting purposes. After a temporary stay of a few months in the administration building of the Carnegie Institution of Washington, a completely separate Carnegie organization, the Endowment purchased three buildings for its quarters at the corner of Pennsylvania Avenue and Jackson Place overlooking the White House and Lafayette Square.

Writing of this period which witnessed the establishment of the Carnegie Endowment, Mr. Robert Lansing, then Counsel for the United States in the American-British Claims Arbitration, in the organization of which Dr. Scott had participated while Solicitor for the Department of State, made the following philosophical observations:

> The future student of history will doubtless look back upon the early years of the twentieth century as a period of momentum in the social development of the human race. Men who live in the time of crises, whether political or social, seldom appreciate the

---

[21] It was the privilege of the writer of this biography to serve as Dr. Scott's assistant in both of those positions from the founding of the Endowment to Dr. Scott's retirement on 30 June 1940. The Trustees elected the writer to succeed Dr. Scott in his several capacities as Trustee, Secretary, and Director.

> full significance of the movements which are taking place; much less are they able to draw accurate conclusions as to what the outcome will be. Yet we, who live at this time, though our sense of proportion may distort events, cannot realize the gravity of the problems which the present generation is called upon to solve. The period is one in which society is seeking to adjust its highly developed institutions, the slow growth of centuries, to new ideas which have all at once become dominant in the world. It is a period of transition, in which the customs and usages of peoples are breaking down before a new sense of obligation and a new conception of duty. Mankind has suddenly awakened to the fact that the methods which have been employed for ages are at variance with the motives which should inspire human actions, and that these must undergo radical change. To work out a social organization which will harmonize with these motives is engaging the thought of those who are students of politics and society.
>
> The fundamental idea which has become dominant and has given impulse to the movement for a change in the very structure of society is in a broad sense altruistic. It seems to have its origin in an appreciation of the interdependence of nations, classes, and individuals comprising the entire human race from the most civilized to the most savage, from the richest to the poorest, from the most virtuous to the most criminal. In the light of altruism the obligations of man to his fellows, of society to the individual, of nation to nation, have been newly interpreted and have furnished a new standard by which human action is to be judged.

Reviewing Dr. Scott's career up to that point, Mr. Lansing concluded that "Mr. Scott's present position as secretary of the Carnegie Peace Endowment furnishes him with unusual opportunities to accomplish the purpose, which he considers to be in accordance with the law of development and in harmony with the spirit of the age. His erudition, earnestness, ability, and industry make him especially fitted to meet the responsibilities and to perform the duties which he has assumed. He has entered upon a larger field of public usefulness than any which he has before occupied, where, doubtless, his labors will bring him new honors and add to the esteem in which he is held by those who know of the services which he has already rendered in the cause of universal peace".[22] Mr.

---

[22] R. Lansing, "James Brown Scott: His Work for the Cause of International Arbitration", *The Green Bag* (April 1912).

Lansing's was only one of many encomiums received by Dr. Scott upon his appointment to the Endowment.

To carry out Mr. Carnegie's purposes the Trustees divided the activities of the Endowment into a number of specific objectives, all of which they considered would promote his general aim. This was obviously Mr. Carnegie's intention, as he said in his letter to the Trustees: "Lines of future action cannot be widely laid down. Many may have to be tried, and, having full confidence in my Trustees, I leave to them the widest discretion as to the measures and policy they shall from time to time adopt, only premising that the one end they shall keep increasingly in view until it is attained, is the speedy abolition of international war between so-called civilized nations".

Three of the specific objectives were formulated in terms to include the continuation of activities in which Mr. Carnegie himself had engaged, and to which he referred in his letter to the Trustees. Although not a lawyer, Mr. Carnegie's faith in arbitration as a substitute for war had made him keenly aware of the vital role of rules of international law in the peaceful conduct of international relations. For example, during the *Alabama* claims dispute, previously mentioned, the British Government maintained that there were no rules of international law under which the United States could predicate the responsibility of Great Britain for damages. On the other hand, the United States maintained that there were such rules, and the British Government eventually agreed to insert those rules in the treaty of arbitration. They subsequently became known as the three rules of the Treaty of Washington. International lawyers and organizations subsequently concluded that those rules were part of the unwritten law of nations at the time the acts complained of by the United States were committed by Great Britain. It is interesting to note in this connection that the only definite suggestion made by Mr. Carnegie to his Trustees when they were drafting the proposed charter of the Endowment was that the codification of international law should be included in its express purposes. To comply with his suggestion it was accordingly provided that the Endowment should "aid in the development of international law, and a general agreement on the rules thereof, and the acceptance of the same among nations". Moreover, to express Mr. Carnegie's and their great confidence in the effectiveness of international arbitration as a substitute for war, it was also provided that the Endowment should "promote a general acceptance of peaceable methods in the settlement of international disputes".

In pursuance of the view of Mr. Root concerning the need for popular understanding of international law, as expressed by him while Secretary of State in the first number of the *American Journal of International Law*, edited by Dr. Scott, the Trustees further directed that the Endowment should seek "to establish a better understanding of international rights and duties in a more perfect sense of international justice among the inhabitants of civilized countries".

All of the foregoing objectives were assigned by the Division of International Law created for that purpose by the Trustees of the Endowment. Dr. Scott was made the Director. There was no man better qualified at that time to advance the purposes assigned to his Division. His first public speech, made while he was practicing law in Los Angeles, California, was on the subject of international arbitration, and he was one of the most active members of the American delegation to the Second Peace Conference at The Hague in seeking to have established an International Court of Arbitral Justice. In 1910, as chairman of a committee of the American Society of International Law, he submitted a report on the codification of international law, pointing out the advantages and difficulties of the proposal and tracing the history of the movement in all countries of the world down to the Hague Peace Conferences.[23]

The foundation of the American Society of International Law and the publication of its quarterly Journal were conceived by Dr. Scott and their success was due primarily to his efforts. Their purpose was to foster the study of international law and promote the establishment of international relations on the basis of law and justice. Indeed, Dr. Scott, by natural abilities, education, experience, and world-wide reputation was so peculiarly best fitted to fill the position of Director of the new Division of International Law of the Carnegie Endowment as to raise the question whether the position was not created for him. There is no question, however, that it was the intention of the trustees who were most responsible for Mr. Carnegie's action and for the selection of Dr. Scott, namely, Elihu Root and Nicholas Murray Butler, that Dr. Scott should be given

---

[23] For the text of that report, see *Proceedings of the American Society of International Law* (1910), pp. 208–227.

the opportunity to put to the most beneficial use his profound knowledge of and experience in the objectives assigned to his supervision and to promote their advancement by his exceptional powers of advocacy, both orally and in writing.

One of Dr. Scott's first acts in his new directorship was to get in communication with prominent international lawyers and publicists in the United States and foreign countries, inviting their counsel, suggestions and cooperation. With many of these men he was personally acquainted as former colleagues in law faculties, fellow members of the bar, co-workers at the Hague Conferences, or associates in international legal organizations such as the American Society of International Law and the Institute of International Law in Europe. Some forty replies were received to those communications.[24] Among them were letters from Simeon E. Baldwin, former Governor and Chief Justice of Connecticut; Professor Eugene Wambaugh, of Harvard Law School; Professor George Grafton Wilson, of Harvard University; and Professor Theodore S. Woolsey, of Yale University. From England, among others, he heard from Professors Thomas Erskine Holland, of Oxford University, and Lassa F. Oppenheim, of Cambridge University. From France, Leon Bourgeois, former Prime Minister and Chairman of the French Delegation to the Hague Peace Conference of 1907; Eduard Clunet, President of the Institute of International Law and founder and editor of the *Journal de droit international privé*; Charles Dupuis, Professor of International Law and Diplomatic History at the École Libre des sciences politiques, in Paris; Paul Fauchille, Director of the *Revue générale de droit international public*; Professor N. Politis, and Professor Antoine Pillet, of the University of Paris, all responded. From Germany, replies were received from Privy Councillor Richard Krauel, Professor Christian Meurer of the University of Wurzburg; and Walther Schucking of the University of Marburg. From Switzerland Dr. Scott received replies from Professor Eugene Borel of the University of Geneva, and Professor Max Huber of the University of Zurich. Professor Heinrich Lammasch replied from the University of Vienna, as did also J. C. C. den Beer Poortugael, Councillor of State of The Netherlands; Dr.

[24] Dr. Scott's circular letter of 12 August 1911 was reproduced in the Endowment's Year Book for that year, as well as all the replies received up to that time (pp. 118–144).

Antonio S. de Bustamante of the University of Havana, Richard Kleen, of the Swedish Ministry of Foreign Affairs, Marquis de Olivart of Spain, and Rafael Fern Seijas, former Minister of Foreign Affairs of Venezuela.

Codification of International Law

The efforts of individuals acting alone or in association with others of like mind in advocating and promoting resort to international law and legal measures for the settlement of controversies between nations have always been in advance of governmental action or commitments. Philosophers and jurists antedating Hugo Grotius and coming down through the centuries have proclaimed the existence of a family or community of nations and have expounded the laws, natural or positive, which should govern the conduct of their interrelationships. In the middle of the nineteenth century a great English jurist cogently expressed in three short paragraphs the consensus of his profession:

> In the great community of the world, in the society of societies, states are placed in relations with each other, as individuals are with each other in the particular society to which they belong ... As it is ordained by God that the individual man should attain to the full development of his faculties through his intercourse with other men, and that so a people should be formed, so it is divinely appointed that each individual society should reach that degree of perfection of which it is capable, through its intercourse with other societies. To move, and live, and have its being in the great community of nations, is as much the normal condition of a single nation, as to live in a social state in the normal condition of single man.
>
> From the nature then of states, as from the nature of individuals, certain rights and obligations towards each other necessarily spring; these are defined and governed by certain laws. These are the laws which form the bond of justice between nations, and which are the subject of international jurisprudence, and the science of the international lawyer.
>
> To clothe with reality the abstract idea of justice, to secure by law within its own territories the maintenance of right against aggression of the individual wrong-doer, is the primary object of the state, the great duty of each separate society. To secure by

> law, throughout the world, the maintenance of right against the aggression of the national wrong-doer, is the primary object of the commonwealth of states, and the great duty of the society of societies. Obedience to the law is as necessary for the liberty of states as it is for the liberty of individuals.[25]

It was not until the First Hague Conference of 1899 that governments formally recognized "the solidarity which unites the members of the society of civilized nations". Nearly a century elapsed following the publication of the above-quoted paragraphs from Sir Robert Phillimore before governments officially proclaimed in the Charter of the United Nations that international aggression is a breach of the international peace.

One of the particular objectives formulated for the Carnegie Endowment by its Trustees and assigned to its Division of International Law read: "To aid in the development of international law and a general agreement upon the rules thereof". This specification of work for the Endowment was not written by Dr. Scott, but was inserted by Mr. Root in accordance with a wish expressed by Mr. Carnegie himself. A fortnight following his gift of 14 December 1910, he met in New York with several of his Trustees to consider the organization and purposes of his Peace Fund. The minutes of that meeting relate that: "Mr. Carnegie brought up the matter of codification and felt that the enumeration of codification among the expressed purposes of the Endowment would be well received and therefore suggested that a reference be made to codification in the statement of purposes".

In surveying the field to be occupied by the Division of International Law, Dr. Scott took the view that: "It should not compete with the work satisfactorily inaugurated or done by individuals, societies or corporate bodies; it should rather strengthen their work and render it more effective; it should endeavor to undertake work which they are unable to do, thus avoiding competition or duplication".[26]

---

[25] R. Phillimore, *International Law* (1854), I, pp. 3–5.
[26] Year Book 1911, p. 103.

Institute of International Law

The most distinguished private group engaged in the work of codifying international law was the Institute of International Law, to which Dr. Scott had been elected in 1908.[27] In his opinion, as reported to the Endowment's Trustees, the Institute "has done more for the systematic and scientific development of international law, and for its popularization, than any agency heretofore created by the learning and ingenuity of man".[28] It was awarded the Nobel Peace Prize in 1904. It is composed of sixty members and an equal number of associate members, all of whom are eminent specialists in international law representing substantially the whole civilized world. It is an exclusively scientific association without official character, the object of which is "to aid the growth of international law" primarily by "endeavoring to state the general principles of the science in such a way as to satisfy the sense of justice of the civilized world" and by "giving assistance to every serious attempt as to gradual and progressive codification of international law".[29]

The Institute was founded at Ghent in 1873 upon the initiative of M. Rolin-Jaequemyns, of Belgium. The organization of such a body was proposed by Francis Lieber, the distinguished German exile who became a citizen of the United States and was entrusted by a commission appointed by President Lincoln to draw up instructions for the government of the armies of the United States in the field. Lieber's instructions were approved and issued as General Orders No. 100 during the American Civil War. They constitute the first codification of the laws and customs of war. As soon as the war was ended, Lieber began a correspondence with American and European friends proposing his "favorite project" that there should be a meeting of the most prominent jurists of the law of nations, one from each country, in their individual and not in any public

---

[27] A scholarly discussion of the problem of the codification of international law, with an historical account of previous attempts at codification, beginning with Jeremy Bentham in 1787, was included in Dr. Scott's report as Director of the Division of International Law published in the Year Book for 1923, pp. 235–253.

[28] Year Book 1911, p. 107.

[29] Article 1, Constitution of the Institute, in *Resolutions of the Institute of International Law* (Carnegie Endowment, 1916), p. xx.

capacity, to settle among themselves great questions of the law of nations – "a private and boldly self-appointed congress, whose whole authority should rest on the inherent truth and energy of their own *proclama*". Letters of this character were written by Lieber to, among others, Andrew D. White and M. Rolin-Jaequemyns. The latter took the initiative in founding the Institute at Ghent after Lieber's death. Lieber had discussed his project with David Dudley Field, of New York, who compiled and published his own *Outlines of an International Code* in 1872.

Lieber's letter to Andrew D. White, dated 15 December 1866, is of special interest as it contained an appeal for a peace endowment nearly a half century before Mr. Carnegie's action. "How fine a thing I would be", Lieber wrote, "for one of the Peabodies, or some such gold vessel, to give, say twenty-five thousand dollars gold, for the holding of a private—i.e., note diplomatic, although international—congress of some eight or ten jurists, to concentrate international authority and combined weight on certain great points, on which we have now only individual authorities".[30]

Following its organization in 1873, the Institute of International Law met biennially, sometimes annually, in large European cities. It has adopted projects, reports, land resolutions on numerous problems of international law which have arisen from year to year during more than three quarters of a century of its existence. Many of the Institute's solutions were later adopted by nations in their practice. The work of the Institute proved especially useful in drafting some of the conventions of the two Hague Conferences. As stated by Mr. Elihu Root: "In practice the work of the unofficial members of the Institute of International Law has made possible the success of the official conferences at The Hague, by preparing their work beforehand and agreeing upon conclusions which the official conferences could accept".[31]

To assist the Endowment in formulating its international law program, and at the same time to encourage the Institute of International Law and strengthen its work, the Trustees invited the Insti-

---

[30] Lieber's letters are collected and quoted in Dr. Scott's preface to the Endowment's English translation of the *Resolutions of the Institute of International Law* (1916).

[31] Presidential address before the American Society of International Law, *Proceedings of the Society* (1913), p. 20.

tute to act as adviser to the Division of International Law. The Institute accepted the Endowment's invitation at its meeting in Christiana on 26 August 1912 and appointed a Consultative Committee of eleven members, to which Dr. Scott submitted the various proposals he had received. Substantially all the future work of the Division fell within the framework of the recommendations of the Institute's Consultative Committee. A subvention of $20,000 per annum from the Endowment was later appropriated by the Trustees "to be expended as the Institute deems proper". The funds were used to reimburse traveling expenses of members in attending general meetings of the Institute and meetings of the Commissions held between general meetings, including the printing of reports, and applied toward the cost of publishing the proceedings of the Institute known as *Annuaires*.

Until the year 1929 the Institute had always held its meetings in Europe. In that year Dr. Scott realized a long-cherished desire and induced the Institute to break with its tradition and meet in the New World. Its thirty-sixth meeting took place at Briarcliff Lodge, New York, on 10–18 October 1929. Special financial arrangements were made by the Endowment to provide for that meeting. All members and associates were invited, including an additional member of each family, to be the guests of the Endowment from the time they left Europe until they returned. Some sixty members, with forty additional members of their families, accepted the invitation. Through arrangements with the United States Steamship Lines they were picked up by the *S.S. George Washington* at Bremen, Southampton, or Cherbourg and landed in New York on 9 October. By courtesy of the United States Treasury Department, they were taken aboard a Coast Guard cutter to Briarcliff. A Conference of American Teachers of International Law and Related Subjects[32] convened at Briarcliff simultaneously with the Institute's meeting. Some seventy-five American professors were in attendance. The courtesy of attending the meetings of each other was extended by both organizations, and advantage was liberally taken of this privilege. Moreover, a number of outstanding publicists of Latin America were invited to the meeting, which assumed the character of a great inter-

---

[32] This was the fourth of a series of like conferences which is referred to elsewhere.

national conference by the most eminent authorities in the field of international law of Europe, the United States and Latin America.

In accordance with the custom of the Institute of electing its President from the country in which each meeting is held, Dr. James Brown Scott presided over the Briarcliff meeting. The Honorable Elihu Root, an honorary member of the Institute, opened the meeting. A formal welcome was extended on behalf of the Carnegie Endowment by its President, Dr. Nicholas Murray Butler. At the close of the meeting the foreign delegates were entertained for four days in New York City and four days in Washington, with visits to Princeton and Philadelphia. In New York they were given a dinner by the Trustees of the Endowment, and receptions by President and Mrs. Butler at Columbia University, and by the Association of the Bar of the City of New York. In Washington they were received at the White House by President and Mrs. Hoover, and given a luncheon at the Pan American Union by the Governing Board to which the entire diplomatic corps in Washington was also invited. The guests left New York for home on 26 October aboard the *S. S. America*.

Of outstanding significance was the adoption by the Institute at its first session in the New World of a Declaration of the International Rights of Man, a notable tribute to Dr. Scott's influence. It states in bold and unequivocal terms the rights of human beings "without distinction of nationality, sex, race, language, and religion" to the equal right to life, liberty and property, together with all the subsidiary rights essential to the enjoyment of these fundamental rights.

In its preamble the Declaration states "That the juridical conscience of the civilized world demands the recognition for the individual of rights preserved from all infringement on the part of the State". After mentioning the declarations of right written into the American and French Constitutions, the preamble quotes the Fourteenth Amendment of the Constitution of the United States that no state shall "deprive any person of life, liberty or property without due process of law, nor deny to any person within its jurisdiction the equal protection of the laws", which the preamble recites "has been applied by the Supreme Court of the United States to every person within its jurisdiction 'without distinction of race, color or nationality'". The text of the Declaration is in six short articles, which in translated form, read as follows:

Article I

It is the duty of every State to recognize the equal right of every individual to life, liberty and property, and to accord to all within its territory the full and entire protection of this right, without distinction as to nationality, sex, race, language or religion.

Article II

It is the duty of every State to recognize the right of every individual to the free practice, both public and private, of every faith, religion, or belief, provided that the said practice shall not be incompatible with public order and good morals.

Article III

It is the duty of every State to recognize the right of every individual both to the free use of the language of his choice and to the teaching of such language.

Article IV

No motive based, directly or indirectly, on distinctions of sex, race, language, or religion empowers States to refuse to any of their nationals private and public rights, especially, admission to establishments of public instruction, and the exercise of the different economic activities and of professions and industries.

Article V

The equality herein contemplated is not to be nominal, but effective. It excludes all discrimination, direct or indirect.

Article VI

Except for motives based upon its general legislation, no State shall have the right to withdraw its nationality from those whom for reasons of sex, race, language, or religion, it should not deprive of the guarantees contemplated in the preceding Articles.[33]

---

[33] For the original French text of the Declaration, see *Annuaire de l'Institut de droit international, Session de New York* (1929), II, pp. 298-

The Institute of International Law thus anticipated by nineteen years the adoption by the General Assembly of the United Nations on 10 December 1948 of its Declaration of Human Rights. To the free world the Institute's declaration was superior for it was not marred by the socialistic and communistic concepts which have dominated the philosophy of international conferences participated in by delegates from behind the Iron Curtain. The statement in the Institute's Declaration of individual rights in terms of American constitutional law unmistakably discloses the hand of Dr. Scott in its drafting. It is there in happy contrast with the later United Nations Declaration of Human Rights stated in terms of the ideology and Constitution of the U.S.S.R.

As he has undertaken, when becoming Solicitor of the Department of State, to make accessible the great works on international law dealing with the philosophy of international law, its sources and customary rules, so, when he entered upon his duties as Director of the Division of International Law for the Carnegie Endowment for International Peace, Dr. Scott planned a similar program to make more accessible the documentary materials which are the basis of international law in its conventional or treaty form. An examination of the catalogs of governmental, educational, and public libraries disclosed the pitiful dearth of authentic source material for official or private study of the work at The Hague with which Dr. Scott was personally familiar because of his services there. None of this material was available in the English language except the Hague Conventions themselves, which had been translated for official purposes only. The proceedings and reports were in French, the official language of the two conferences.

Encouraged by the President of the Endowment and other members of the Board of Trustees, who also had personal knowledge of the achievements of the Hague Peace Conferences and who understood their value as progressive steps in the development of international law and organization, Dr. Scott began a series of publications to make the work of the conferences better understood. The first of these volumes was an English translation of the official texts of the conventions adopted by the Conference. It was published in 1915 under the title *The Hague Conventions and Declara-*

---

300. A complete English translation appears in the *American Journal of International Law*, XXXV (1941), pp. 663–664.

tions of 1899 and 1907. In addition the volume contained tables of signature, ratifications, and adhesions of the various Powers and the texts of their reservations whenever made. This supplementary material was certified as correct by the Department of State and the official depository at The Hague, the Dutch foreign office. Before the appearance of this book, information regarding the status of any of the conventions could be obtained only by writing to one of those two official sources. The usefulness of the work was promptly shown by the general demand for it from Government officials, international lawyers, professors and teachers. It was adopted as a textbook in courses on international law in some of the large universities. To supply the demand, a second edition was immediately published and a third became necessary in 1918. A Spanish edition was published in 1916 and a French edition in 1918.

The next volume in this series was published in 1916. It contained the instructions to the American delegates to the Hague Peace Conferences of 1899 and 1907 and their official reports. These documents were available in scattered places, but Dr. Scott wished to make them accessible for study together.

It is the practice of international conferences to appoint commissions from their membership for detailed examination of all proposals offered for consideration, and it is the task of the reporter of each commission to accompany the draft conventions recommended by it with such explanatory and interpretative commentary as may be necessary to a correct understanding of the document. The reports of national delegations to their respective governments do not necessarily bind other participating governments when questions arise as to the meaning of conventions. To make accessible to the English-speaking world the official commentaries on the work of the Hague Conferences, the Division of International Law under Dr. Scott's direction published in English in 1917 a volume entitled *The Reports to the Hague Conferences of 1899 and 1907*, "being the official explanatory and interpretative commentary accompanying the draft conventions and declarations submitted to the Conferences by the several commissions charged with preparing them, together with the texts of the final acts, conventions and declarations as signed, and of the principal proposals offered by the delegations of the various powers as well as of other documents laid before the commissions". As had happened upon the issuance in English of previous volumes in this series, there was a demand for a French edition, and such an edition was published by the Endowment in 1920.

To each of the foregoing volumes Dr. Scott wrote an informative introduction to guide the reader in their use.

At the request of Secretary of State Lansing, and pursuant to the offer by the Carnegie Endowment to the Government of the services of the Division of International Law following the entry of the United States into World War I, the Division undertook the translation into English of the entire proceedings of the Peace Conferences held at The Hague in 1899 and 1907. It was assumed at that time that the experience of the Hague Conferences would be drawn upon at the close of the war in formulating the plans for future peace. The official proceedings of the two Hague Conferences published in French consisted of four large volumes. The proceedings of the first conference were comprised in one volume, but those of the second conference required three volumes, one covering the plenary sessions and two volumes covering the meetings of the four commission into which the work of the conference was divided.

The Endowment's English translation reproduced the original French editions volume for volume. For the English translation two very comprehensive analytical indexes were prepared, one for each of the Conferences. With the aid of these indexes the reader is able to trace the course of proposals through the several committees, commissions, and plenary sessions and thus gain a knowledge of the positions taken by the several governments through the statements of their delegates. The indexes were published in a separate volume of 272 pages, thus adding to the convenience of using the volumes for reference and study. The four volumes of translated texts comprised 3,834 large pages.

Preliminary copies of the entire set were printed in time for the meetings of the American Commission at the Paris Peace Conference in 1919. In a brief prefatory note to the first volume, dated at Paris, 28 February 1919, Dr. Scott, who was one of the principal legal advisers to the American Commission, reminded his colleagues who might see the volumes that "The Peace Conferences held at The Hague were the first truly international assemblies meeting in time of peace for the purpose of preserving peace, not of concluding a war then in progress. They marked an epoch in the history of international relations. They showed up on a large scale that international cooperation was possible, and they created institutions – imperfect it may be, as in the work of human hands –

which, when improved in the light of experience, will both by themselves and by the force of their example promote the administration of justice and the betterment of mankind". The volumes were published in final form in 1920 and 1921.

A Third Hague Conference

The Second Peace Conference at The Hague in 1907 recommended the calling of a third conference within a period corresponding to that which had elapsed since the preceding conference. At the same time, it recommended that some two years before the probable date of the next meeting a preparatory committee be appointed by the governments with the task of collecting the various proposals to be submitted to the conference and of preparing a program. These recommendations were adopted upon the urging of Mr. Joseph H. Choate, head of the American delegation, acting upon Secretary Root's instruction to "keep always in mind the promotion of this continuous process through which the progressive development of international justice and peace may be carried on". When the time arrived for the appointment of such a preparatory committee, Mr. Choate proposed and the Trustees of the Endowment adopted on 18 April 1913, a resolution urging that the formation of the international committee should be pressed without delay by the United States State Department upon the other governments and that the Secretary of State be requested to appoint a committee on behalf of the United States to prepare an American program. President Root and Secretary Scott were designated to present the Endowment's resolution to the Secretary of State, who at that time was the Honorable William Jennings Bryan. Dr. Scott later reported that the new Secretary of State "was busied with his proposed treaties for the advancement of peace" and "was not at that time thinking in terms of a Third Conference".[34]

Later that year, on 10 December 1913, Mr. Root wrote to Secretary Bryan inquiring whether an impulse could not be given to greater activity in the official preparations for a Third Hague Conference, whereupon Secretary of State Bryan sent instructions to the diplomatic officers of the United States directing them to re-

---

[34] Year Book, 1920, p. 102.

mind the governments to which they were accredited of the recommendation for a Third Hague Conference, and to inform them that the preparatory Committee of the United States had been appointed by the President and submitted a preliminary report.[35] The replies received from the foreign governments led Secretary Bryan to send a second instruction in June 1914 suggesting that the date of the Third Hague Conference be fixed for June 1916.

As the result of these negotiations, the Governments of The Netherlands and Russia on 6 July 1914 sent to the Department of State a memorandum containing a joint proposal inviting all the Powers that were represented at the Second Peace Conference to appoint a member of the preparatory committee for the Third Conference and that the committee meet at The Hague on 1 June 1915.

Dr. Scott had been in frequent conference with Secretary Bryan on this subject during the spring and summer. He had also been in correspondence with many distinguished publicists in other countries, especially with members of the Institute of International Law. He embodied his views and those of his foreign associates in a memorandum to Secretary Bryan which was delivered on 31 July 1914. The Secretary of State requested Dr. Scott to take charge of this work on behalf of the United States. The outbreak of war in Europe on the following day made of Dr. Scott's memorandum, as he subsequently reported, "unfortunately, the final action in the matter of the Third Hague Conference".[36]

The Paris Peace Conference and the Advisory Committee of Jurists

The outbreak of war on 1 August 1914 did not kill the hopes of the small but persistent group of advocates of peace through justice whom Mr. Carnegie had gathered together to administer his Peace Fund. The incompatibility of the two-fold purposes of the Paris

---

[35] Mr. Root's letter of 10 December 1913 to Secretary Bryan and Mr. Bryan's instruction of 31 January 1914 are printed in the Year Book, 1914, pp. 122–124.

[36] Year Book 1920, p. 105. Dr. Scott's memorandum of 30 July 1914 is reprinted in the Year Book for 1920, pp. 126–134.

Peace Conference of 1919, namely, to settle world-wide political problems and at the same time establish a permanent international organization for the administration of justice, was recognized in many quarters. Upon Dr. Scott's return from that conference, where he served as one of the legal advisers of the American delegation, he had this to say in his report to the Trustees of the Endowment:

> Congresses and conferences which have met to end the wars to which groups of nations had been parties have ordinarily confined themselves to such provisions as were necessary to restore peace between the belligerents. In the present instance, however, the Conference of Paris sought not only to impose terms upon the enemy, but also to agree upon the means of preserving the peace which had been created, and of preventing a recourse to arms in the future, both between the belligerents and the other nations of the world; in other words, to superimpose upon a Congress of Vienna a Peace Conference of The Hague. This procedure was as difficult as it was novel, inasmuch as the war congress and the peace conference are animated by different purposes. The war congress is dominated by the victor who seeks to impose his will upon the vanquished, in which process the sword thrown upon the scales outweighs justice. This is inevitably so, because the representatives of the Powers at war meet in an atmosphere of passion, and in which they seek, and necessarily so, the interests of their various countries irrespective of the nations which have not been parties to the war. The peace conference of the type of The Hague meets in an atmosphere of peace, when the sword sleeps in the scabbard, and the representatives of the nations, not unmindful of their special interests, nevertheless consider projects in the light of their bearing upon the nations at large.[37]

The President of the Endowment was among the distinguished critics of the proceedings at the Paris Conference. Mr. Root suggested six amendments to the proposed Covenant of the League of Nations which were cabled by the Department of State to Secretary Lansing at Paris. One of the amendments provided that the League Council "shall call a general conference of the Powers to meet not less than two years nor more than five years after the signing of this convention for the purpose of reviewing the condition of interna-

---

[37] Year Book 1920, p. 86.

tional law, and of agreeing upon and stating in authoritative form the principles and rules thereof. Thereafter regular conferences for that purpose shall be called and held at stated times".[38] This amendment was not adopted at Paris.

The following year Mr. Root was a member of the Advisory Committee of Jurists which formulated the Statute of the Permanent Court of Justice as provided by Article 14 of the League Covenant. Dr. Scott was his technical adviser on that occasion. In addition to the Statute of the Court, formulated at The Hague on 20 December 1920, the Advisory Committee of Jurists recommended "That a new conference of the nations in continuation of the first two conferences at The Hague be held as soon as practicable . . . to restate the established rules of international law . . . To formulate and agree upon the amendments and additions, if any, to the rules of international law . . . To endeavor to reconcile divergent views . . . To consider the subjects not now adequately regulated by international law". The resolution recommended that the proposed conference be named "Conference for the Advancement of International Law" and that it be followed by "further successive conferences at stated intervals to continue the work left unfinished".[39]

The foregoing resolutions were rejected by the League of Nations. The opposition was voiced by Lord Robert Cecil: "He did not think that a stage had yet been reached in international relations at which it was desirable to attempt the codification of international law".[40]

The Codification of International Law in America

Ten years prior to the First Hague Conference of 1899, to which only two Latin American States were invited—Brazil and

---

[38] For the text of all of Mr. Root's proposed amendments, with his personal explanation of their formulation and transmission to Paris, see *Proceedings of Executive Council of the American Society of International Law*, 17 April 1919, pp. 50–53.
[39] For the full text of these resolutions with Mr. Root's personal statement of what they were intended to do and of his experience at the Jurists' meeting at The Hague in 1920, see *Proceedings of Executive Council, American Society of International Law*, 13 November 1920, pp. 16–35.
[40] *Journal of the First Assembly of the League of Nations*, pp 298–299.

Mexico[41]—a series of Pan American Conferences was initiated pursuant to an Act of Congress of the United States approved 24 May 1888,[42] by which the President was authorized and requested to invite the Governments of the Republics of America to join the United States in a conference at Washington to agree upon a plan of arbitration for the settlement of disputes that might thereafter arise between them. The conference was also to consider the improvement of direct means of communication, business intercourse and reciprocal commercial relations.

The conference met upon the invitation of Secretary of State James G. Blaine from 2 October 1889 to 19 April 1890. Andrew Carnegie was one of the official delegates of the United States. The Conference initiated the series of International Conferences of American States of which eleven have been held, and which have developed the Pan American Union into the Organization of American States. It adopted a model treaty of obligatory arbitration, which it recommended not only to their own governments, but to the European Powers. Accompanying the Arbitration Plan was a recommendation to outlaw conquest during the continuance of the arbitration treaty and to declare "That all cessions of territory made during the continuance of the treaty of arbitration shall be void if made under threats of war or in the presence of an armed force".[43] That official recommendation, although it never became effective, was, in fact, the real origin of the more recent so-called doctrine of non-recognition.

Secretary of State Blaine closed the Conference of 1889 with the following ringing statement:

> If, in this closing hour, the Conference had but one deed to celebrate, we should dare call the world's attention to the deliberate, confident, solemn dedication of two great continents to peace, and to the prosperity which has peace for its foundation. We hold up this new *Magna Charta,* which abolishes war and

---

[41] Through the good offices of Secretary of State Elihu Root, invitations to the Second Hague Conference of 1907 were sent to all the American Republics.

[42] U. S. Statutes at Large, XXV, p. 155.

[43] The Plan of Arbitration and Recommendation on the Right of Conquest are reprinted in *International Conferences of American States* (1931), pp. 40, 44.

> substitutes arbitration between the American Republics, as the first and great fruit of the International American Conference.[44]

It remained for later generations to adopt the principles of these original proposals and incorporate them in the Covenant of the League of Nations, the abortive Geneva Protocol, the Pact of Paris for the Renunciation of War, and the Charter of the United Nations.

Successive international conferences of American States have been held as follows: Mexico City, 1902; Rio de Janeiro, 1906; Buenos Aires, 1910; Santiago, Chile, 1923; Habana, 1928; Montevideo, 1933; Lima, 1938; Bogota, 1948, and Caracas. Each conference produced a plethora of resolutions, recommendations, declarations, treaties and conventions on a great variety of subjects – legal, political, social, economic, humanitarian, and cultural. Mr. Carnegie demonstrated his great personal interest in the success of the Pan American Union by donating funds for its headquarters building in Washington.

The proceedings and documents of the Pan American Conferences, like those of the Hague Conferences, were published in the official languages of the conferences, Spanish or Portugese. The editions were limited and soon disappeared. To make them available for official as well as private and research purposes, under Dr. Scott's direction authentic texts from official sources were collected and issued in English in two volumes, *The International Conferences of American States, 1889-1928* and *First Supplement, 1933–1940*. In the latter were included the records and documents of the Inter-American Conference for the Maintenance of Peace held at Buenos Aires in 1936, and the two meetings of the Ministers of Foreign Affairs of the American Republics held at Panama in 1939, and Habana in 1940.[45]

The codification of international law had been acted upon at almost every Inter-American Conference. The Second, held at Mexico City in 1902-1902, provided for the appointment of an international committee of jurists to draft codes of public and private international law for the American nations, but the committee

---

[44] Minutes of 19 April 1890, *International American Conference, Washington 1889-1890*, p. 857.

[45] A Spanish edition of these two volumes, brought up to date to include the meeting of the Ministers of Foreign Affairs held at Rio de Janeiro in 1942, was published by the Endowment in 1943.

was not appointed. The Third, held at Rio de Janeiro in 1906, provided for the establishment of an International Commission of Jurists for the codification of international law. That commission met at Rio de Janeiro in July1912 and organized and assigned its work to six committees. The outbreak of World War I in the summer of 1914 postponed indefinitely the work of the Rio Commission.

5

THE AMERICAN SOCIETY AND JOURNAL OF INTERNATIONAL LAW

The idea of publishing a journal of international law in this country originated with Dr. Scott while he was Dean of the Law School of the University of Illinois. He discussed it with President Draper, but nothing came of it until after he left Illinois and joined the faculty of the Columbia University Law School in New York City. The facts were related afterwards by Dr. Scott himself:

> Shortly before that period, I had been invited to a chair of law in the Columbia University Law School. President Draper, of the University of Illinois, was anxious to have me remain and he was willing to make certain concessions, none of which interested me because of their financial character. I stated that I should be glad to remain, and to remain as long as the university cared to have me carried upon its rolls, if he would request the trustees of the University of Illinois to permit the establishment of a journal of international law. He said that he did not see the feasibility of such a journal. Therefore, I accepted the appointment to Columbia University which had been offered to me.[1]

After moving to New York, Dr. Scott was placed upon the invitation list to the Annual Conferences on International Arbitration held by invitation of Mr. and Mrs. Albert K. Smiley in their Lake Mohonk Mountain House in Ulster County, New York. Those conferences began in 1895 and continued for some years. At the Eleventh Annual Meeting, held 31 May–2 June 1905, Dr. Scott with George W. Kirchwey and Robert Lansing, acting as an informal committee, proposed and obtained the approval of the conference in favor of a "movement to establish a society of international

---

[1] Remarks at Luncheon in Celebration of the 25th Anniversary of the Society, *Proceedings*, 1931, p. 242.

law in the United States and an American journal of international law". Some twenty-four members interested in the professional and theoretical study of international law met on the afternoon of 2 June and appointed a committee to draft a form of organization with power to call a subsequent meeting. Dr. Scott was appointed secretary and treasurer of the organizing committee. New York members of the committee, including Dr. Scott, met a number of times at the residence of Hon. Oscar S. Straus, its chairman, and drew up a proposed constitution. Upon the invitation of the committee, Dr. Scott submitted a plan for the publication of the journal of international law, which was approved.

Upon the call of the Committee on Organization, a meeting to effect the permanent organization of the Society was held on 12 January 1906, in the rooms of the Bar Association of the City of New York. The Constitution previously approved by the committee was adopted with slight emendation and the project for the publication of the journal of international law was approved. Elihu Root was elected President, with twelve very distinguished men as Vice-Presidents, namely, the Chief Justice of the United States, Melville W. Fuller; two associate justices of the Supreme Court, David J. Brewer and William R. Day, Andrew Carnegie, Joseph H. Choate, former Attorney-General John W. Griggs, Judge William W. Morrow, former Secretary of State Richard Olney, Oscar S. Straus, and Secretary of War, William H. Taft. Twenty-four members equally distinguished in Government, public affairs, or education were elected to serve on the Executive Council with the Vice-Presidents. All of these gentlemen and their equally prominent successors accepted their elections and most of them took an active interest in the affairs of the Society by participating in its annual meetings, serving on committees, and contributing to the columns of its journal.

The organization of the Society was completed in Washington on 29 January 1906, at a meeting of the Executive Council. James Brown Scott was elected Recording Secretary, Charles Henry Butler, the Corresponding Secretary, and Chandler P. Anderson, the Treasurer. At a second meeting of the Executive Council held at the Lake Mohonk Conference on 1 June 1906, Dr. Scott was appointed Managing Editor of the *American Journal of International Law*, with authority to name an Editorial Board to assist him, and to proceed with the publication of the journal in accordance with the plan previously approved. The plan contemplated that the journal should contain original articles of a historical or critical nature and articles dealing with important principles of international law involved in present questions; editorial comments in which the journal might express its view on international matters; a chronicle of international events, the texts of decisions of domestic and foreign courts based upon or affecting international law; a summary or symposia of the literature of international law; a bibliography of American, English, and foreign publications relating to international law as they issue from the press, and book reviews written by specialists; and a supplement containing the texts of significant treaties, conventions, and the like. It should be remembered that at that time there were no publications of the Department of State giving current information on such matters. Its official reports to the public were confined to the series known as *Foreign Relations of the United States*, in which such information was published from fifteen to twenty-five years *post facto*. As will be seen later in this biography, the American Society of International Law was instrumental in having established the Division of Publications in the Department.

Because the preparation of the journal would involve great industry and labor, patience and time, Dr. Scott recommended that it be issued quarterly. Such a journal, his plan urged, "would be of great service to students and specialists, as well as to the lay reader, for it would be the only journal in the English language exclusively devoted to the interests of international law. It would also be of importance in the development of international law, for it would offer an ever ready means of reaching and instructing the public. Its contributors would naturally be specialists in international law, such as professors, international law practitioners, diplomatists, and students of diplomatic history. Articles should be solicited from the great foreign authorities and publicists of France, Germany, Italy, Spain, not to omit Russia. When received, these articles should be translated and published in English.[2]

Dr. Scott's case for the establishment of the Society was stated in a prospectus defining its aim and scope. The prospectus was published in pamphlet form and sent to prospective members in Government service, the diplomatic corps of the United States and foreign countries, judges, professors of international law and re-

---

[2] *Proceedings*, 1907, p. 30.

lated subjects, lawyers with an international practice, and other specially interested persons. The prospectus called attention to the keen interest of the people and government of the United States in the common law of nations as shown by the Constitution, Acts of Congress, the conduct of foreign affairs from the beginning of its existence, and the decisions of its courts. The need for the Society was indicated by the lack in the English-speaking world of any periodical devoted exclusively to international law.[3]

The first number of the journal was published in January 1907. Owing to the lack of funds in the Society's treasury, the cost of that number as well as of the second quarterly issue of April 1907 was paid personally by Dr. Scott. He was subsequently reimbursed by the Society.

The responses to the Society's invitations were many and gratifying. It soon had a membership whose annual dues of five dollars, which included subscription to the journal, provided funds sufficient to pay the cost of publication. Neither Dr. Scott nor any other officers of the Society ever received any compensation for their services and contributions to the journal were always gratuitous.

The journal declined to dilute its professional character by extraneous advertising. The office of the Society was in Dr. Scott's home until after the founding of the Carnegie Endowment for International Peace, when its trustees provided the Society with office space in its Washington buildings.

The first annual meeting of the Society was held in Washington 19-20 April 1907, under the presidency of Mr. Root. In the meantime Dr. Scott had been appointed Solicitor for the Department of State. He received much encouragement and valuable assistance from the Secretary of State. Mr. Root contributed the first article to the Society's journal, in which he emphasized the "need of popular understanding of international law". Mr. Root enlarged upon this theme in his first presidential address before the Society on 19 April 1907:

> In opening this meeting of the American Society of International Law, which I hope will be the first of many meetings in unbroken succession to continue long after we personally have

---

[3] For the text of the prospectus, see *Proceedings of the Society*, 1907, pp. 35–37.

cased to take part in affairs, let me welcome you to the beginning of your labors for a more thorough understanding of this important and fascinating subject. It is impossible that the human mind should be addressed to questions better worth its noblest efforts, offering a greater opportunity for usefulness in the exercise of its powers, or more full of historical and contemporary interest, than in the field of international rights and duties. The change in the theory and practice of government which has marked the century since the establishment of the American Union has shifted the determination of great questions of domestic national policy from a few rulers in each country to the great body of the people, who render the ultimate decision under all modern constitutional governments. Coincident with that change, the practice of diplomacy has ceased to be a mystery confined to a few learned men who strive to give effect to the wishes of personal rulers, and has become a representative function answering to the opinions and the will of the multitude of citizens, who themselves create the relations between states and determine the issues of friendship and estrangement, of peace and war. Under the new system there are many dangers from which the old system was free. The rules and customs which the experience of centuries had shown to be essential to the maintenance of peace and good understanding between nations have little weight with the new popular masters of diplomacy; the precedents and agreements of opinions which have carried so great a part of the rights and duties of nations toward each other beyond the pale of discussion are but little understood. The education of public opinion, which should lead the sovereign people in each country to understand the definite limitations upon national rights and the full scope and responsibility of national duties, has only just begun. Information, understanding, leadership of opinion in these matters, so vital to wise judgment and right action in international affairs, are much needed. This Society may serve as a *collegium*, in the true sense of the word, in which all who choose to seek a broader knowledge of the law that governs the affairs of nations may give each to the other the incitement to be earnest and faithful study and may give to the great body of our countrymen a clearer view of their international rights and responsibilities.[4]

Mr. Root continued as the Society's President for eighteen years, during which time he delivered a series of annual presiden-

---

[4] Proceedings, 1907, pp. 43–44.

tial addresses that added to the Society's prestige and enhanced its President's international reputation.

At times, the *American Journal of International Law* was utilized as a ready medium for the dissemination of official and other material to selected readers bearing on international law and international relations. For instance, when the Department of State decided to publish its diplomatic correspondence concerning neutral rights and duties prior to World War I, it arranged with the Society for prompt publication of the texts in Supplements to the journal. On such occasions the Carnegie Endowment contributed to the expenses of publication of the material. Similar provision was made for the publication and circulation of projects for the codification of international law by the League of Nations, the American Institute of International Law, and the Harvard Research in International Law. Dr. Scott's title on the journal was soon changed to Editor-in-Chief with a Board of Editors to assist him. He continued in that capacity and as Recording Secretary of the Society until Mr. Root retired from the presidency in April 1924. Dr. Scott decided at the same time that he should retire from the positions he then held. His retirement was received with the deepest regret and with profound appreciation of his services, as shown by the following minute entered upon the records of the meeting of the Society on 26 April 1924:

> After eighteen years of faithful and untiring service, Dr. James Brown Scott has indicated a desire to retire from his long service as Recording Secretary of the Society and as Editor-in-Chief of its Journal. The Executive Council does not wish the occasion to pass without an expression of its profound regret at the loss of Dr. Scott's services in both these offices, and desires the members of the Society to understand that only after persistent efforts to have him reconsider his purpose and his determined refusal so to do that it has been willing gracefully, though reluctantly, to accept the situation.
>
> Dr. Scott was not merely one of the founders of the Society, but the one upon whom the chief burden fell in executing the plan and in carrying it forward to success. He brought to the Society from the beginning, and has continued to evidence throughout, a genius for organization, high scholarly ideals and an untiring industry without which the Society could not have been the force that it now is in the study of international law and

> in the establishment of better international relations on the basis of law and justice.
>
> As Dr. Scott is by no means retiring from his activities in the Society, but only from the burdens of active office, it is not intended to review his achievements or public services but only to emphasize that he has never permitted other positions in government and unofficial service to interfere either with the efficient administration of the Society's affairs as Secretary, nor with the scholarly direction of its Journal, to which he contributed not only numerous articles but the chief body of its editorial comment. That both phases of the Society's activities should have continued successfully through the difficult years of the war is due to the wise counsel of our distinguished President, Mr. Root, and others, but particularly to him upon whom, in large measure, the detail work fell. We are especially indebted to Dr. Scott for systematically and ably bringing to the notice of our members the problems confronting our government and the solutions arrived at in that period, so momentous in its effects upon international law.[5]

Dr. Scott was elected Honorary Editor-in-Chief of the Journal, which position he retained until his death. He was elected President of the Society in 1929 and continued in that position for ten years, when he was made Honorary President. He retained that office until his death in 1943.

It was the privilege of the writer of this biography to serve as Dr. Scott's chief assistant in all of his work in the American Society of International Law and with the *American Journal of International Law* beginning in the latter part of the year 1909.

Dr. Scott took part in the celebration of the 25th anniversary of the founding of the Society in Washington in April 1931. A number of prominent members of the Society who had been with it for many years were present and the celebration took the form of a tribute to Dr. Scott's services and leadership. Mr. George Wickersham recalled that he was President of the Association of the Bar of the City of New York, in whose building the Society was born in June 1906, and that three years later, when he came to Washington as Attorney General of the United States, "the first thing that happened to me was an invitation of Dr. Scott to attend one of the meetings of this Society. I told him I was not a member. He said he

---

[5] *Proceedings of the American Society of International Law*, 1924, p. 148.

would soon correct that, and I quickly found myself a member and an interested participant ... I have followed the deliberations and the work of the Society with constant interest ever since". He then paid the following tribute to the Journal:

> I have always marveled that this *Journal* has maintained such high excellence and has had such an increasing influence and position in international thought, but I reflect that Horace Walpole once said that virtue is the compensation given to the poor for the lack of riches. The cooperative effort of a body of men giving their services without reward to this great task, for a society that had very little in the way of material resources, has eventuated in establishing a journal of primary importance in the world touching the subjects with which it concerns itself, until today the *Journal* of this Society enjoys an authority second to none and has a practical adaptability and usefulness which I think is primary over all others. My interest in that work has been quickened by the fact that its direction was in the hands of a man whom I first met some forty-odd years ago and with whom I have enjoyed a friendship ever since which has been one of the bright things in my life and experience.[6]

Dr. David Jayne Hill recalled that Dr. Scott discussed the Journal with him at The Hague in 1907, when they were both members of the American Delegation to the First Peace Conference in that city. While he could not date back his connection with Journal to its cradle, "I helped to wash and dress and give medicine to the child later on". Dr. Hill was for many years a member of the Board of Editors of the Journal. Looking back over the 25 years of existence of the Journal, Dr. Hill said:

> I have seen it grow in value and in authority. I cannot conceive of any leadership that could have accomplished more or even that could have accomplished so much, because here there was a background of adequate learning, of absolute zeal and devotion, and above all a permanent and deeply-rooted idea that justice, if we could only ascertain what it is and how it is to be determined and applied, should rule the nations as well as individual men.

---

[6] Ibid., 1931, p. 246.

One of the original members of the Society present at its founding in New York on 12 January 1906 then spoke as follows:

> As I look back over the first 25 years of our existence, I am sure the various Secretaries of State, the heads of departments, and even the Presidents, must have felt that we have at least made a worthy contribution in organizing the legal minds of our country for the expression of what is the best and the highest in that science from the point of view of American practice and American policy. In organizing such a group, placing it upon an active basis, and continuing with its labors over a quarter of a century in the notable manner in which you, Dr. Scott, and your associates have done, you have made a memorable contribution to the life and work of our nation and our Government. As a younger member I bring that tribute and lay it at your feet today.[7]

Dr. Scott, who was presiding at the luncheon meeting at which these remarks were made, expressed his surprise that those present had "indulged in personal observations or views". He ended their encomiums by referring to a memorable incident in the history of Greece:

> There was an occasion upon which the friends of one Miltiades, who was in command of the coming of Hellas, at the time in question, wished to erect a monument to him. The Greeks, a very intelligent people, a very reasonable people, replied that they would be delighted to do so if Miltiades could prove that he was the only person at Marathon. The statue has still to be erected.
>
> Gentlemen, this is a collective movement, this is a cooperative movement in which I happened to bear perhaps the laboring oar, but all of us pulled together, all of us in the same boat, and all of us at the end of life's tempestuous journey, swinging slowly, gracefully and peacefully at anchor.

---

[7] Proceedings, 1931, p. 247.

6

THE AMERICAN INSTITUTE OF INTERNATIONAL LAW

From the inception of the Pan American Conferences at Washington in 1889, the American Republics have endeavored to subject their international relations to juridical regulation and to bring about, by means of international conventions, uniformity in the principles of international law. At the first conference, to which, it may be noted in passing, Mr. Andrew Carnegie was an official delegate of the Government of the United States, a Plan of International Arbitration was adopted for the settlement of international disputes to which it was intended that European powers were to be invited to become parties. A formal treaty to put the plan into effect was signed on 28 April 1890, by eleven American States, including the United States, but the treaty lapsed through failure of all of its signatories to exchange ratifications within the required time.

The Conference at the same time, on 18 April 1890, adopted a recommendation urging the governments to declare that during the continuance of the Treaty of Arbitration the principle of conquest should not be recognized as admissible under American public law and that all cessions of territory should be void if made under threats of war or in the presence of an armed force.[1]

The Second Pan American Conference, held at Mexico City in 1901–1902, adopted a convention providing for the appointment of an international committee of jurists to draft codes of public and

---

[1] J. B. Scott (ed. & intro.), *International Conferences of American States, 1889–1928* (1931), p. 44. This volume contains a collection of the conventions, recommendations, resolutions, reports, and motions adopted by the first six international conferences of American States, and documents relating to the organization of the conferences. A supplementary volume, including similar documentary material for succeeding conferences, with an appendix of synopses of technical Pan American Conferences and Commissions, was edited and published by the Division of International Law in 1940.

private international law to govern the relations between the American nations. That committee was not appointed because the convention was not ratified by a sufficient number of signatories.[2] The attempt was more successful at the Third Pan American Conference held at Rio de Janeiro in 1906. There an identical convention was adopted, which was ratified by seventeen states, including the United States, which established an International Commission of Jurists for the codification of international law. The Commission was organized and held its first meeting in Rio de Janeiro from 26 June to 19 July 1912.[3]

Genesis of the American Institute of International Law

Dr. Scott's active participation in the work of the Institute of International Law in Europe and his knowledge of the services it had rendered to the official conferences at The Hague and elsewhere led him to think of the desirability of establishing an American Institute of International Law to render similar services to the American International Conferences. Only a few members from Latin America were elected to the European Institute, and problems of special concern to the Western Hemisphere were not specifically discussed at its meetings.

An opportunity to discuss his idea with a well-known jurist who was his counterpart in South America occurred in the spring of 1911 when Dr. Alejandro Alvarez, Jurisconsult of the Chilean Ministry of Foreign Affairs, made a brief visit to Washington. Dr. Alvarez had a wide reputation for his efforts to promote what he called American International Law. He had been a delegate to the Third and Fourth Pan American Conferences, was a member of the Permanent Court of Arbitration at The Hague, and counselor to the Chilean diplomatic missions in Europe. He also represented his government on the International Commission of Jurists at Rio de Janeiro.

Dr. Alvarez spent the better part of two days in Washington with Dr. Scott, then newly appointed Director of the Division of

---

[2] Ibid., p. 69.
[3] Ibid., p. 144.

International Law of the Carnegie Endowment. An account of their conversations was given by Dr. Scott in a letter to Mr. Root, President of the Endowment, dated 3 June 1911:

> Our relations with Latin America were much discussed. I stated my great desire to see the nations of North and South America drawn more closely together as the result of an interchange of thought and the creation of a better understanding . . . Dr. Alvarez seemed to feel that the Pan American Union could serve as an intermediary between the Governments, although in the last two years its influence had not been so great owing to the aggressive policy of the United States.
>
> I expressed the view that if we could bring the peoples of the various countries in closer touch, diplomatic relations would take care of themselves, and suggested that the interchange of thought and the better understanding created by an exchange of professors and students would, in the course of time, draw us together intellectually, and that it was possible to set on foot a movement for the dissemination of those principles of law and justice which should regulate the foreign relations of the countries, especially their intercourse in times of peace. I suggested the establishment in the capital of each Latin American country of a local society of international law which might work in harmony with our society [American Society of International Law—*GF*], and Mr. Alvarez expressed himself as heartily in favor of the idea. After reflection and very much discussion, we came to the conclusion that the best way to draw the leaders of thought together would be to create an American Institute of International Law, in which each country should have equal representation, say five members; that the members of each country should organize at their capital a local society of international law; that the Institute should hold annual meetings, preferably at Washington, and discuss scientific questions of international law, especially those relating to peace, so that, little by little, a code of international law might be drafted which would represent the enlightened thought of American publicists and be the result of their sympathetic collaboration. Mr. Alvarez informed me that he was on his way to Paris to prepare a draft code of international law to be presented to the committee appointed pursuant to the resolution of the Pan American Conference.
>
> Knowing that the delegates of the Governments would not represent international law but the views of the Governments appointing them, that is to say, that the code would be political instead of scientific, I suggested that a much more satisfactory

> code could be produced by the painstaking study of unofficial publicists, and that a code produced under such circumstances would not merely be better in itself but would stand a better chance of adoption in whole or in part by the Governments, either expressly at some Pan American Conference or silently and piecemeal in the practice of the various foreign offices. Mr. Alvarez was very much impressed by these ideas and said that he would communicate with his friends in South America, that an Institute of the kind proposed would be, in his opinion, the very best method of bringing the various peoples together in a non-political way, and that the headquarters of the Institute should be at Washington which was really the capital of the Americas.[4]

In his letter to Mr. Root, Dr. Scott added: "if a political or diplomatic union of a closer nature than the Pan American Union at Washington and the Pan American Conferences seems to be out of the question, it is nevertheless possible to being a movement whose purpose should be to determine and promote the principles of law and justice which should regulate the international relations of the American countries and especially their relations in time of peace". Mr. Root approved the project as outlined by Dr. Scott and later consented to become the Honorary President of the new organization.

Following the preliminary discussions in Washington, Dr. Alvarez proceeded to Paris, where he remained for some months. In October of that year Dr. Scott followed him to that city to attend a meeting of a committee of the European Institute of International Law. While there together, on 10 October 1911, they jointly signed and sent a confidential letter explaining the nature and scope of the proposed American Institute to representative publicists with whom they were acquainted in each of the American Republics and inviting their cooperation. The project met with enthusiastic approval and with promises of cooperation.

Before proceeding further, to quote Dr. Scott, "the proposers of the Institute were unwilling to trust their own judgment, although approved by their friends in Latin America. They felt that they might be unconsciously the victims of enthusiasm. They, therefore, addressed representative members of the Institute of International

---

[4] See a memorandum dated 3 June 1911 in Dr. Scott's papers, and J. B. Scott, "The American Institute of International Law", *University of Pennsylvania Law Review* (June 1913).

Law, whose experience and detachment would enable them to weigh rightly the benefits reasonably to be expected from such an Institute and the difficulties in the way of its creation". The consultations with the Europeans took various forms, Dr. Scott and Dr. Alvarez had personal contacts with some of them while in Europe and obtained expressions of opinion in writing.

Other opinions were obtained through correspondence with distinguished members of the profession in various European capitals. Articles outlining the plan and purposes of the new Institute were written by Professor A. de Lapradelle of the Law Faculty of the University of Paris and published in the *Revue générale de droit international public* and by M. Paul Fauchille, Director of the Revue, together with opinions from Europeans.[5]

Only a few friendly criticisms were received. It was suggested that the name of the new Institute might be confused with the Institute already existing in Europe; and the concept of regional international law, such as American international law, as distinct from universal international law, was challenged by one or two writers. Dr. Scott answered these criticisms in identical letters, dated 7 November 1912, to leading members of the European Institute:

> The name "American" has been used for geographical reasons, to distinguish this Institute from the (international) Institute of International Law, of which you are an honored member, not to suggest that there is or can be an American International Law. There are indeed American problems to be solved by the application of the generally-recognized principles of international law, and, if these principles do not suffice, it may well be that they will be required to be developed in the future, as in the past, to meet new and changed conditions. I make this statement, in order that there may be no mistake as to our purpose, which is to contribute, to the full extent of our abilities, to the development and the dissemination of a system of international law, as it has been created by the weight and wisdom of European publicists.

Following these consultations, Dr. Scott decided to proceed with the organization of the American Institute. He drafted a Constitution and By-Laws based upon those of the European Institute

---

[5] These opinions were published by the American Institute in a volume entitled *Institut Americain de droit international: historique, notes, opinions* (1916).

and sent them on 4 July 1912 on behalf of himself and Dr. Alvarez to the American publicists to whom they had addressed their first communication. The recipients were asked, if they approved the project, to sign and return the proposed Constitution and By-Laws and by so doing to become charter members of the new Institute. They were further asked to authorize the proposers to effectuate a temporary organization.

In the meantime Dr. Alvarez had attended the meeting of the International Commission of Jurists at Rio de Janeiro during the same month of July, and after the adjournment of the Commission he returned to Washington to confer with Dr. Scott about the American Institute. While in Rio, he had succeeded in obtaining a formal resolution commending the initiative taken to found the Institute and recording the opinion of a committee of the Rio Commission that the Institute would be of great usefulness in the work of codification which the statesmen of the New World had in view.

The Latin American recipients of the letter of 4 July approved the Constitution and By-Laws of the proposed Institute and authorized Dr. Scott and Dr. Alvarez to proceed with the temporary organization. This they did by declaring the American Institute of International Law founded on Columbus Day, 12 October 1912. The following provisional officers were designated: Elihu Root, Honorary President; James Brown Scott, President; Alejandro Alvarez, Secretary General; Luis Anderson (for Minister of Foreign Affairs of Costa Rica), Treasurer. A circular note signed by Messrs. Scott and Alvarez was sent to the charter members, notifying them of the Institute's founding and requesting that they proceed at once with the establishment of a Society of International Law in each country as required by the Constitution of the new Institute.

A second note sent to them on 18 December 1912 by Dr. Scott informed the charter members that the time for collaboration had arrived, and that the founders believed themselves justified in calling upon the charter members in each country to aid in the task of founding the national societies, which, Messrs. Scott and Alvarez admitted, was too heavy for them. As the next few years would prove, the task was also beyond the unaided capabilities of the charter members. It was an undertaking of continental proportions and was eventually accomplished only by a conjunction of events and by bringing to bear upon the objective effective influences which happened to be available to Dr. Scott at that time and which he knew well how to master.

The Carnegie Endowment for International Peace was founded by Andrew Carnegie on the understanding that Elihu Root would be its first president. His reputation for sympathetic understanding of the Latin American countries was at its peak due to the success of his visit to Latin America while Secretary of State at the time of the Third Pan American Conference, at Rio de Janeiro, in 1906. Mr. Root had made that visit largely for the purpose of counteracting the unfavorable impressions of the Big Stick policy of the United States. The results of that policy and the success of Secretary Root's mission were communicated to Congress in a message that President Roosevelt sent to Congress on 3 December 1906 after Mr. Root's return:

> In many parts of South America there has been much misunderstanding of the attitude and purposes of the United States toward the other American republics. An idea had become prevalent that our assertion of the Monroe Doctrine implied, or carried with it, an assumption of superiority, and of a right to exercise some kind of protectorate over the countries to whose territory that doctrine applies. Nothing could be further from the truth. Yet that impression continued to be a serious barrier to good understanding, to friendly intercourse, to the introduction of American capital and to the extension of American trade. The impression was so widespread that apparently it could not be reached by ordinary means.

It was part of Secretary Root's mission to dispel this unfounded impression, and there is just cause to believe that he has succeeded. In an address to the Third Conference of Rio on the thirty-first of July—an address of such note that I send it in, together with this message—he said:

> We wish for no victories but those of peace; for no territory except our own; for no sovereignty except the sovereignty over ourselves. We deem the independence and equal rights of the smallest and weakest member of the family of nations entitled to as much respect as those of the greatest empire, and we deem the observance of that respect the chief guaranty of the weak against the oppression of the strong. We neither claim nor desire any

rights or privileges or powers that we do not freely concede to every American republic.

The Bacon Mission

The Carnegie Endowment for International Peace wished to enlist worldwide interest and cooperation in its program. Its president, Elihu Root, especially desired to secure the interest and sympathy of the leaders of opinion in South America. To that end, Robert Bacon, who had been Assistant Secretary of State under Mr. Root, was invited by the Endowment to visit South America as its representative. Mr. Root's letter of instruction, dated 20 July 1913, explained the organization of the Endowment into three divisions of work, together with the specific objectives assigned to each. Mr. Root said to Mr. Bacon that he would observe "the respect and friendship which the trustees of the Endowment entertain for the peoples of Latin America and for the many distinguished Latin Americans with whom many of the trustees have the most agreeable relations of personal friendship". These relations, Mr. Root wrote, "lead us to desire that the work of the Endowment may have the same active and useful cooperation in South America that it has already secured in Europe".[6]

Mr. Bacon was asked to seek to bring about cooperation in South America in certain specific projects of each of the Endowment's Divisions. Among such projects of the Division of International Law was the formation of national societies of international law to be affiliated with the American Institute of International Law.

When he accepted the Endowment's initiative, Mr. Bacon was on his way home from the Orient and he decided to leave for Latin America from Lisbon. Dr. Scott and Dr. Alvarez met him in Paris and furnished him with all the information he needed regarding the American Institute and the national societies to be affiliated with it. Dr. Scott wrote some of the speeches on that subject to be delivered in South America. The time at Mr. Bacon's disposal for such an extended journey by sea and land transportation did not permit a

---

[6] The texts of Mr. Bacon's instructions and of his report on the visit were published in a volume entitled *For Better Relations with Our Latin American Neighbors* (1916).

visit to all the capitals of South America. He started his Latin American tour at Rio de Janeiro and spent a week more or less there and at Buenos Aires, Montevideo, Santiago de Chile, and Lima. The party had left Lisbon on 23 September and reached New York from Panama on 27 November.

The Bacon mission was well prepared in advance of its arrival in Latin America by appropriate information sent through diplomatic channels. He was cordially received everywhere by the highest officials of government and given every opportunity during the time at his disposal to fulfill his mission. He had interviews with the Ministers of Foreign Affairs and other important officials in each of the countries visited and was received by the Presidents of Brazil, Uruguay, Chile, and Peru. He was invited to address distinguished audiences in university and legal circles. In some places Mr. Bacon met former colleagues of Dr. Scott at the Second Hague Peace Conference who paid high tribute to him. As a result of Mr. Bacon's efforts, committees to organize a national society of international law were appointed in each of the capitals he visited.

Second Pan American Scientific Congress

In the meantime Dr. Alvarez and Dr. Scott were on the alert for some opportunity for a meeting of the Institute in order formally to organize and begin its activities. The great distances to be traveled between the various American capitals, and the time and expense involved, had to be taken into consideration if a sufficient number of members were to be present to constitute a quorum. In this connection Dr. Scott and Mr. Root came up with the suggestion that the American Institute of International Law might formally meet in Washington in connection with the holding of the Second Pan American Scientific Congress scheduled to take place in December 1915. A circular letter containing this suggestion was sent by Dr. Scott on 25 August 1914 to the organizing committees and charter members in Latin America, urging that they take all steps necessary to complete the organization of the national societies and recommend their members for election to the Institute, so that they might be properly represented at the meeting to be held in 1915. The importance of these letters was sought to be emphasized by sending them in care of the American diplomatic missions in each of the countries.

The outbreak of war in Europe was not calculated to encourage activities in the field of international law. *Inter arma silent leges.* The European Institute of International Law, divided in membership between friends and enemies, was of course obliged to discontinue its meetings. The friends of Dr. Scott and Dr. Alvarez in Latin America needed considerable more encouragement under the circumstances than that provided by Mr. Bacon's visit, to proceed with the organization of their national societies. While the purpose of the American Institute was similar to its European precursor, its structure was different. The European Institute was unitary in organization and its members and associates were chosen by it. The American prototype was organized on the federative principle. Its full membership could only be composed of candidates recommended by the national societies in each American country. It was accordingly not in a position to function properly until such societies had been organized and made nominations to fill the Institute's quota of five members from each.

Sensing the feeling of discouragement in Latin American due to the outbreak of the war in Europe, Dr. Scott and Dr. Alvarez undertook to meet the situation in a long letter to the charter members dated 22 February 1915. The letter restated the steps that had been taken to organize the Institute and its associates in the national societies. They argued that the war in Europe was the most important event in the history of mankind, that because of its economic and political effects it was sure to mark in history the end of the system under which Europe was living; that one of the lessons it taught was the necessity of subjecting national relations more and more to legal rules armed with effective sanctions, and that war made clear the fact that public opinion is one of the most effective sanctions; that the efforts of the European belligerents to win the good opinion of American neutrals abroad showed the need for a continental conscience or opinion; and that thus the idea of an American Institute of International Law based upon societies of international law in each American country had acquired great force and timeliness: "Today, when European civilization is passing through a formidable crisis", they urged, Latin America "must organize in order to become the spokesman of law and justice in international relations".[7]

It is doubtful that even these efforts would have been completely successful had it not been for the financial aid extended to the participants in the Second Pan American Scientific Congress by the Carnegie Endowment for International Peace. Favorable responses to the official invitations issued by the Government of the United States were disappointing and fears for the success of the Conference seemed well-grounded. To avoid such a failure, Mr. John Barrett, then Director General of the Pan American Union, appealed for assistance to Mr. Root as President of the Carnegie Endowment for International Peace. Mr. Root had been Chairman of the Governing Board of the Pan American Union during his tenure of office as Secretary of State of the United States, and he decided to come to the rescue of the Scientific Congress. Upon his initiative, the Endowment decided to invite as its guests, with provision for traveling expenses, three delegates to be selected by each of the Latin American Governments, one delegate to be a specialist in the field of activity of each of the three big divisions of the Endowment, namely, an educator, an economist or historian, and an international lawyer. The Endowment's generous invitations were communicated by cablegram to each of the Latin American countries through diplomatic channels, and it was intimated that in appointing an international lawyer as an official delegate to the Scientific Congress, the charter member or other permanent member of the national society of international law would be especially welcomed.

In the meantime, Robert Lansing, a personal friend of Dr. Scott of long standing, became Secretary of State of the United States. Mr. Lansing was, with Dr. Scott, one of the founders of the American Society of International Law, and had been recommended and elected a member of the American Institute of International Law from the United States. Mr. Lansing became Secretary of State about the time arrangements were being made for the Second Pan American Scientific Congress to meet in Washington upon the invitation of the Government of the United States in December 1915. Dr. Scott was appointed a member of the Program Committee of the Congress, Vice-Chairman of its Executive Committee, Reporter General of the Conference, and Chairman of its Section

[7] Year Book of the Carnegie Endowment, 1915, pp. 121–130.

on International Law, Public Law, and Jurisprudence. Working together, Secretary Lansing and Dr. Scott lost no time in manifesting the interest of the Department of State in the successful formation of national societies of international law and the creation of the American Institute. The official program of the Second Pan American Scientific Congress sent to the Ministers of Foreign Affairs of all the American Republics included the following passages:

> It is hoped that the American Institute of International Law, which is composed of representatives of the different national societies in the Pan American countries, may be formally inaugurated and hold its first session in Washington, under the auspices of the Second Pan American Scientific Congress.
>
> National societies have been formed in Brazil, Chile, Mexico, Nicaragua, Peru, and Uruguay, and are in process of formation in others. It is believed that in this way international law, consisting not merely of the rights but of the duties of nations, will be brought home to the peoples of the different countries through the national societies composed of persons interested in the subject, versed in its principles, and competent to expound and to popularize them.
>
> The Institute, composed of five publicists from each American country, recommended by the national societies, will, it is hoped, do for international law in the Americas what the older Institute of International Law has done for international law in general, and the scientific co-operation of American publicists will not only advance the cause of international law and base the actions of governments upon its principles, but will strengthen the bonds of sympathy which exist between and among the American Republics.
>
> The formation of these societies in all of the countries of Central and South America will materially aid in this educational process, and any encouragement or co-operation which the Governments of the American Republics can extend will give the movement an official impetus.

The time for the meeting of the Scientific Congress in Washington was fixed at 27 December 1915.

Repeated requests of the same character were sent by Dr. Scott on 7 April 1915 to the heads of American Embassies and Legations accredited to the American Republics, enclosing communications to the respective Ministries of Foreign Affairs, members of organizing Committees and charter members. With these communications was enclosed a copy of a decree of the President of Uruguay, dated 29 December 1914, appointing a committee to organize a national society of international law, which the decree declared should have legal status as an institute of public interest.

Presidential decrees similar to the Uruguay decree were issued in a number of countries; in others, the initiative was taken directly by the Minister of Foreign Affairs, and in a few capitals the personal urging of Secretary of State Lansing through diplomatic channels was required. In either event, the formation of a national society in each American Republic was completed in time to be represented when the Second Pan American Scientific Congress convened in Washington on 27 December 1915. Prior to that date, the American Institute was officially welcomed by the Governing Board of the Pan American Union in the following resolution adopted 1 December 1915:

> Considering that the official inauguration of the American Institute of International Law, founded in Washington 12 October 1912, is soon to take place under the auspices of the Second Pan American Scientific Congress; and
>
> Considering that said Institute, consisting of representatives of every one of the American republics, recommended by the international law associations of their respective countries, will result in strengthening, through the active cooperation of jurists and thinkers of the whole continent, the bonds of friendship and union now existing between these republics, and will contribute to the development of a common sentiment of international justice among them, the Governing Board of the Pan American Union,
>
> *Resolves*, To tender to the founders and members of the American Institute of International Law a vote of commendation and encouragement for the foundation of the said organization, which represents a step of the highest importance in the moral advancement of the continent and in the strengthening of the sentiments of friendship and harmony among the republics.

Declaration of Rights and Duties of Nations

The American Institute of International Law met for the first time on the afternoon of 29 December 1915 in the beautiful marble building of the Pan American Union at Washington, a gift from

Andrew Carnegie as a Temple of Peace to the American Republics. The meetings of that Institute on that and in the following days were integrated into the program of the Section on International Law of the Second Pan American Scientific Congress and of the Annual Meeting of the American Society of International Law, which had been postponed from the preceding April in order to meet with these two organizations in December.

The meeting of the American Institute was attended by four members from the American Society of International Law, namely, Robert Lansing, who as Secretary of State welcomed the Institute on behalf of the Government of the United States; Elihu Root, as Honorary President of the Institute; James Brown Scott, its President, and Robert Bacon, who had toured Latin America on behalf of the Institute. Three members were present from the national societies of international law of Haiti and Honduras; two members represented each of the societies in Argentina, Bolivia, Brazil, Chile, Ecuador, Guatemala, Peru, and Uruguay; and there was one representative each from Colombia, Costa Rica, Cuba, Dominican Republic, Mexico, Nicaragua, Panama, Paraguay, Salvador, and Venezuela. All of the delegates were men of the highest distinction in the field of international law or government in their respective countries. One of the Chilean delegates was also President of the Scientific Congress.

Dr. Scott presided at a preliminary meeting which transacted the necessary business of formally adopting the Constitution and By-Laws making permanent the temporary officers previously designated, and electing the full quota of members from each of the national societies. When this business was out of the way, Dr. Scott introduced Elihu Root to open the solemn session, which he did in a brief address, in the course of which he said:

> We all know that there is throughout the American Republics a feeling for the better safeguarding of our liberty and of justice, for the better establishment and enforcement of those laws of nations which are the protection of national independence and peace. That feeling requires an institution through which to become effective, and this Institute furnishes the institution that is necessary for the continued life of the feeling. If it did not respond to a general demand, existing in the intelligence and feeling of the American peoples, it would come to naught. If it does respond to the intelligence and to the feeling of the American

> peoples, it will be a great and lasting agency for the good of mankind. I believe that it does; I believe that through it there may be consolidated and created and perpetuated a united sentiment, opinion, feeling, and purpose, which will make for the benefit of all our countries. At all events, it is worth an effort. The good intentions, the strong desires, toward what is best throughout the Americas should not be allowed to go without an opportunity to become effective. It is an effort in a noble cause which we are organizing, and I firmly believe that in future years our children will look back to the organization of this Institute as one of the important steps in the great new departure which the influence of the democratic governments of the New World has added to the debt of mankind and to the cause of liberty and justice.[8]

A number of proposals were submitted to the Institute, including a memorandum from Secretary of State Lansing suggesting a study of the rights and duties of neutrals.[9] Dr. Scott had in the preceding January, in anticipation of the successful inauguration of the Institute, filed with the Secretary General memoranda proposing a series of studies to be undertaken after the Institute got started. Among them was the preamble from the Declaration of Independence of the United States, which he offered "as the American conception of the origin, nature and purpose of the State and as to the function of the Government established within each State. He proposed a study to determine to what extent and in what form the principles of the American Declaration are applicable to the State as a moral, that is, an artificial person, because, if the State be the creature of the subject, if the government be the creature of law and responsible to law, it is a moral or artificial person and as such subject to law. His conclusion, expressed in the memorandum, was that "if this conception should meet with the approval of the Institute, we could begin to develop an American international law, based upon an American conception of the State and an American conception of the government thereof".[10]

---

[8] Papers of Dr. Scott. A French version of Mr. Root's address is included in the published proceedings of the Institute entitled *Procès Verbaux de la première session tenue à Washington* (*1915–1916*) (1916), pp. 10–11.
[9] Mr. Lansing's memorandum was published in the Carnegie Endowment Year book 1916, p. 127.
[10] Scott Mss.

The foregoing proposal of Dr. Scott became the basis of the principal accomplishment of the inaugural meeting of the Institute. On 6 January 1916 it adopted a Declaration of the Rights and Duties of Nations, in which Dr. Scott elaborated his earlier proposals. The Declaration consisted of a preamble of eight paragraphs premising the analogy of the rights and duties of nations with those of individuals and six substantive articles.[11]

The Declaration was accompanied by an commentary of Dr. Scott, in which he undertook to demonstrate that it was a "statement of the fundamental rights, as well as duties, stated in terms of international law, based upon the fundamental rights now recognized by the municipal law of civilized nations to life, liberty and the pursuit of happiness, legal equality, to property and the right to the enjoyment of the aforesaid rights", and that "these fundamental rights of national jurisprudence are convertible in terms of international law and apply to the relations of the members of the Society of Nations, one with another, just as they have been applied in the relations of citizens or subjects of the states forming the Society of Nations".[12]

The Declaration of the American Institute was received with wide acclaim in the United States and abroad. Mr. Root expressed the opinion that the six postulates of the Declaration "are the fundamentals of international right. They involve the existence of a democratic community of nations in which each individual nation has the same rights and full liberty for their enjoyment, limited and limited only by the equal rights of every other member of the community. The body of rules of action which long experience and general consent have worked out for the assertion and preservation of these rights and the application of the universal limitation upon them in the practical relations between nations constitutes international law".[13]

Charles Evans Hughes, when he became Secretary of State a few years later, declared: "It cannot be doubted that this declaration embodies the fundamental principles of the policy of the United

---

[11] The Declaration and Official Commentary were printed separately in English, French, Spanish, and Portuguese by the Institute.

[12] See Dr. Scott's Report as Director of the Division of International Law, Carnegie Endowment Year Book, 1923, p. 249.

[13] *Proceedings of the American Society of International Law* (1916), p. 4.

States in relation to the Republics of Latin America. When we recognized these Republics as members of the family of nations, we recognized their rights and obligations as repeatedly defined by our statesmen and jurists and by our highest court".[14]

At the close of the Second Pan American Scientific Congress on 8 January 1916, a resolution was included in its Final Act extending a cordial welcome to the American Institute of International Law into the circle of scientific organizations of Pan America.

Leading French authorities on international law were especially laudatory in their approval of the Declaration. Professor Louis Renault, of the University of Paris, welcomed the American Institute and its Declaration with joy as "proclaiming certain essential principles that dominate the law of nations everywhere. All might be quoted and might find their application in present conditions". He mentioned particularly the first article, which, he said, condemned "the so-called right of necessity which Germany invoked against Belgium", the consequences of which were "irreconcilable with the idea of a true law of nations, based, not upon force, but upon justice".

Professor Charles Dupuis, of the École libre des sciences politiques, in Paris wrote:

> The Declaration of the Rights and Duties of Nations is at the same time American and universal: American in its manner, its form, its adaptation of the principles of internal law to the relations between States; universal in its content and in the motives which inspired it. Mr. James Brown Scott has well demonstrated in his concise, deep, and original argument, that principles which have been tested and recognized as just and beneficent in the relations between men, should be considered equally just and beneficent in relations between States, and that international law may make profitable use of the experiences of internal law . . . The philosophers of the 18th century, admirers of the philosopher king, spread the opinion in Europe that thenceforth the light would come from the North . . . the jurisconsults of the 20th century may say, and with better right, that in the West is rising a warmer light, which, lighted by the torch of Christianity and of

---

[14] Address in Commemoration of the Centenary of the Monroe Doctrine, Philadelphia, Pennsylvania, 30 November 1923, quoted in Carnegie Endowment Year Book 1924, p. 95.

> the best traditions of humanity, illumines anew the essential verities which German culture has veiled and darkened in old Europe . . . To the *will for power* America opposes the *will for justice*. It is in this will for justice that the principle of life for the society of nations, as for all society, lies.

Habana Session of American Institute of International Law

Upon the invitation of the Government of Cuba, the American Institute of International Law met in the city of Habana in January 1917 under the auspices of the Cuban Society of International Law. The President of Cuba opened the meeting, the Cuban Congress adopted resolutions of welcome and voted $10,000 for the entertainment of the members, the Secretary of State welcomed the Institute on behalf of the Government, and the City Council gave its members the freedom of the city. Projects were presented to the Institute, discussed, and referred to the national societies for the expression of their opinions, on the fundamental bases of international law, rights and duties of nations, fundamental rights in the American continents, neutrality in naval war, the organization of a court of arbitral justice, and a union or league of nations for the maintenance of peace.

A Final Act was adopted on 23 January 1917 containing what it called "Recommendations on International Organization". The recommendations called for period meetings of the Hague Conferences and the ratification and observance of their conventions, official acceptance of the principles of law contained in the Institute's Declaration of the Rights and Duties of Nations, the settlement of non-justifiable disputes by an international council of conciliation, or by resort to good offices and arbitration in such cases, and the creation of a judicial union with a permanent court for the settlement of justifiable disputes.[15] These recommendations were also

---

[15] The Proceedings of the Havana Meeting were published by the Institute in Spanish and French.

the work of Dr. Scott, who proposed and supported them with a detailed commentary appended to the text adopted.[16]

Dr. Nicholas Murray Butler, President of Columbia University, trustee and later President of the Carnegie Endowment, said of the recommendations of Habana:

> They provided a platform upon which all American governments and peoples can stand. Representative jurists from many different American Republics united in formulating and publishing this impressive Declaration. It may now be offered to the peoples of Europe and of Asia as America's positive contribution to the solution of the problem of providing a form of international cooperation which will avoid the creation of a super-government and rest international cooperation upon respect and reverence for law. This is the path of progress to which the traditions of American foreign policy point and this is the path upon which the Government of the United States may well invite other nations speedily to enter.[17]

Central American Court of Justice

The first permanent international court to be established in the world was the Central American Court of Justice created by the Central American Peace Conference held at Washington D. C. in 1907 under the presidency of the Secretary of State, Elihu Root. Dr. Scott was at that time Solicitor for the State Department, Mr. Andrew Carnegie was a guest at the Conference and made an address of encouragement to the delegates. He donated funds for the building of a court house in San José, Costa Rica, and when the building of the Central American Court of Justice was destroyed by earthquake a few years after its construction, he duplicated his gift to rebuild it.

The Court rendered a decision on 30 September 1916, holding that the treaty of 5 August 1914 between the United States and

[16] See American Institute of International Law, *Acta Final de la Sesion de la Habana* (Habana, 1917).

[17] "Introduction", *American Foreign Policy* (1920). The Recommendations of Habana were incorporated in the platform of the Republican Party of the State of New York in its convention held 20 February 1920. *New York Times*, 21 February 1920.

Nicaragua for the construction of an interoceanic canal violated the territorial rights of Costa Rica and other neighboring states. Nicaragua refused to accept the decision. The Government of the United States was prepared to accept it and settle the dispute diplomatically in order to save the Court. The American Institute of International Law was requested to use its influence to that end by sending an appeal to the societies of international law in the Central American countries urging them to secure the renewal of the treaty providing for the Court. Such an appeal was sent by the Institute on 1 March 1918, but to no avail. The Court went out of existence on 17 March of that year upon the termination of the ten-year period for which it had been created.[18]

Informal Contacts in Latin America

The American Institute of International Law avoided the discussion of political questions at its meetings, but there could be no inhibition on the exchange of personal views upon any subject they considered agreeable or fruitful to take about among the members themselves. Such personal contacts were often used by Dr. Scott to keep his friends in the State Department advised of the trend of opinion abroad on public questions before them. His opportunities for services of that character were set forth in a letter he wrote to his friend, William Phillips, Assistant Secretary of State, on 8 March 1917, in which he said:

> For the past ten years it has been my good fortune to meet prominent representatives of Latin America both at home and abroad. At the Second Hague Peace Conference I came into intimate and daily contact with them during the period of four months. At various times since I have met some of their most distinguished publicists. Last year at the Second Pan American Scientific Congress I met large numbers of them and in the sessions of the American Institute, where the exchange of views is very informed, I have got to know what they feel in private as well as what they express in public.

---

[18] A full account of this incident is contained in Dr. Scott's report to the Trustees of the Carnegie Endowment, Year Book, 1918, pp. 118–120.

The letter of 8 March followed a previous one of 3 March to Mr. Phillips transmitting a telegram, dated 28 February 1917, addressed to Dr. Scott and Mr. Alvarez, a month after the Habana meeting of the American Institute, by the five members from Colombia, urging the approval by the North American Senate of the treaty signed 6 April 1914 by Colombia and the United States "to remove all misunderstandings growing out of the political events in Panama in November 1903". Those events, well known in history, were the revolt of Panama against Colombia, the immediate recognition of the new government of Panama by the Government of the United States, and the prompt conclusion of the Panama Canal Treaty by the two last-named governments. Objections to certain provisions of the treaty of 1914 with Colombia were raised in the United States Senate and the treaty remained unapproved in that body for seven years.

With reference to the telegram of 28 February from Bogota, Dr. Scott informed the Assistant Secretary of State:

> The publicists of Latin America with whom I have come into contact seem to regard the failure to adjust with Colombia the difficulties over Panama as a very great obstacle in the way of a closer union of the American republics, and, until the controversy between Colombia and the United States is settled to the satisfaction of each, the critics of the United States in Latin America, of whom there are not a few, will in my opinion be afforded a plausible justification for their activity in preventing closer relations and friendly cooperation which advocates of Pan Americanism desire to see brought about".

Dr. Scott's letter was written less than a month before the United States found it necessary to declare war against Germany. He cited President Wilson's action, taken three days previously on 5 March, in personally urging upon Congress the repeal of the exemption of American coastwise trade from the payment of tolls when passing through the Panama Canal. Dr. Scott said in his letter of 8 March that "I know of no action of the President which reflected greater credit upon the United States, and he continued "The President refused to discuss the interpretation of the treaty, contenting himself with the statement that right or wrong the powers of the world were opposed to us in this matter, and stated that the repeal was necessary in the interest of the United States".

Dr. Scott concluded his letter by suggesting that the President make a similar appeal for Senate approval of the Colombian treaty "in the interest of better relations with Latin America" and "to remove that great obstacle standing in the way of the United States and the Latin American Republics".

A few weeks later, on 6 April 1917, the United States was in World War I as a belligerent, and it was promptly followed by a number of the other American Republics. Action upon the Colombian treaty was held up until the war was over.[19] On 20 April 1921, the Senate gave its advice and consent to ratification with some amendments and an understanding which were later accepted by Colombia.

The Institute received and accepted an invitation from the Government of Uruguay to hold its third session in Montevideo in 1918, but the participation of the United States and other American Republics in World War I postponed indefinitely further meetings of the Institute.

Dr. Scott and Dr. Antonio S. de Bustamante, of Cuba, the latter having become Vice President of the American Institute, both represented their governments at the peace negotiations at Paris in 1919. There they frequently discussed the possibility of resuming the activities of the Institute. After their return home, they called a meeting of the Executive Council in Dr. Bustamante's office in Habana. The Council decided to urge all members to reactivate or reorganize their national societies in anticipation of an early meeting of the Institute and to recommend new members for election by the Institute to fill vacancies due to losses of membership, of which there were a number. A long list of topics was suggested by the Council for study by the national societies according to their respective choices. The Council also decided that there should be established a journal published in the Spanish language to serve as the organ of the Institute. An offer of Dr. Bustamante to edit such a journal in Habana was accepted.

The desirability of a printed bulletin or other regular medium of contact for the members of the Institute had been seen from the beginning. The Carnegie Endowment for International Peace sought to meet the need by financing a Spanish edition of the

[19] For Dr. Scott's analysis and comment upon the dispute, see his editorial comment in the *American Journal of International Law*, XV (1921), p. 430.

American Journal of International Law beginning in 1912. After ten years, it was obvious that there was not sufficient demand for the translated edition to justify its continuance, and publication was terminated at the end of the year 1921. The Endowment transferred limited financial support to the new *Revista Americana de Derecho Internacional*, edited by Dr. Bustamante in Habana. It began publication as a quarterly in 1922 and continued through the 1950s. Deficits during Dr. Bustamante's lifetime were met by him.

Suggestions that the Institute meet in Mexico, or Panama, or Chile, in 1922 turned out to be impracticable, as did an idea of Dr. Scott that the American Institute meet with the Institute of International Law in Europe when the latter celebrated its fiftieth anniversary in Brussels in September 1923.

The Covenant of the League of Nations incorporated in the peace treaties ending World War I contained a provision for the establishment of a Permanent Court of International Justice, and the Council of the League appointed an Advisory Committee of Jurists to prepare a plan for the court. Mr. Elihu Root accepted membership on the Advisory Committee, and he requested Dr. Scott to accompany him as technical adviser to The Hague, where the committee met in the summer of 1920. After formulating the Statute of the Permanent Court of International Justice, the Advisory Committee of Jurists felt that provision should be made for what it terms "the advancement of international law" to be applied by the Court. It accordingly recommended that the Hague Conferences be resumed for that purpose and that certain private institutions established for the same purpose be invited to prepare projects for consideration by the proposed conferences after submission to the participating governments. The American Institute of International Law was one of the private institutions named by the Advisory Committee of Jurists at The Hague to share in these preparatory labors. The entire recommendation was rejected by the Assembly of the League of Nations.[20] As Dr. Scott correctly observed at the time, the initiative in the codification of international law passed from the Old to the New World.[21]

---

[20] *Journal of the First Assembly of the League of Nations*, pp. 298–299.

[21] See his scholarly report on the history of the codification of international law in the report to the Trustees of the Carnegie Endowment, Year Book, 1923, pp. 235–253.

Fifth International Conference of American States

The Fifth International Conference of American States met at Santiago, Chile, in 1923. Dr. Alejandro Alvarez was a delegate of the Government of Chile. He presented to that Conference a memorandum entitled "The Codification of American International Law". The Conference adopted a resolution recommending that codification should be gradual and progressive, and requesting each of the American Governments to appoint two delegates to reconstitute the Commission of Jurists and resume the work of codifying international law. The Commission was asked to convene at Rio de Janeiro in the year 1925. A vote of appreciation was extended to the American Institute of International Law and the hope was expressed that the Institute "may continue to exercise in the future its beneficent influence in favor of the principles of international law on the American continent".[22]

Hon. Charles Evans Hughes was then Secretary of State of the United States and *ex officio* Chairman of the Governing Board of the Pan American Union. He read in the report of the Santiago Conference that "codification requires the cooperation of specialists, ample time and an environment of tranquility ... characteristic of scientific bodies". He accordingly, through Dr. Scott, turned to the American Institute of International Law and asked it to prepare a series of projects on international law to be laid before the International Commission of Jurists at Rio de Janeiro. Upon his initiative, the Governing Board of the Pan American Union on 2 January 1924 adopted a resolution requesting the American Institute to undertake that preparatory work.

Dr. Scott promptly repaired to Habana to confer with Dr. Bustamante. They agreed upon the steps to be taken to enable the Institute to accept and fulfill the important responsibilities with which it had been officially honored by the Pan American Union.[23] They were again concerned with reinvigorating the national societies so that they would act in time to enable the Institute to function effectually. Dr. Bustamante undertook to enlist the help of the Cuban Department of State, and on 3 March Dr. Carlos Manuel de

---

[22] *International Conferences of American States, 1898–1928*, p. 283.

[23] A memorandum summarizing the results of their discussion was left with Dr. Bustamante by Dr. Scott when he departed from Habana on 9 February.

Cèspedes, Secretary of State of Cuba, sent circular instructions to the chiefs of all Cuban diplomatic missions in Latin America, requesting them to ask the Minister of Foreign Affairs in each country to take an interest in the reorganization of their respective national societies to the end that they might collaborate effectively in the work of the American Institute at its next meeting.

Third Pan American Scientific Congress

Inasmuch as the Institute had held its first session in connection with the Second Pan American Scientific Congress, it was felt that it should meet again in connection with the meeting of the Third Pan American Scientific Congress, which was to convene at Lima, Peru, in December 1924. The Institute was officially invited to attend the Congress. Dr. Scott, Dr. Alvarez, and Mr. Luis Anderson met in Paris during the summer of 1924 as an informal committee to prepare for the work of the forthcoming meeting. Taking as the basis Dr. Alvarez's projects of codification submitted to the Santiago Conference the year previously, and some additional texts drafted by Dr. Scott, they formulated some thirty projects of codification covering a wide range of topics dealing with the international law of peace.

The Third Pan American Scientific Congress met at Lima from 22 December 1924 to 5 January 1925. A call for a special meeting of the American Institute at the same time and place was sent from Paris on 12 October 1924[24] by Dr. Scott as President and Dr. Alvarez as Secretary General to permit the Institute to comply with the resolution of the Governing Board of the Pan American Union adopted on 2 June of that year. When the members reached Lima, they were confronted with an embarrassing situation. Due to the strained relations between the Governments of Peru and Chile over the Tacna-Arica controversy, Chile was the only American Republic not represented by an official delegation at the Scientific Congress. Moreover, the Government of Peru had not invited the Government of Chile to take part in the celebration then being held at Lima of the Centenary of the Battle of Ayacucho, which success-

---

[24] Printed in pamphlet of the Pan American Union (1925), p. 15.

fully terminated the wars of liberation of the South American colonies of Spain. Under the circumstances, Dr. Alvarez, a distinguished official of the Chilean Government, felt it impossible for him to proceed to Lima for the Institute's meeting.[25]

More embarrassing still was the attitude of President Leguia of Peru, who did not wish the Institute to meet in formal session lest views be expressed which might be embarrassing to the governments in dispute. Whereupon, Dr. Scott invited the members present in Lima to be his guests at a series of luncheons in the private dining room of the Gran Hotel Bolivar. At the first of the luncheons, which began on 20 December, Dr. Scott observed that there could be no objection on the part of the Government of Peru to the members of the Institute lunching informally together during the sessions of the Third Pan American Scientific Congress and exchanging views upon codification of international law, the subject uppermost in the minds of all international lawyers present at the time in Lima. Dr. Scott's proposal was unanimously approved, and the members proceeded to discuss the projects of codification drafted at Paris for the Lima meeting. The discussions continued at luncheons every other day through 31 December.[26] The projects were discussed in detail, revised or amended, and the Council of Direction, to be enlarged for the purpose, was authorized to put the projects in final form for submission as a report of progress to the Governing Board of the Pan American Union.

Upon Dr. Scott's return to Washington, he reported personally to Secretary of State Hughes on 22 January 1925 upon what had happened at Lima. "Secretary Hughes is immensely pleased with the result of our labors", Dr. Scott wrote to one of his colleagues.[27] "He believes that we accomplished infinitely more in the informal meetings than we would have done if circumstances had been apparently more propitious". Mr. Hughes expressed the wish to have the progress report of the Institute ready for submission to the Pan American Union before he retired from office on 4 March 1925. Dr. Scott accordingly issued by cablegram a call for a meeting of

---

[25] Letter from Dr. Alvarez dated Santiago, Chile, 9 December 1924 addressed to Dr. Scott as President of the Institute at Lima.

[26] See American Institute of International Law, *Informal Conversations at Lima* (1925).

[27] Letter of José Matos, Guatemala, 24 January 1925.

the Council of Direction, enlarged by members from Brazil, Haiti, and Guatemala, to be held in Habana beginning 19 February. The meeting convened as requested, with only two members unable to be present, and on 23 December 1925, the report was presented to the Governing Board of the Pan American Union at its meeting on 3 February 1926, by the new Secretary of State, the Honorable Frank B. Kellogg. The new project was directed to be transmitted to the respective governments in the same way as was done with the previous projects on public international law.[28]

The thirty projects discussed at Lima[29] were rearranged and finished in the four official languages of the Americas – Spanish, English, Portugese, and French. Dr. Scott brought them to Washington and transmitted them to the Pan American Union on 2 March 1925 under cover of a letter recounting their background and summarizing their purpose. A special meeting of the Governing Board was held the same afternoon to which the projects were submitted by Chairman Hughes. They were not presented, he said, either for approval or criticism. "What is far more important than any particular text or proposal", he continued, "is the fact that at least we have texts and projects, the result of elaborate study, for consideration. We have the inspiration and stimulus of this action full of promise for the world. We feel that, thanks to American initiative, we are on the threshold of accomplishment in the most important endeavor of the human race to life itself out of the savagery of strife into the domain of law breathing the spirit of amity and justice".[30]

The Governing Board directed that the projects be sent to the respective member governments for submission to the International Commission of Jurists at Rio de Janeiro. In conclusion Mr. Hughes said:

> I believe that this day, with the submission of concrete proposals which take the question of the development of international law out of mere amiable aspiration, marks a definite step in the progress of civilization and the promotion of peace, and for that

---

[28] For the text of the code and resolution and other pertinent documents, see pamphlet published by the Pan American Union in 1926.
[29] The texts of the projects were printed by the Pan American Union in a pamphlet entitled *Codification of American International Law* (1925), and also in *Special Supplement to the American Journal of International Law*, XX (1926), pp. 300–384.
[30] Ibid., p. 5.

> reason will long be remembered. For in this effort we are not unmindful of the larger aspects of the question, and it is our hope that the American Republics by taking advantage of this opportunity may make a lasting contribution to the development of universal international law.[31]

The projects were made public by the Pan American Union on 31 March 1925. They received nation-wide and generally favorable comment in the press. Editorially, the *Christian Science Monitor* said on 2 April that "It is significant that on the same day the announcement of the Pan American Union was made, representatives of many of the progressive nations of the world met in Geneva to consider the codification of international law". The editorial continued: "Both these activities afford hopeful indications of the trend of world thought. Civilization has progressed beyond the war era. The lesson has been learned, apparently, and nothing but ignorance, abetted by selfishness and greed, can ever again plunge humanity into armed conflict and destructive strife".

The progress of the movement for the codification of international law in the Western Hemisphere after World War I had a favorable reaction in the League of Nations, which had rejected the idea in 1920. Due at least in some measure to the insistence of the Latin American delegates, the Fifth Assembly of the League of Nations, on 22 September 1924, adopted a resolution expressing the desire of the League to increase its contribution to the "progressive codification of international law", and requesting the Council of the League to appoint a Committee of Experts to report with a view to preparing eventually for official conferences on the subject. The Committee of Experts, which was duly appointed, was directed to consult the most authoritative organizations devoted to the study of international law. The Director of the Legal Section of the League, on 7 March 1925, communicated the text of the Assembly's resolution to the American Institute of International Law and requested its opinion and such data as it might have to communicate. In reply, Dr. Scott, on 2 April 1925, sent through the Pan American Union a copy of the projects that had been laid before the Governing Board on 2 March.

---

[31] Ibid., p. 3.

Mr. Hughes' interest in the codification of international law was deeply aroused by his experience with the American Institute of International Law. He was reluctant to dissociate himself with the movement at the end of his term of office. In the interview with Dr. Scott on 22 January they discussed the continuation and enlargement of the work done at Lima. On 17 February 1925 Secretary Hughes wrote to Dr. Scott on the eve of his departure for Habana inquiring whether the Institute would be willing to undertake to prepare a project of a convention formulating the international law of peace for the consideration of the nations of the world. The Council of Direction at its meeting in Habana welcomed such a task with satisfaction and offered to appoint a Committee for the General Codification of the International Law of Peace to represent the different regions and the four official languages spoken in America. The chairmanship of the proposed committee was offered to Mr. Hughes after he laid down the duties of the Secretaryship of State. On his last day in that office, 4 March 1925, Mr. Hughes wrote to Dr. Scott accepting the position of President of the Codifying Committee of the American Institute. "I am sure", he wrote, "that their labors cannot fail to be of the greatest benefit in promoting the development of the body of American international law and thus aiding the formulation of the principles and rules of the universal law of nations".

The Governing Board of the Pan American Union at its meeting on 2 March 1925 adopted also a resolution requesting the American Institute of International Law to prepare a project or series of projects embodying the principles and rules of private international law for the consideration of the Commission of Jurists. A special committee which had been appointed at the Lima session of the Institute to consider this subject met in Habana in December 1925 and approved a project in the form of a Code of Private International Law which had been prepared by Dr. Bustamante.

The meeting of the International Commission of Jurists scheduled for Rio de Janeiro in the year 1925 was postponed until 1927. The Council of Direction decided to hold a plenary meeting of the American Institute. The Uruguayan Government then renewed, through diplomatic channels, its invitation of 1917 to hold the plenary meeting in Montevideo which had earlier to be abandoned because of World War I.

Montevideo Session of the American Institute of International Law

The fourth meeting of the American Institute was accordingly held in Montevideo on 21-26 March 1927. This meeting provided the first opportunity for the Institute to review in formal plenary session the projects discussed at Lima and transmitted by the Pan American Union by the Council of Direction following its meeting in Habana, as well as the Code of Private International Law prepared for the Institute by Dr. Bustamante. The Institute also considered at this meeting separate projects drafted by members from Argentina, Uruguay, Bolivia, and Peru.

The time allotted for the meeting did not permit such a detailed examination of the projects article-by-article as would be required for their approval in particular. The Institute limited its action to a declaration that the thirty projects of conventions drafted by the American Institute, as well as those separately presented by members from the four national societies previously mentioned, were to be considered "as a scientific contribution of the Institute to the preparation of American international law legislation" to be undertaken by the Pan American Conferences and which presently would occupy the American jurists at Rio de Janeiro. All of the projects on public international law received the approval of the Institute "in so far as they tried to make international solidarity more intense and more susceptible of rules, and to unite more closely the American Republics in the advancement and perfection of the organization of their continental relations". Commenting upon this action of the Institute, Dr. Scott, who presided as president of the Institute, wrote that "it was intended to be, and was in fact, an approval of the projects of public international law".[32]

A difference of opinion developed in Montevideo over the Bustamante Code of Private International Law between the partisans of two conflicting legal theories, namely, those who advocate that the status and capacity of aliens and in general all their legal relations of a personal character shall be governed by the law of the territory in which they are domiciled, and those who prefer that all

---

[32] J. B. Scott, "The Gradual and Progressive Codification of International Law", *American Journal of International Law*, XXI (1928), pp. 432–433.

such matters should be governed by the laws of the aliens' nationality. Dr. Bustamante was unable to be present at Montevideo, and a committee was appointed to work out an acceptable formula which was later adopted upon Dr. Bustamante's suggestion by the Commission of Jurists at Rio de Janeiro.

The Institute had been handicapped in the final formulation of its projects of codification by the difficulty of holding plenary sessions due to the great distances between the various American capitals and the time and expense involved in assembling the membership in any one of them. Advantage was taken of the plenary meeting at Montevideo to revise the Constitution and By-Laws in two respects: first, to enlarge the scope of the Institute's purposes so as to include the consideration of private, as well as public international law – a modification made necessary so as to embrace the field of Dr. Bustamante's Code; and, secondly, to enlarge the Council of Direction and authorize it to represent the Institute in the intervals between meetings. The resolution on this amendment states that the "scientific contribution of the Institute to the development and regulation of international law requires a constant labor of investigation, and as frequent meetings of the Council of Direction as is possible".[33]

The members of the Institute took advantage of the plenary session at Montevideo to reconsider the procedure of codification and adopted a series of resolutions to which they gave the collective name "Rules of Montevideo for the Formation and Development of Positive International Law in America". It was recommended that the forthcoming meeting of the Commission of Jurists create permanent technical organs to be devoted to the work of systematizing and developing international law in America, but that in advance of any deliberations by official delegates, matters selected for codification "be the object of investigation and scientific reports on the part of bodies on the Continent devoted to the study of international law".[34]

---

[33] Scott, ibid., p. 432.

[34] Scott, ibid., p. 433. An excellent account of the meeting at Montevideo is contained in the *Paginas Diplomaticos* of Victor M. Maurtua, to which Dr. Scott contributed a Prologue, published by Manuel Augusto Olaechea, Lima, Peru, 1940, pp. 1–39.

Rio Meeting of International Commission of Jurists

Dr. Scott was the principal delegate of the United States to the International Commission of Jurists which convened at Rio de Janeiro on 18 April and adjourned on 20 May 1927. He went directly from Montevideo to Rio for that meeting. The other American delegate was Professor Jesse S. Reeves, of the University of Michigan. Again, the time at the disposal of the Commission to complete its labors did not allow of the consideration of all the projects submitted. The President of the Commission, the distinguished Brazilian delegate, Epitacio Pessao, was a judge of the Permanent Court of International Justice at The Hague and had to arrive in that city by 15 June for a session of the Court. After an exchange of views on procedure, upon the suggestion of the delegates of the United States a committee of five was appointed to select the projects that could be considered adequately within the time available. Twelve were selected by the committee and provisions from them were embodied in the ten projects adopted by the commission and recommended to the consideration of the Sixth International Conference of the American States to be held at Habana in the following year. Those projects dealt with the fundamental bases of international law; states, their existence, equality, and recognition; status of aliens; treaties; exchange of publications; interchange of professors and students; diplomatic agents; consuls; maritime neutrality; and pacific solution of international conflicts. Two additional projects, not included among those of the American Institute, namely, on asylum and duties of states in case of civil war, were also adopted and recommended to the forthcoming conference at Habana.[35]

Upon the return from Rio de Janeiro of the American members of the International Commission of Jurists, they submitted a report to the Secretary of State under date of 10 June 1927. The report was obviously the handiwork of Dr. Scott. It was written in his usual literary style and gave a complete history of the Commission, details of its composition and organization, the activities of the American and some of the other principal delegates, and the results accomplished.

---

[35] The Report of the International Commission of Jurists, with texts of the projects adopted, was printed and published by the Pan American Union in 1927.

Dr. Scott also enlightened the lay reader on some technical aspects of the meeting. For example, the word "codification" was used in a twofold sense: strictly, as a statement of the law actually in force; and popularly, as a statement, not merely of the law in force, but such as it should be, in the opinion of those undertaking its formulation and statement. The delegates of the United States so understood "codification" in its first and strict sense, and the sense in which they believed that the Commission likewise understood it. The projects, therefore, of public international law are in general, it is believed, an acceptable statement of the practice, not only of any one republic, but of the American Republics, in their relations with one another.

Again he explained, that the Commission "was a body of experts in international law, public and private – not a conference of diplomatists vested with political powers by the Republics appointing them, but jurists representing what our Latin American friends and neighbors so happily call the juridical conscience of the Americas. Their purpose was to state international law, public and private, in the form of articles – not to make law as a legislature, or to adopt conventions which, when ratified by the treaty-making Powers of their respective countries, would become law for the High Contracting Parties. Their task was humbler, but still honorable: to state in the form of articles, principles of international law and the conflict of laws, to recommend them to the favorable consideration of the Sixth Conference of the Americas, to meet in Habana on 16 January 1928 in order that the diplomatic representatives of the American Republics taking part in that conference might, through the exercise of political power, invest them, in their original or modified form, with the force of conventional law. The diplomatic representatives, acting under instructions from the governments of their respective Republics, would bind their countries to the extent of their instructions, and the countries would bind themselves and each to each, by subsequent ratification of the conventions adopted by the Conference". From the foregoing, Dr. Scott concluded that "the Commission of Jurists could not, therefore, bind the governments which they represented, nor could the Delegation bind the government appointing it".

Another typically characteristic feature of Dr. Scott's report was the inclusion extracts from the principal addressed delivered upon the opening and closing of the Conference and at significant periods during its proceedings; but he mentioned only in passing his own address delivered at the closing banquet on Saturday evening, 21 May, given to the delegates and their ladies by the Minister of Foreign Affairs on behalf of the Government of Brazil. In accordance with the custom on such occasions, one of the guests – on this occasion Dr. Scott – was requested by the Minister of Foreign Affairs to propose a toast to the President of Brazil. Dr. Scott performed the honor with such notable success and ability that the American Ambassador made his personal achievement the subject of a report to the Department of State. In a dispatch sent three days after the banquet, Ambassador Edwin D. Morgan wrote to the Secretary of State as follows:

> Dr. Brown Scott's address on Saturday evening was exceptionally gratifying to the guests assembled around the Foreign Minister's hospitable board because not only did it express appreciation of the courtesies which the delegates had received from the Brazilian Government but its sentimental and elevated tone was the one which Latin-American orators employ and which they deplore that Anglo-Saxon orators do not adopt more often on festive occasions. In this respect it resembled a recent address of Mr. Rudyard Kipling before the Brazilian Academy, in which with rare penetration for an Anglo-Saxon he voiced the sentiments which Dr. Brown Scott admirably expressed. The fact that the address of the latter was delivered without notes and in the French language agreeably impressed his hearers, whose definition of culture includes a knowledge of French literature and of the French language, which frequently is forgotten, indeed unappreciated, by the Anglo-Saxons who only speak the English tongue.

Sixth International Conference of American States

The Sixth International Conference of American States met at Habana on 16 January and adjourned on 20 February 1928. Dr. Scott was again an official delegate of the United States Government. In the organization of the Conference he was a member of the Committee on Public International Law and Vice President of the Committee on Private International Law. He was reporter of a project on the Status of Aliens, one of the sub-topics for the implementation of the Declaration of the Rights and Duties of Nations.

Of the conventions adopted by the Conference, projects drafted by the American Institute of International Law as approved by the Rio Commission of Jurists, figured in the following final texts: Status of Aliens, Treaties, Diplomatic Agents, Consuls, Maritime Neutrality, and Obligations of States in Event of Civil Strife.[36]

The Conference adopted the Bustamante Code. Private international law is the term used abroad to describe the systems of jurisprudence governing persons and property usually referred to in the United States as the conflict of laws. It embraces all aspects of personal and property rights, interests and relationships in the daily lives of the people within the state. In the United States such matters are governed by the laws of the respective States of the Union. Because their local laws were at variance with some of the provisions of the Code of Private International Law, a number of reservations were made by Latin American States when it was adopted at Habana. Dr. Scott formulated a reservation which was approved by the United States Delegation, stating that it could not approve the Code "as in view of the Constitution of the United States, the relations among the members of the Union and the powers and functions of the Federal Government, it finds it very difficult to do so". The reservation expressed the hope that after carefully studying the code in all of its provisions the Government of the United States might later adhere to at least a portion of it.[37]

Some projects of the American Institute as approved by the Rio Commission of Jurists were laid over for future action by the Habana Conference. Those on the Fundamental Bases of International Law and on States—their existence, equality and recognition—were referred to the next conference, following an extended debate over a provision inserted at Rio on the subject of intervention. The Chairman of the American Delegation at Habana, Hon. Charles Evans Hughes, explained why no action was taken upon those two projects. The reason, he said, "lay in the fact that one of these projects contained a fragmentary and inadequate declaration on the

---

[36] For the texts of the Conventions and other acts of the Conference, see *International Conferences of American States, 1889-1928*, published for the Carnegie Endowment by the Oxford University Press, New York, 1931, pp. 295–444.

[37] Ibid., p. 371.

subject of intervention. It declared briefly and simply that 'No State may intervene in the internal affairs of another'. No distinction between action that was justified in certain exigencies, and action that was unjustified, was attempted. The learning, and the discriminating postulates, of international law found no place in the text. The manifest defect of the project lay in its failure to set forth the rights and duties of states in any manner that could be regarded as satisfactory and could thus provide an appropriate context".[38]

Dr. Victor Maurtua, of Peru, proposed to incorporate the American Institute's Declaration of the Rights and Duties of Nations as the essential basis of a statement of principles with respect to fundamental rights, but this proposal also met with objections. In supporting Dr. Maurtua's proposal, Mr. Hughes stated that the Declaration was the work of the most distinguished jurists of all the American Republics, which had been repeatedly approved by the leading jurists of the world, and he commented:

> Strange as it may seem to an impartial observer, the submission of this fair and comprehensive statement provoked a debate. It was unwelcome to some who desired the adoption of the incomplete statement of the original project. Occasion was afforded for eloquent assertions of the rights of sovereignty of the sacredness of independence, which no one had any desire to challenge. The declaration of the American Institute with its appropriate reference to the duties of states seemed to some to qualify the attributes of sovereignty. The balanced precepts of international law were thus in danger of being forgotten in the zeal for a trumpet call in defense of the ideal of liberty to which we are all devoted . . .[39]

The debate, Mr. Hughes continued, showed the very great difficulty of distinguishing between international law and political doctrine. "There is no one here", he continued, "who does not have enjoyment in the free air of independence. My country was nurtured in the desire for independence. One hundred years ago we declared the policy that all the American Republics should be rec-

---

[38] C. E. Hughes, "Address before the American Society of International Law", *Proceedings*, 26 April 1928, p. 9.

[39] *Report of the Delegates of the United States to the Sixth International Conference of American States*, Habana, 1928.

ognized in their independence. We have given our arms and our blood for the independence of the American Republics and are always ready to do so. We yield to none in the establishment of the ideal of sovereignty and independence for every one of the American Republics from the greatest to the smallest. And I have the right, speaking here on behalf of the Delegation of the United States, to declare the policy of my country. I joined readily in the resolution of the Delegation of Mexico against aggression. We want no aggression. We want no aggression against ourselves. We cherish no thought of aggression against anybody else. We desire to respect the rights of every country and to have the rights of our own country equally respected. We do not wish the territory of any American Republic. We do not wish to govern any American Republic. We simply wish peace and order and stability and recognition of honest rights properly acquired so that this hemisphere may not only be the hemisphere of peace but the hemisphere of international justice".[40]

Turning directly to the situation in Nicaragua, whose Minister of Foreign Affairs was a delegate to the Conference, Mr. Hughes continued:

> I can tell you that we desire nothing more than the independence and peace of this country and that we are there simply to aid them in obtaining free elections, in order that they may have a sovereign and independent government. I mention that merely because I speak in a spirit of entire frankness. Now what is the real difficulty? Let us face the facts. The difficulty, if there is any, in any one of the American Republics, is not of any external aggression. It is an internal difficulty, if it exists at all. From time to time there arises a situation most deplorable and regrettable in which sovereignty is not at work, in which for a time in certain areas there is no government at all—in which for a time and within a limited sphere there is no possibility of performing the functions of sovereignty and independence. Those are the conditions that create the difficulty with which at times we find ourselves confronted. What are we to do when government breaks down and American citizens are in danger of their lives? Are we to stand by and see them killed because a Government in circumstances which it cannot control and for which it may not be

[40] Ibid.

> responsible can no longer afford reasonable protection? I am not speaking of sporadic acts of violence, or of the rising of mobs, or of those distressing incidents which may occur in any country however well administered. I am speaking of the occasions where government itself is unable to function for a time because of difficulties which confront it and which it is impossible for it to surmount.
>
> . . . the United States cannot forego its right to protect its citizens. No country should forego its right to protect its citizens. International law cannot be changed by the resolutions of this Conference. International law remains. The rights of nations remain, but nations have duties as well as rights. We all recognize that. This very formula, here proposed, is a proposal of duty on the part of a nation. But it is not the only duty. There are other obligations which courts, and tribunals declaring international law, have frequently set forth; and we cannot codify international law and ignore the duties of States, by setting up the impossible reign of self-will without any recognition upon the part of a State of its obligations to its neighbors.[41]

The Declaration of the Rights and Duties of Nations was not without its friends in the Conference. During the discussion, Dr. Orestes Ferrara, a delegate of Cuba, spoke with deep feeling of his country's history and declared that intervention as applied to the acts of the United States in his country was a word of glory and justice, which he could not forget. He regarded Dr. Maurtua's proposal as a declaration responsive to the ideals of justice.

The failure to include the Declaration of the Rights and Duties of Nations in the conventions of the Conference "was not", in the opinion of Mr. Hughes, "without its compensations. It gave opportunity for frank interchanges in committee, in subcommittee, and finally in plenary session, which cleared the air, promoted a fairer appreciation of opposing views and made us at the close of the conference much better friends than we were at the beginning. We did not codify this part of international law, but we did better than that. We strengthened the ties which are deeper than the law and made firmer the mutual respect and confidence without which the law is of slight avail".[42]

---

[41] Ibid.

[42] *Proceedings of the American Society of International Law* (1928), p. 10.

Dr. Scott's services at the Sixth Conference were not limited to his technical work in commissions and committees. After his return to New York from the Conference, Mr. Hughes wrote a letter to Dr. Scott in which he said: "It was not simply your learning, and complete knowledge of all that had been done in relation to the matters under discussion, but what I may call your highly intelligent zeal and sympathetic interest, which bound us together as co-workers in a brotherly effort on behalf of your country".[43]

The Institute's project for the Pacific Settlement of International Disputes was disposed of at Habana in the form of a resolution condemning war as an instrument of national policy, favoring arbitration and conciliation of such disputes, and recommending that the American states call a separate conference to draft a convention on the subject "with a minimum of exceptions they may consider indispensable to safeguard the independence and sovereignty of the States, as well as matters of domestic concern".

Pursuant to the foregoing resolution, an International Conference of the American States on Conciliation and Arbitration met in Washington on 10 December 1928. The Conference adjourned on 5 January 1929 after signing a General Convention of Inter-American Conciliation, a General Treaty of Inter-American Arbitration, and a Protocol of Progressive Arbitration.[44]

The Sixth Conference at Habana also adopted a resolution concerning the future codification of international law. Three permanent committees were to be organized, one in Rio de Janeiro, for work relating to public international law; another at Montevideo for work dealing with private international law; and another in Habana, for the study of comparative legislation and uniformity of law. Those committees were to be constituted by the governments at the respective capitals from members of their national societies of international law. Projects drafted by those committees were to be submitted through the Pan American Union to the Executive Council of the American Institute of International Law "to the end that through a scientific consideration thereof the latter may make a

---

[43] Letter dated 29 February 1928. Scott Mss.

[44] For the texts, see *International Conferences of American States, 1889–1928*, pp. 455–468.

technical study of such draft projects and present its findings and formulas, in a report on the matter".[45]

The American Institute of International Law was thus officially recognized as an adviser to the Pan American Union for the scientific and technical study of draft projects to be presented to future official Inter-American Conferences. On 16 May 1928 Dr. Scott as President of the American Institute wrote to the Honorable Leo S. Rowe, Director General of the Pan American Union, placing the Institute at the disposal of the Union "for any purpose which you may consider to be in the interest of international law, its codification, and its development, especially in connection with the Seventh International Conference of American States, which is to meet shortly in the City of Montevideo". Dr. Rowe accepted the offer in a letter to Dr. Scott the following day.

On 1 May 1929 the Governing Board of the Pan American Union requested the Governments of Brazil, Uruguay, and Cuba to appoint the committees contemplated by the Habana resolution, and to forward any projects formulated by them to the Union for transmission to the Executive Committee of the American Institute of International Law. At the same time, the Institute was requested to continue its work and to send its projects of codification to the Governing Board of the Union.[46]

Towards a Cuban Temple of Justice

The future of the American Institute as an integral part of the organization for the codification of international law in the Americas seemed to be thus assured. Its headquarters at Washington in the offices of the Carnegie Endowment, closely accessible to the Pan American Union, seemed an ideal arrangement. Nevertheless, the difficulty that had been experienced in arranging plenary sessions, the burden of work that had consequently devolved upon a few members of its Executive Council, and the tendency of the national societies to function only intermittently, seemed to shake Dr. Scott's confidence concerning the future. He advanced the idea

---

[45] Ibid., pp. 439–440.

[46] Letter of Hon. Henry L. Stimson, Chairman of the Governing Board, to James Brown Scott, President of the American Institute of International Law.

that the Institute should be reorganized and permanently located in Habana. He mentioned these possibilities to his close Cuban friend, Dr. Cosme de la Torriente, when they met in New York early in 1929, and on 21 January 1929 Dr. Scott wrote to Dr. Bustamante urging the same idea: "If we can only have the Institute", he said, "permanently established in Habana, under your guidance, protection and supervision, its ultimate success will be assured.

A meeting of the Executive Council at Habana was called to consider Dr. Scott's proposal, but lacking a quorum, Dr. Scott, Dr. Bustamante, Dr. Victor M. Maurtua, and Dr. Pedro Martinez Fraga met as a special committee in Dr. Bustamante's office from 28 February to 7 March 1929. Among other things, they decided to propose that Habana be made the headquarters of the Institute, and that there be established in that city an American Academy of International Law similar to the academy established at The Hague under the auspices of the Carnegie Endowment for International Peace.

It was agreed to seek to enlist the interest of the President of Cuba in these propositions. President Gerardo Machado received the members of the special committee on 4 March in the presence of Dr. Carlos Miguel de Cespedes, Secretary of Public Works. A few days later, the special committee left a memorandum with the President giving further details of the proposals. President Machado was duly impressed with these overtures. To him and to his Secretary of Public Works, they signified "the establishment in the capital of the Republic of Cuba of the international scientific center of America, and implies a splendid homage to the people and Government of Cuba".

On 8 March 1929 the President issued a decree authorizing the establishment of a Palace of the American Institute of International Law "as the contribution of the Republic of Cuba to the very excellent work which the American Institute of International Law is realizing in behalf of inter-American culture and peace, and in just response to the honor which this body concedes to the City of Habana, by establishing therein the center of its activities". In accordance with the recommendations of the Institute's special committee, the Palace was to provide permanent quarters for the Executive Council of the Institute and its Secretariat, an American Academy of International Law analogous to that which functions at The Hague, as well as for the Cuban Society of International Law, and for a Latin American center of the Carnegie Endowment for International Peace. The decree directed the Secretary of Public Works "to designate for the site of the said edifice adequate grounds from those which have been reclaimed from the sea by the works recently effected at the entrance of the port of Habana".[47]

The cornerstone of the Palace was laid with elaborate ceremonies on 19 May 1929. Dr. Scott was a guest of honor and delivered an address. Dr. Nicholas Murray Butler, then President of the Carnegie Endowment, was also invited but asked to be excused because of the state of his health.

In accordance with the decision to make Habana the headquarters of the Institute, the Executive Council met in that city from 29 October to 1 November 1929. At the opening of the meeting, Dr. Alvarez resigned as Secretary General, an office he had held from the foundation of the Institute. He gave as his reason the necessity of his continuous residence in Europe. Dr. Victor M. Maurtua, of Peru, was elected Secretary General *ad interim*, a choice which was later made permanent.

Among the many items of business transacted was the ratification of the proposals of the special committee made to the President of Cuba as stated in his presidential decree of 8 March. Another decree was signed by President Machado on 29 October appropriating $1,200,000 to the Department of Public Works for the construction of the Palace. Provisional quarters for the Institute and the proposed Academy were provided in the National University. Dr. Bustamante was elected Director of the Academy.

Due to subsequent economic and political complications in Cuba, the Palace of the American Institute of International Law was never constructed.

Women's Rights and Codification

The Institute at Montevideo in 1927 accepted an invitation from the Argentine group to hold its next plenary meeting at Buenos Aires in advance of the meeting of the Seventh International

---

[47] The decree, No. 339, was published in the *Gaceta Oficial* of 12 March 1929. An English translation appeared in the Year Book of the Carnegie Endowment for International Peace, 1929, pp. 197–198.

Conference of American States scheduled to meet at Montevideo in December 1932. Although that Conference had to be postponed for a year, Dr. Rowe, the Director General of the Pan American Union, wrote to Dr. Scott as President of the American Institute of International Law urging the Institute to meet in Buenos Aires as planned. In his letter to Dr. Scott, dated 29 February 1932, Dr. Rowe stated:

> I consider it most essential that a meeting of the American Institute of International Law be held because of the close relationship that has been established between the Institute and the International Conferences of American States and the Pan American Union. As you know, the resolution on the future codification of International Law adopted at Habana in 1928 provided for the establishment of three permanent committees; one at Rio de Janeiro on Public International Law; one at Montevideo on Private International Law, and another at Habana on Comparative Legislation and Uniformity of Legislation. At the same time, the American Institute of International Law was made an integral part of this organization by the stipulation that all material and draft projects formulated by the Permanent Committees should be submitted to the American Institute for scientific consideration and report.
>
> Furthermore, in view of the probable delay in the initiation of the work of the Permanent Committees, the Governing Board of the Pan American Union has requested the American Institute of International Law to continue its work in the field of codification and to send to the Board any projects that may be formulated by the Institute. The continuation of the work of codification on the American Continent depends in large measure, therefore, on the cooperation and activity of the American Institute of International Law.

Through its officers and committees, the Institute continued to make preparations for the session at Buenos Aires. The Executive Council had met in Washington from 29-31 October 1931 and approved some twenty-two subjects for study and named reporters and commissions for each. Among these were Nationality, with Dr. Scott as Reporter, Responsibility of States for Damages to Foreigners, with Dr. Maurtua as Reporter, and the Territorial Sea, with Dr. Bustamante as Reporter. These three studies were undertaken following the meeting of the special committee at Habana in March 1927 as scientific contributions of the Institute to the official conference on the Codification of International Law held at The Hague in 1930.

In anticipation of the Buenos Aires meeting, the Institute issued in Spanish a volume of over 400 pages containing the projects and reports drawn up in preparation for that session.[48]

For various reasons it was found impracticable to hold a meeting of the Institute at Buenos Aires prior to the meeting of the Seventh International Conference of American States at Montevideo, which met 3–26 December 1933. In lieu of such a meeting, the Supervisory Committee of the Pan American Union, by resolution dated 27 September 1933, requested the American Institute to create a technical committee to advise and assist the conference at Montevideo with reference to matters of international law. The technical committee was appointed and attended the Conference. Dr. Scott was not a delegate of the Government of the United States, nor did he attend the Conference in any capacity.

A dozen projects from those prepared for submission to the Institute's postponed session at Buenos Aires were officially selected and made available to the delegates at Montevideo in mimeographed form by the Institute and the Pan American Union. Conventions and resolutions on some of them were adopted by the Montevideo Conference.

The projects relating to the Inter-American Commission of Women, the nationality of women, and equality of rights were at first opposed by the American delegation, but the delegation's attitude was changed as a result of pressure brought upon the Administration in Washington by the National Woman's Party. A convention was adopted by the Conference agreeing that "There will be no distinction based on sex as regards nationality". The Conference, however, declined to adopt the proposed treaty providing for equal political and civil rights of men and women on the ground that this was not a proper subject matter for consideration by an international conference but belonged exclusively to the sovereign body of each state. However, a resolution was adopted recommending to the government of each American Republic that it establish a maximum of equality so far as the peculiar circumstances of each country would permit. The representatives of four of the govern-

---

[48] American Institute of International Law, *Trabajos Preparatorios de la Sesion Plenaria de Buenos Aires* (Habana, Molina y Compania, 1931). 431 p.

ments in attendance at the Conference did sign an equal rights treaty, which Dr. Scott later called the "Stevens Treaty" in recognition of Miss Doris Stevens' activities in procuring its signature. Another resolution was adopted thanking the Inter-American Commission of Women for its work and recommending its continuance. The United States Delegation did not vote for that resolution.

The bitter struggle at the Montevideo Conference over the proposals of the National Woman's Party of the United States sponsored by the American Institute produced outspoken dissatisfaction and resulted in the adoption of a long detailed resolution in regard to future procedures for the codification of international law at Inter-American Conferences. They were said to be not the considered judgment of the organization as a whole, but the proposals of a few of its most active members. The resolution reorganized the International Commission of Jurists established at Rio de Janeiro, and each American Government was recommended to appoint its own national codification members. The preparatory work of the International Commission of Jurists was to be done by a smaller Commission of Experts composed of seven jurists officially selected, and a Juridical Section was established in the Pan American Union at Washington to coordinate and administer the codification machinery. No mention was made of future activities by the American Institute of International Law.

The resolution reaffirmed that codification must be gradual and progressive and asserted that it is "a vain illusion to think for a long time of the possibility of carrying it out completely". The resolution asserted that codification must be done by jurists who were not only specialists in international law, but who should be provided with plenipotentiary powers to sign treaties. It was accordingly provided that the members of the International Commission of Jurists are to have the character of official plenipotentiary delegates at their meetings and that the results of their labors are to be incorporated in conventions between the American States. That conclusion was predicated upon the doubtful premise that "if it is desired to do practical work with actual results, it is indispensable to seek the conjunction of the juridical viewpoints, theoretical and universal in essence, with the political viewpoints, positive and localistic by nature".[49]

---

[49] *International Conferences of American States, First Supplement*, pp. 84–87.

The unsoundness of that conclusion was demonstrated by the attitude of the Conference itself toward the American Institute of International Law, by discontinuing its function as an adviser to the Pan American Union expressly bestowed upon the Institute by the preceding conference. Thus, when the Institute attempted at Montevideo to include political and local aspects regarding women's rights along with its juridical projects of a theoretical and universal nature, it lost its official standing before the Inter-American Conferences. To soften the blow, the Montevideo Conference paid tribute to the jurists who had participated in the work of the past. The name of Dr. Scott was included in the list together with many of his associates in the founding and previous activities of the Institute. Another resolution adopted at Montevideo left a loophole for the future work of private organizations by requesting the Pan American Union "to take the necessary measures to secure the preparation of projects on topics included in the programs of international conferences, and to send these projects to the government members of the Union".

The Committee appointed by the American Institute of International Law at the request of the Pan American Union to advise and assist the Conference of Montevideo consisted of Alejandro Alvarez, Luis Anderson, Victoro M. Maurtua, Rodrigo Octavio, and Cicero Peregrino da Silva. Messrs. Maurtua and Octavio were unable to go to Montevideo but the other three members put in their appearance. Miss Doris Stevens, who had gone to Montevideo as Chairman of the American Commission of Women, was made a member of the Institute's committee in that city. She had been elected a member of the Institute by its Executive Council in 1931.

Demise of American Institute of International Law

In the report of its mission to Montevideo, the Institute's Committee stated that "from the outset the attitude of the Conference was not favorable to the Institute. Certain delegates from the South expressed regret that the plenary session of the Institute in Buenos Aires had not taken place and thus provided an opportunity for the plenary approval of the Institute's projects presented to the

Conference by the Pan American Union.[50] As a matter of fact, most of the projects were of long-standing and had been specifically approved by the Executive Council by correspondence before they were transmitted to the Pan American Union by Dr. Scott in May 1933. The projects of conventions on the nationality of women and equal rights were twice formally approved by the Executive Council in duly convened meetings on 31 October 1929 and 31 October 1931. The Executive Council had also recommended at the latter meeting the continuance of the Inter-American Commission of Women "until men and women, throughout all the American Republics, shall have equal rights". In transmitting these projects to the Pan American Union in June 19311, Dr. Scott reminded the Director General that they came within the eleventh topic of the official program of the Seventh International Conference of American States entitled "Political and Civil Rights of Women".

An additional report on what happened at Montevideo was sent by Dr. Alvarez. He reiterated the unfriendly feeling toward the Institute by some of the delegates at Montevideo, who, he said, were intent on depriving the Institute of its character as juridical adviser to the Pan American Conferences. Moreover, he informed Dr. Scott that certain leading delegates had revealed themselves as mortal enemies of the Institute "and declared that it was a dead organization".[51]

Following the Montevideo Conference, a correspondence ensued between Dr. Scott, Dr. Alvarez, Mr. Anderson, Dr. Bustamante, and Mr. Maurtua regarding the future of the American Institute. In answer to the criticism made at Montevideo that the Institute did not meet often enough in plenary session, Dr. Scott reminded his colleagues of the great distances at which the members lived from one another, requiring large sums to meet traveling and other expenses; that the Institute received neither dues nor financial support from any American government but had to rely entirely upon subventions from the Carnegie Endowment for International Peace; that the meeting at which the Institute was formally organized during the Second Pan American Scientific Congress had

---

[50] Report to Dr. Scott dated Montevideo, 16 December 1933, signed by Messrs. Anderson, Alvarez, and da Silva.

[51] Letter of Dr. Alvarez to Dr. Scott written 22 December 1933 on board the steamer after he left Montevideo.

cost the Endowment over $100,000. He might have added that the various contributions made by the Endowment to finance the plenary meetings of the Institute, meetings of the Executive Council, and expenses of publications amounted to over $150,000, in addition to over $92,000 expended by the Endowment for the publication of a Spanish edition of the *American Journal of International Law* for the use and benefit of the members of the Institute, and that when that project was abandoned the Endowment paid nearly $70,000 in annual installments toward the expenses of publishing the *Revista de Derecho Internacional*, at Habana, the Institute's official organ.

Dr. Scott also called attention to the fact that the Endowment at the same time was granting a subvention of $20,000 to every meeting of the Institute of International Law in Europe, and he intimated that the Endowment's trustees might have to decide which of the two institutes it should continue to support. He recalled that the previous activities of the American Institute had caused the League of Nations to take up the codification of international law which, in turn, resulted in the Pan American Conferences committing themselves to gradual and progressive codification. He accordingly raised the question whether the American Institute had not rendered the services for which it was founded, namely, to advance codification in the Western Hemisphere; and, he concluded, "that being the case, whether it might not gracefully leave the field to the Pan American Conferences".[52]

Whether the critics of the American Institute of International Law at the Montevideo Conference advanced the codification of that subject by turning future activities over to official agencies is a matter of doubt; but they succeeded, probably somewhat beyond their calculations, in drying up a source of financial support for the codification of international law in America which had been made available through the activities of the American Institute. The trustees of the Carnegie Endowment made no further grant of funds to that organization.

The dampening effect of the action of the Montevideo Conference upon the immediate activities of the American Institute of International Law was written by Dr. Scott himself in his annual report to the trustees of the Carnegie Endowment: "Following the

---

[52] Letter to Dr. Alvarez at Paris, 1 September 1934.

action of the Seventh International Conference of American States at Montevideo in 1933, creating national commissions for the codification of international law and an official Commission of Experts, the American Institute of International Law held in abeyance further activities which might seem to preempt the functions of the official agencies of codification".

It is a recognized weakness of official international conferences to pass high-sounding resolutions, create governmental agencies to carry them out, and then bury the results of their deliberations in an official report. Dr. Scott commented upon this aftermath of the Montevideo Conference as follows: "But there seems to be, unfortunately, an inertia or ineffectiveness inherent in attempts at codification by official action, and actual progress in the matter of the adoption of conventions has not gone beyond the accomplishments of the Sixth Conference which had before it the projects of the American Institute. The same lack of results is in evidence in the efforts of the League of Nations through its Committee of Experts for the Progressive Codification of International Law, established under resolution of the Assembly of 22 September 1924. The failure of the first official conference for the codification of international law held at The Hague in 1930 as the result of the work of the committee has apparently postponed indefinitely the work of codification outside of America".[53]

During the period while the American Institute was, in Dr. Scott's words, "resting on its laurels", he found an outlet for his interest and energy in the work of the American Bar Association, particularly its newly-founded Section of International and Comparative Law. Upon the recommendation of that Section, the Association at its Sixtieth Annual Meeting, held in Kansas City, Missouri, 27 August–1 September 1937, recommended that the American Institute of International Law resume its activities and take advantage of the forthcoming Eighth International Conference of American States at Lima in 1938 to hold a formal session on that occasion. Later the Peruvian Government, as host to the official conference, became interested in having the American Institute meet at the same time in Lima and invited it to do so. It went further and placed a meeting of the Institute upon the official program of the Conference.

---

[53] Carnegie Endowment Year Book.

"Under the circumstances", Dr. Scott wrote, "it seemed to the officers of the American Institute of International Law that the time had come for the Institute to consider the resumption of its work of codification".[54] The invitation of the Government of Peru was accepted and advantage was taken of the presence in Lima, as delegates of their governments to the Eighth International Conference of American States, of a number of members of the Institute to hold a meeting in that city for the purpose of reviving the activities of the Institute. Upon their arrival in Lima, Dr. Scott as President, and Dr. Ricardo J. Alfaro as Secretary General,[55] issued a call for a meeting to be held on 19 December.

Twenty-one out of a possible twenty-four members were present at the meeting. They were from Argentina, Bolivia, Brazil, Costa Rica, Cuba, United States, Guatemala, Haiti, Mexico, Panama, Peru, El Salvador, Dominican Republic, and Uruguay. A number of vacancies in membership were filled, steps were taken to reorganize the Institute so that it might function effectively without too much dependence upon the active participation of the national societies, and the approval of Institute action by correspondence with the members was expressly authorized whenever it was impracticable or impossible to hold plenary sessions. A list of subjects for codification was approved, and the Executive Council was empowered to assign these topics for study among the members interested in them.

A second meeting of the Institute of a more formal nature was held on 24 December, as a part of the official program of the International Conference of American States. This second meeting, like the first, was held in the University of San Marcos. It was attended by Dr. Carlos Concha, the Minister of Foreign Affairs of Peru and President of the International Conference, by Dr. Arturo Garcia Salazar, the Secretary General of the Conference, by Dr. Alfredo Solf y Muro, the Rector, who welcomed the Institute to the University, and by the heads and members of many of the official delegations. Such interest was taken in the meeting that it was prolonged

---

[54] Carnegie Endowment Year Book 1939, pp. 122–123.

[55] Dr. Maurtua died suddenly on 26 May 1937 aboard the steamer *Northern Prince* just before reaching Rio de Janeiro, where he was Peruvian Ambassador to Brazil. Dr. Alfaro, Panama, was elected *ad interim* to succeed him by the Executive Council early in 1938, which action was confirmed at the Lima plenary session.

several hours beyond the scheduled time for the convening of the official conference and its delegates were kept waiting until the Institute's meeting was over.

Dr. Scott was not an official delegate to the Conference, but was present as a guest of the Peruvian Government in his capacity as President of the Institute. So also were Dr. Ricardo J. Alfaro, the Secretary-General of the Institute, and the writer of this biography as the Assistant Secretary-General of the Institute. Dr. Scott and the writer were, moreover, authorized by the Trustees of the Carnegie Endowment to attend the Conference as observers and to promote unofficially the work in which the Endowment was engaged in Latin America.

In his Report on the Results of the Eighth International Conference of American States, Dr. Rowe, Director General of the Pan American Union, stated that "There was a general feeling that the previously existing system of carrying on the work of codification was unsatisfactory; that in the words of the Committee of Experts, it was unnecessarily complicated and hindered rather than facilitated codification; and also that there was a lack of coordination between the different codifying bodies"[56] The Conference approved a comprehensive resolution of fifteen paragraphs "to coordinate the action of the agencies now entrusted with this task and to establish precisely the duties which each is to perform". The American Institute was not reinstated as a part of the revised codification machinery, and its work during the few remaining years of its activity was of a strictly private character.

The topic of the political and civil rights of women which had created such commotion at the Seventh Conference was retained in the program of the Eighth. The Inter-American Commission of Women submitted a report. The action of the Conference upon it has already been stated in the preceding chapter entitled "Equal Rights for Women"[57]

In connection with his visit to Lima, Dr. Scott was invited to deliver a series of lectures at the venerable University of San Marcos on the background and development of international law in

---

[56] Report to the Governing Board, Pan American Union, Congress and Conference Series No. 27, 1939, p. 11.

[57] [Despite references in the manuscript to this Chapter, the text has not been found—WEB].

America. The lectures were prepared before Dr. Scott's departure from Washington, but because of a slight throat infection which developed on the voyage, he was not able to deliver them in public as had been arranged. He delivered the manuscripts to the Rector of the University and they were published by the University in book form and distributed to all the delegates at the Lima Conference as well as to all the universities and institutes of law throughout Latin America.[58]

The Executive Council of the Institute met in Washington on 8 November 1939 and designated the reporters and commissions for the drafting of the projects agreed upon at the session in Lima on 19 December 1938. At the same time, the Executive Council drafted regulations to accelerate and facilitate the execution of the work by the reporters and commissions. These assignments were communicated to the members and were generally accepted by them.

Eighth Pan American Scientific Congress

On the invitation of the Government of the United States, the Eighth Pan American Scientific Congress was held in Washington from 10–18 May 1940. Dr. Scott was appointed a member of the Organizing Committee and was an official delegate of the Government of the United States to the Conference. He was also a delegate of the Carnegie Endowment for International Peace as well as the American Institute of International Law. He became Chairman of Section IX dealing with International Law, Public Law and Jurisprudence. He delivered a paper before the section on the subject "The Inter-American Community". Secretary of State Cordell Hull sent an invitation through Dr. Scott to the members of the American Institute of International Law to participate in the Conference. Dr. Scott promptly accepted the invitation and transmitted it to the members of the Institute. Nineteen of them also accepted and participated in the Conference. Some were already in Washington as members of the diplomatic corps and others came as official dele-

---

[58] *Conferencias del president del Institute Americano de derecho internacional, preparados en homenaje a la Universidad mayor de San Marcos* (Lima, Peru, 1938). 178 p.

gates of their governments to the Conference. For example, Dr. Alejandro Alvarez was chairman of the Chilean Delegation.

The crowded program of the Conference, which was divided into eleven sections, with representatives of the twenty-one American Republics and delegations from 650 educational institutions and scientific bodies throughout the Americas, containing a total of 3,800 persons participating in the work of the Conference, did not allow time for a separate meeting of the American Institute of International Law, but during the Conference Dr. Scott on 16 May gave a luncheon to the members of the Institute in attendance. He and Dr. Alvarez made brief remarks concerning the Institute.

The twenty-fifth anniversary of the founding of the Institute occurred in December of the year 1940. The anniversary was celebrated on 16 December at a luncheon attended by members of the Institute then present in Washington. The feature of the luncheon was the submission by Dr. Alvarez of a report entitled "The American Continent and the New Social and International Order". He had prepared the report looking to the future activities of the Institute. There was an exchange of views about it among the members present and with Dr. Alvarez, and it was decided to send the report to all members of the Institute for their consideration and comment. This direction was promptly complied with by the Secretary-General.

Several informal meetings were held in Washington during the years 1941–1942 attended by Dr. Scott, Dr. Alfaro, and others looking toward the strengthening of the organization of the Institute so as to increase its effectiveness, but even these activities ceased with the death of Dr. Scott on 25 June 1943. The vacancy in the presidency of the Institute caused by his death was never filled.

7

SERVICES FOR THE GOVERNMENT DURING WORLD WAR I

Upon the outbreak of war in Europe on 1 August 1914, the question of neutrality during that war was uppermost in the official thinking of the United States Government and in the minds of the American people. It will be recalled that President Wilson advised the American people to remain neutral in spirit as well as deed. In the summer of 1914 Dr. Scott, with the permission of the Trustees of the Carnegie Endowment for International Peace, accepted appointment as special adviser to the Department of State in matters of international law arising out of the war. In November of that year, an official Neutrality Board was established, consisting of representatives of the State and Navy Departments. Dr. Scott was appointed chairman on behalf of the State Department and two admirals of the Navy were appointed by that Department. The Trustees of the Endowment also offered the facilities of its offices and staff in Washington to assist in the work of the Neutrality Board. The Board met almost daily for two years in the offices of the Endowment in Washington and prepared opinions and memoranda advising the Government on the many delicate and complex questions concerning the rights and duties of the United States as a neutral power. The officers and staff of the Endowment's Division of International Law gave freely of their time and talents to this work and the unique facilities of the Endowment's Library in Washington were in constant use by the members of the Board.

In addition to the performance of his official services as Chairman of the Neutrality Board, Dr. Scott, as Director of the Carnegie Endowment's Division of International Law, initiated and supervised a comprehensive program of research and studies covering practically the whole field of neutrality and the laws of war.

The diplomatic disputes between the United States and Germany during that period resembled in some respect the controversy over neutral rights between the United States and France from 1797 to 1800. The Division, accordingly, collected and made available to the interested authorities a collection of American state papers and judicial decisions concerning that old controversy. They were published in volume form in 1917. The Division made likewise available the opinions of the Attorneys General and judgments of the Supreme Court and Court of Claims of the United States relating to the controversy with France, and the opinions of the Attorneys General and decisions of the Federal Courts and diplomatic correspondence respecting the Treaties of 1785, 1799 and 1828 between the United States and Prussia. In President Wilson's address to Congress of 26 February 1917 reporting upon what he regarded as unwarranted infringements of American neutral rights by Germany, he suggested "that there may be no recourse but to armed neutrality". In the same year, the Division published a collection of official documents bearing in the armed neutralities of 1780 and 1800, as well as extracts from American and foreign works on international law concerning those neutralities.

The Declaration of London of 1909 on maritime neutrality was taken up by the Division article-by-article and discussed with the utmost thoroughness. Studies were made of the official attitudes of many governments on such matters as contraband of war, visit and search, convoy, transfer of flag, and the sinking of neutral ships and cargoes. Examination was made of the positions of the governments represented at the Hague Conferences on subjects covered by those conventions, such as the dropping of bombs and explosives from aircraft, the laying of submarine mines, the transfer of merchant vessels of belligerents, internment of enemy ships in neutral ports, use of wireless apparatus, strategic war areas, military occupation of invaded territory, use of neutral flags by belligerent vessels, the position in international law of government-owned ships, and so on. Many of these comprehensive memoranda were later formulated into valuable treatises or pamphlets by the Division.

The collection of all of these materials was in line with the policy of the Endowment of assisting the Government to preserve the peace of the United States during that critical period. It fell upon the United States to bear the brunt of the inevitable attack upon neutral rights incident to a war of large proportions. The United States Government was forced to conduct a correspondence with the governments at war in defense of neutral rights and commerce and to protest against their infringement in an effort to cause the warring nations to confine their activities within the limits of their legitimate belligerent rights and to have regard for their belligerent duties.

It was deemed to be in the best interests of the promotion of international peace through the maintenance of international law to give the widest possible public knowledge to the neutral position of the United States. At that time, the Department of State had no public relations services and Dr. Scott arranged with Secretary of State Lansing to publish the official correspondence of the United States on these subjects as special supplements to the *American Journal of International Law*. Through this form of publicity the actual text of the American correspondence was made available to statesmen, diplomats, legislators, teachers, the press, and other persons interested in questions of international law. When the United States entered the war on 6 April 1917, it ceased to be a neutral and became a belligerent. There was accordingly no further need for the services of the Neutral Board and it was disbanded by a letter from Secretary of State Lansing to Dr. Scott dated 4 May 1917. As a result of his own work on the Neutral Board, Dr. Scott wrote a "Survey of International Relations between the United States and Germany" which was published by the Oxford University Press in New York in 1917. Moreover, the Carnegie Endowment published in its legal series several volumes dealing with neutrality in World War I.

It will be recalled that Dr. Scott had served as a private in the California Volunteer Infantry in the war with Spain in 1898. When Congress passed an act to raise a national army, which was approved on 4 June 1916, Dr. Scott applied for a commission as major of the Judge Advocate General's section of the Officers Reserve Corps. At that time, the Judge Advocate General was Brigadier General Enoch H. Crowder, under whom Dr. Scott had served in 1898. The commission was granted to Dr. Scott in November 1916 by his good friend and associate in the peace movement, the then Secretary of War, Newton D. Baker. Dr. Scott's first act after receiving his reserve commission was to prepare at the request of the Judge Advocate General an extended memorandum of the history and legal status of the militia, a subject then earnestly under consideration in Congress and by the people at large. The memorandum consisted of extracts from the Journals and Debates of the Federal Convention of 1787, the State Conventions on the Ratification of the Federal Constitution, the Debates in and Acts of Congress, the Federalist Papers, and other pertinent papers such as extracts from the correspondence of General Washington to the Congress during the War of the Revolution, and sundry views of the framers of the Constitution on the establishment of the militia. The memorandum was transmitted through military channels to the Chairman of the Senate Military Affairs Committee and was printed as a public document early in 1917.[1]

Following the declaration of war against Germany and the disbanding of the Neutrality Board, Major Scott was assigned to active duty on 15 May in the office of the Provost Marshal General, who also happened to be General Crowder. Major Scott's principal duties there were in relation to the organization and administration of the Selective Service System. His great aid in building up the superstructure of that system was later recognized by General Crowder in a personal inscription to Dr. Scott in the General's Final Report as Provost Marshal General. Major Scott's other assignments in that office were in the appeals division, the correspondence division and the aliens division.

At the start of the last year of the war, the Department of State decided it was time to begin active preparations for the peace conference which would inevitably take place when hostilities had ceased. The Secretary of State requested the Secretary of War to have Major Scott relieved of his duties with the Army and detailed to the Department of State for special research work. Accordingly, on 8 February 1918 orders were issued to that effect and Dr. Scott transferred his activities back to his office in the Carnegie Endowment, where he remained in charge of special work for the State Department until he left for Paris on the S.S. *George Washington* on 4 December 1918 as one of the legal advisers of the American Commission to Negotiate Peace. He retained his commission in the Army while serving at Paris until 14 April 1919, where he was honorably discharged with a number of other officers whose services were no longer required by the Army.

---

[1] Senate Document, No. 695, 64th Congress, 2d Session.

8

An American Academy of International Law and Inter-American Bar Association

The proposal to establish an American Academy of International Law at Habana was coupled with Dr. Scott's desire to move the headquarters of the American Institute of International Law to that city, and the offer of the President of Cuba to construct a palace in Habana for this and other related purposes (see Chapter 6 above). Due to subsequent economic and political complications in Cuba, the palace was never constructed. Before those unfavorable conditions were foreseen, however, the Academy was formally opened in its temporary quarters in the aula magna of the National University at Habana on 30 October 1929, in the presence of the President of Cuba, the Secretary of State, and other Cabinet officers, members of the diplomatic corps and of the Executive Council of the American Institute of International Law, as well as of the Rector and professors of the University and other distinguished personalities. Dr. Scott was the principal speaker. He concluded his opening address with the following peroration:

> Thirty-one years ago today I was serving in the Army of the United States, in the war with Spain for the liberation of this beautiful Island. I had heard the cry of *Cuba Libre* everywhere resounding throughout the States to the North. I forsook the Deanship of the Law School of the University of Southern California to answer the call of President McKinley for volunteers. I responded in April 1898, enlisting in the Infantry of the United States. Although no longer young—indeed, I have passed the average life of man or woman—I still seem to hear within my heart the distant echo of *Cuba Libre*, and today, in the presence of the President of Cuba, its officials, and the Diplomatic Corps accredited to Havana, I cry with all the force of my being, and "con to-

dos mis esfuerzos": *Viva Cuba Soberana, libre y independiente de todas las naciones y de cada una de ellas, del mundo entero!*

According to press reports of the occasion, Dr. Scott received a tremendous ovation. President Machado arose from his seat and embraced him, whereupon the entire audience came to their feet and applauded wildly for five minutes, a demonstration rarely equaled in Cuba.[1]

The Secretary of State, Dr. Rafael Martinez Ortiz, presided as chairman of the session. Other speakers were Dr. Antonio S. de Bustamante, Director of the new Academy; Dr. Octavio Averoff, Rector of the University; and Dr. Victor M. Maurtua, Peruvian Ambassador to Brazil.

After the formal opening, six lectures were delivered on as many succeeding days by members of the Executive Council of the American Institute. Dr. Alvarez led off on the subject of "The Reconstruction of International Law". He was followed the next day by Dr. Carlos Saavedra Lamas, of Argentina, who discussed a "Third Hague Conference". A justice of the Supreme Court of Brazil was next on the subject of "A. de Cusmao and Panamericanism". Then came Dr. Maurtua, who lectured on "Responsibility of States and Indemnification for Injuries". Dr. Luis Anderson, former Secretary of Foreign Relations of Costa Rica, followed with a lecture on "International Recognition of the Rights of Man". The lecture series was concluded by Dr. Scott on 7 November with a discussion on "Nationality".[2]

A more imposing and promising start could not be imagined for any academic institution, but the first was also the last session of this Academy.

The project remained dormant for several years. In September 1936 Dr. Scott and Dr. Bustamante met at The Hague where the latter was serving as a judge of the Permanent Court of Arbitration. Dr. Scott expressed the hope that "in the near future, an Academy somewhat similar to that of The Hague might be established in Havana". From London Dr. Scott elaborated on this subject in a memorandum which he sent to Dr. Bustamante. "Of course", he

---

[1] See *Diario de la Marina*, the *Heraldo de Cuba*, *El Mundo*, the *Havana Evening Telegram*, and other newspapers of Habana published on 31 October 1929.
[2] The schedule of lectures was published in the *Diario de la Marina*, 31 October 1929.

wrote, "the existence of the Academy at Havana would rehabilitate the American Institute of International Law; for it could be installed in the Academy at Havana".[3]

The Inter-American Conference for the Maintenance of Peace was held in Buenos Aires in December 1936. Dr. Scott was not a delegate to that Conference nor did he attend it in any capacity, but there were members of the American Institute of International Law on other official delegations. On 16 December the Conference adopted a resolution recommending that the American Academy of International Law be established as soon as possible. No details such as location, expense of maintaining and operating the Academy, were given, except that the Academy should be established "upon an adequate basis". The resolution stated that the Conference was "convinced of the important contribution which the Academy of International Law at The Hague, in cooperation with the Carnegie Endowment for International Peace, is making to the cause of world peace"; and that the Conference was also "convinced that similar benefits would be derived from the establishment of such an Academy in America, in which questions of great current interest to this continent might be authoritatively considered, with facilities for easier access and more prompt dissemination among the citizens of the American Republics".[4]

Dr. Scott commented as follows upon the resolution of the Buenos Aires Conference in his next annual report to the Trustees of the Carnegie Endowment:

> Here, indeed, it may properly be said that imitation is the sincerest flattery. Without the slightest suggestion from the Endowment, the Conference, wholly on its own initiative, stated its conviction that the Academy at The Hague is making an important contribution to world peace, and that the establishment of such an institution in the Western World would be of similar benefit with respect to the relations between the American Republics. The creation of the American Academy of International Law would, indeed, have far-reaching consequences in the development of international law on the American Continent. The Academy would be in the nature of a clearing house for American conceptions regarding American international problems; the

---

[3] Memo prepared at London, September 1936, in Scott papers.
[4] *International Conferences of American States, 1933–1940*, p. 146.

> courses offered by it would be of interest not only to advanced students and teachers of international law, but to the officials of foreign offices throughout the Americas; and the result should be a clearer perception both of the basic principles of international law and of the variations in their concrete application to questions peculiar to the American republics.

Upon the recommendation of the Section of International and Comparative Law, the resolution of Buenos Aires of 1936 was approved by the American Bar Association at Kansas City in September 1937. The Association's resolution expressed the hope that the American Academy would be established in the capital city of a Latin American country in the near future.

Upon his return from the annual meeting of the American Bar Association at Kansas City, where he submitted a report as Chairman of the Association's Committee on International Law containing several recommendations, Dr. Scott got in communication with Dr. Pedro Martinez Fraga, the Cuban Ambassador at Washington, and repeated his suggestion that the proposed Academy be located in Habana. He recalled the action of the Cuban President in 1928 in decreeing the erection of a palace for the American Institute and Academy. In the course of a luncheon at the Cuban Embassy, Dr. Scott and the Ambassador enlarged their visions to foresee a "university center" or "university city" in Habana. On 3 November, Dr. Scott sent the Ambassador a memorandum entitled "Habana as a Center of Inter-American Culture". In that memorandum Dr. Scott described the ancient Greek academies of Plato and Aristotle, quoted Cardinal Newman's portrayal of a university, and gave a summary account of the development of the mediaeval University of Paris into an international cultural center; all of which he seemed to envision within the framework of the beautiful capital of Cuba. These highly ideal plans for an international center at Habana were again not realized.[5]

On his way back to Washington from Lima early in 1939, Dr. Scott stopped over in Habana and discussed briefly with Dr. Bustamante the plans they had in common to make of Habana an inter-American cultural center. At attempt was made to revive the

---

[5] A copy of the original memorandum is in his papers. So also there are copies of his letters to the Cuban Ambassador dated 4 October and 2, 3, and 4 November 1937.

plan of 1929 in the Cuban Congress in 1940,[6] but the attempt with no better success than the previous one.

The Inter-American Bar Association

The idea of a closer relationship and cooperation between the bar associations of different countries did not originate in the United States. An International Union of Advocates was organized in Belgium in 1919. The American Bar Association in 1933 appointed a special Committee on International Bar Relations, under the chairmanship of Col. John H. Wigmore. It submitted a report the following year giving information regarding the organized bar associations throughout the world.[7]

Upon its recommendation, the Association adopted a resolution declaring the time to be ripe "for some sort of affiliation between the organized bars of all nations and directing that the subject be hereafter allotted to the Section of International and Comparative Law".[8] At the annual meeting of the Association held in Kansas City in 1937, upon the recommendation of the Section, a resolution was adopted "in favor of cooperation with the other twenty-one associations of the American continent" and recommending "that on the occasion of the Eighth International Conference of American States, to be held at Lima, Peru, in 1938, delegates or representatives of said bar associations of the Americas meet with a view to taking proper steps for the preparation at subsequent meetings, to be held in connection with later Inter-American Conferences, of projects of certain phases of comparative law problems pertinent to America".

In this connection the Association adopted at the same time resolutions favoring the establishment of an American Academy of International Law and the revival of the American Institute of International Law.[9] Later the Section of International and Comparative Law of the Association requested Dr. Scott and the writer of

---

[6] See Report to the Cuban House of Representatives, 22 July 1940, signed by a number of members.

[7] A.B.A. Report 1934, pp. 620–633.

[8] Ibid., pp. 216–217.

[9] A.B.A. Report, 1937, pp. 393–394.

this biography to inquire into the feasibility of the project of an Inter-American Bar Association when they were in Lima, Peru, in attendance upon the Eighth International Conference of American States. They reported to the Section's Committee on the Development of International Law through International Conferences, of which Dr. Scott was chairman. The Section submitted a recommendation to the American Bar Association at its meeting in San Francisco in July 1939 favoring the establishment of an Inter-American Bar Association and authorizing the Section to support fully the efforts to establish it. Owing to a crowded calendar, the resolution was not reached at the annual meeting in San Francisco, but it was adopted at the mid-winter meeting at Chicago in January 1940.[10]

Upon the basis of the report of Messrs. Scott and Finch regarding the inquiries at Lima, and in consequence of the effective work of a Committee of the Section under the chairmanship of Colonel William Cattron Rigby, a draft constitution of the Inter-American Bar Association was made ready for signature during the Eighth American Scientific Congress at Washington in May 1940. It was approved and opened for signature by the Section on International Law, Public Law and Jurisprudence, under the chairmanship of Dr. Scott, and signed by a sufficient number of representatives of bar associations to bring the association into being.[11]

At its first session, held at Habana, 24–28 March 1941, the Inter-American Bar Association approved the establishment in that city of an Inter-American Academy of International and Comparative Law. The writer of this biography was chosen as its President and he has served continuously in that capacity. The Academy has functioned for several weeks during the winter months in intermittent years since its establishment. Its faculty is invited to serve for each session from lecturers on international law and comparative law from the United States and Latin American countries. Its student body has a like complexion. Financed at first jointly by the Cuban Government and the Carnegie Endowment, in later years it has been dependent upon the former for support. It is managed by

[10] A.B.A. Report, 1939, pp. 399, 412.

[11] See Proceedings of the Eighth International Conference of American States, Washington, 1940, I, pp. 202, 205, 212, 214, 215, 217.

an international council and its academic activities are guided and controlled by an international curatorium.

In the Inter-American Academy of International and Comparative Law there have been realized, at least in some small degree, the dreams of Dr. Scott and his colleagues in the American Institute of International Law of the establishment of an international academy and cultural center in the beautiful city of the Pearl of the Antilles.

9

AMERICAN BAR ASSOCIATION

While he was Dean of the Law School of the University of Illinois, Dr. Scott was elected to membership in the American Bar Association at its 24th annual meeting in Denver, Colorado, held from 21-23 August 1901. He maintained his membership in the Association throughout his life. At the meeting of the Association held at Hot Springs, Virginia, in August 1903, he delivered on the 27th of that month an address on the subject of "The Place of International Law in Legal Education".[1]

In 1907 he was appointed a member of the Association's Committee on International Law and served continuously on that committee until 1931. For the last eleven years of that period he was the Chairman of the Committee. The reports of the committee under his chairmanship assumed the character of scholarly accounts of important current international events in many of which Dr. Scott had personally taken part. His comments upon them were for that reason particularly enlightening.[2]

In his first report as Chairman, which he presented to the 45th annual meeting of the Association in San Francisco on 10 August 1922, he stated his concept of the function of the report: "The method of preparing the report has been somewhat different this year from the times past. The committee has remembered that the American Bar Association is a body composed of lawyers, and, therefore, that the international events to be discussed would better be those of a legal nature, and that the international events or the international agreements should be those to which the United States was a party". Due to limitations of space, the reports were necessar-

---

[1] For the text, see the printed Report of the American Bar Association, 1903.

[2] His reports were published in the printed annual Reports of the American Bar Association as follows: 1922, pp. 323–352; 1923, pp. 308–324; 1924, pp. 332–340; 1925, pp. 401–405; 1926, pp. 420–427; 1928, pp. 403–418; 1929, pp. 346–351; 1930, pp. 441–453; 1931, pp. 395–402.

ily restricted to a few selected events of outstanding significance. The contents of the reports were selected in the first instance and the original drafts prepared by the Chairman. The drafts were then submitted to the other members of the committee either by mail or at personal meetings. The chairman always sought unanimity in the committee on the report and usually succeeded by modifications of details. Members who could not then agree without reservation were permitted to append personal statements explaining their positions. This procedure was especially employed during the years when the Committee had to deal with the proposed adherence by the United States to the Permanent International Court of Justice, a subject which, like the unsuccessful attempt to take the United States into the League of Nations, became so bitterly controversial that favorable action could not be obtained in the United States Senate.

Dr. Scott had attended with Mr. Elihu Root the meeting of the Advisory Committee of Jurists which drafted the Statute of the Court at The Hague in the summer of 1920. The Statute was opened for signature on 20 December 1920; but, as is well known, the Government of the United States never accepted membership in what opponents referred to as the "Court of the League of Nations" in spite of several attempts to obtain the advice and consent of the Senate by proposed reservations.

Dr. Scott's experience with his first report on international law submitted to the American Bar Association in the year 1922 taught him a practical lesson on the difficulty of dealing with international questions in the United States at that time. A section of the report dealt with the treaties which it had become necessary to conclude between the United States and Germany putting an end to the state of war between those two countries following the rejection of the Treaty of Versailles by the United States Senate. Exception was taken on the floor of the American Bar Association to a paragraph in Dr. Scott's long report by Judge C. N. Goodwin, of Illinois, as follows:

> The question of whether President Wilson was unwilling to accept reasonable reservations in the Treaty of Versailles, and whether his action, whatever it was, was the cause of the rejection of that treaty, is a controversial political question on which this Assembly is divided. It has no place here. We are met for the improvement of the law; we are not here to bring about a more

> efficient and satisfactory administration of justice; we are met to produce better conditions in the bar, and we cannot bring about those results if controversial questions, political questions on which we are divided, are brought into this Assembly, and therefore I ask, on behalf of those who feel as I do in this matter, Mr. Scott, that you withdraw that portion of your report.[3]

Notwithstanding that the statement objected to was fully justified by the record of the debate on the League of Nations in the Senate,[4] Dr. Scott, in the interest of harmony, consented to withdraw that paragraph of his report. When accepting reappointment as Chairman of the Committee in 1926, he wrote the President of the Association: "For some years past the Bar Association has been divided on the League of Nations, and it has been a very difficult matter to present a report from year to year without giving offense to any section of the Association".

The establishment of the Permanent International Court of Justice at The Hague and the successive attempts to obtain the adherence of the Government of the United States were from the beginning prime subjects of Dr. Scott's reports as Chairman of the Committee on International Law. A resolution recommended in his first report was adopted by the Association as follows:

> *Resolved*, that the American Bar Association, at its 45th Annual Meeting, held in the City of San Francisco, on the 10th day of August 1922, expresses the hope that a way may be found by which the Government of the United States may avail itself of the Permanent Court of International Justice.[5]

Another resolution recommended by his committee expressing the hope of the Association "that the recommendations of the Committee of Jurists assembled at The Hague, in 1920, proposed by the Hon. Elihu Root, that a new conference of the nations in continuation of the first two conferences at The Hague be held as soon as practicable" for the specified purposes of stating and advancing international law was approved at the same time by the Association. The resolution instructed the Committee on Interna-

---

[3] See Proceedings of the Association, Report, 1922, pp. 54–59.
[4] G. A. Finch, "The Treaty of Peace with Germany in the United States Senate", *American Journal of International Law*.
[5] Proceedings of the Association, Report, 1922, pp. 54–59.

tional Law to present a report to the next meeting of the Association concerning each of the said recommendations. An amendment added upon motion of Chief Justice William H. Taft instructed the Committee "to formulate such amendments or changes in the Statute which now constitutes the Court which in the judgment of the Committee might make it possible for the United States to accept it.[6]

The report of the Committee on International Law for the 1923 annual meeting of the American Bar Association was prepared by Dr. Scott after much correspondence with the other members of the Committee, but he was not able to submit it to the meeting at Minneapolis in August of that year. He was then at The Hague taking part in the inauguration of the Academy of International Law. Because of the controversy then raging in the United States over adherence to the Permanent International Court of justice, that subject was treated separately in a special report of the Committee.

Former Secretary of State Robert Lansing, a member of the Committee, opposed any report on the subject because it would inject a political controversy into the discussions of the American Bar Association.[7] Mr. George W. Wickersham[8] and Professor Manley O. Hudson[9] insisted that the Committee should recommend that the Association approve adherence to the Court upon the terms and conditions recommended by Secretary of State Hughes and President Harding in the preceding February. Dr. Scott's own position was stated in a letter of 3 March 1923 to Prof. Hudson, in which he said: "I should think that the Committee on International Law would not need to go beyond this report [Hughes-Harding to the Senate] inasmuch as it is the judgment of the duly constituted authorities as to what should, in their opinion, be done. The report would be a report of fact, and discussion by the Committee might open us to a charge of taking sides, for it is probable that the question will by this time have become more or less political.[10]

The special report dealing with American adherence to the Permanent Court was drafted at Dr. Scott's suggestion by Judge George Donworth of Seattle, Washington, following an exchange

---

[6] Ibid.

[7] Letter to Dr. Scott, 16 April 1923. Scott Papers.

[8] Letter to Dr. Scott, 7 March 1923, Scott Papers.

[9] Letter to Dr. Scott, 5 March 1923. Scott Papers.

[10] Copy of letter in Scott Papers.

of correspondence and personal meetings between them. It was Dr. Scott's thought that a member of the Committee on International Law residing on the West Coast away from the partisanship of the East would be able to approach the subject of the World Court with more objectivity. Concerning the Taft resolution of 1922, the special report states: "In view of the fact that after the meeting [in 1922] the President of the United States transmitted to the Senate with his approval the recommendation of the Secretary of State presenting a definite plan whereby the United States should accept the Permanent Court, the Committee did not feel it incumbent upon them to carry out the resolution of the Assembly and present a plan of its own; obviously, it would not only be a work of supererogation but of impropriety on the part of the Committee to present a resolution of its own when the Government had presented such a simple plan and resolution and method as were embodied in the message of the President".

Dr. Scott joined with Judge Donworth and Mr. Wickersham in adding to the report a personal statement that they were "unequivocally in favor of the participation of the United States in the present Permanent International Court of Justice upon such terms and conditions, not inconsistent with the character and functions of the court, as the President and Secretary of State may suggest and the Senate of the United States approve".

The report was presented to the Association by Mr. Wickersham as acting Chairman in Dr. Scott's absence. Upon Mr. Wickersham's recommendation, the Association adopted a resolution joining "in what it believes to be the wise judgment of the American people that the United States ought to become one of the supporters of the Permanent Court of International Justice at The Hague, and that our Government, therefore, should adhere to the Protocol establishing the Court, in the manner set forth by the President in his message to the Senate of 24 February 1923". This resolution was in the language identical with a resolution adopted by the committee on international law of the Association of the Bar of the City of New York, of which Mr. Elihu Root was chairman. In a letter transmitting to Dr. Scott the report and resolution of that New York Association, Mr. Wickersham stated that they were drafted by Mr. Root himself.[11]

---

[11] Letter of 7 March 1923, Scott Papers.

A second paragraph of the same resolution put the Association on record as favoring the calling of a new conference of the nations in continuation of the two former Conferences at The Hague for the purpose of further stating and clarifying the rules of international law. Professor Manley O. Hudson, who was also in Geneva in the service of the League of Nations, sent a dissent from the second recommendation on the ground that he did not see the necessity for a new conference at The Hague.[12] Dr. Scott sent Prof. Hudson's statement to the Secretary of the American Bar Association for publication in its Report.[13]

The Committee on International Law in its report submitted to the 1926 meeting brought the Association up to date on the Senate resolution authorizing the United States to adhere, with reservations, to the Permanent Court of International Justice. The final report on that subject by Dr. Scott's committee was submitted to the 1929 meeting of the American Bar Association at Memphis, Tennessee. It gave the history and discussed the provisions of the Root formula agreed upon at Geneva, 11–19 March 1929. As to that formula, the report stated:

> These provisions would seem to provide full protection to the interests of the United States with respect to advisory opinions, and to carry out fully the purport of the Senate Reservations, while at the same time reserving to the United States and other signatory states, respectively, the right at any time to terminate the connection, if they should deem it advisable. If the Council of the League should act favorably upon this recommendation, as is anticipated, it is earnestly to be hoped that the United States Senate shall take its place as a signatory of the Court Protocol.

The report was adopted upon a motion which declared that "The adoption of this report carries with it the approval of the American Bar Association of the World Court as to the terms and conditions set forth in the report".[14]

---

[12] Prof. Hudson's dissent went also to the special report on the Permanent Court, but he had no opportunity to consider the additional statement signed by Dr. Scott, Judge Donworth and Mr. Wickersham.
[13] For discussion of the reports, see Report for 1923, pp. 60–64; for the text of the two reports and additional statements, see ibid., pp. 308–324.
[14] Proceedings, Report, 1929, p. 135.

Other subjects dealt with in reports of the Committee on International Law while Dr. Scott was its chairman were, principally, the Washington Conference on the Limitation of Armaments, the Tacna-Arica and Chaco disputes in Latin America, the Vatican agreement with Italy, the Locarno treaties, the different Central American and Inter-American Conferences during that period, the codification of international law by the American Institute of International Law and the Committee of Experts of the League of Nations, the meeting of the Inter-American Commission of Jurists at Rio de Janeiro, and treaties of the United States for the maintenance of peace.

The last report prepared by Dr. Scott on behalf of its Committee on International Law was that submitted to the American Bar Association at Atlantic City in September 1931. The main portion of the report dealt with the participation of the United States in the Permanent Court of International Justice. The following recommendation of the report was approved by the Association:

> Your Committee, believing that the Permanent Court of International Justice is the greatest of international instrumentalities for the preservation of peace and justice between nations, recurs to the approval given to the participation of the Government of the United States in the World Court upon the terms and conditions set forth in the Protocol of Accession of the United States. It requests the American Bar Association to reaffirm at its forthcoming session at Atlantic City the action taken at the meeting of the Association in Memphis in 1929: that the Government of the United States shall adhere to the Permanent Court of International Justice, upon the terms and conditions as stated in the Protocol of Adherence, to which it is a signatory; and the Association respectfully requests and earnestly urges the Senate of the United States to advise and consent to the Protocol of Signature of the Statute of the Permanent Court of International Justice, executed 26 December 1920 , and the Protocol of Revision of the Statute of the said Permanent Court and to the Protocol of Accession of the United States, signed 14 September 1929, to which the Government of the United States became signatory on 9 December 1929, which protocols were transmitted to the Senate on 10 December 1930 by the President of the United States.[15]

---

[15] A.B.A. Report, 1931, pp. 54–56, 395–402.

When the American Bar Association held its annual meeting in Washington D. C. in October 1914, Dr. Scott was appointed by the President of the District of Columbia Bar Association a member of its Committee of One Hundred on Entertainment. He went to the London meeting of the American Bar Association in July 1924. He took an active part in the professional activities there and with Mrs. Scott fully enjoyed the many interesting social events and entertainments provided so generously by the English lawyers and other hosts. He was appointed a member of a subcommittee of five members of the American Bar Association to accept an invitation from the Paris Bar Association. He and Mrs. Scott accompanied a large group of American lawyers to that city, responded in French to addresses of welcome on several occasions and presided at a reception for the visitors and French hosts given on the evening of 31 July by the Carnegie Endowment for International Peace at its Paris quarters, 173 Boulevard St. Germain.[16]

From 1936 to 1938 Dr. Scott served on the Committee on Resolutions of the Association.

Two years after Dr. Scott retired from service on the Committee on International Law, the Association, at its meeting in Grand Rapids, Michigan, in August 1933 amalgamated the committee with the Comparative Law Bureau into a Section of International and Comparative Law, under the Chairmanship of Professor John H. Wigmore.[17] Dr. Scott subsequently served on several committees of the Section. In 1936 he accepted the chairmanship of its Committee on the Pacific Settlement of International Disputes and Current Development of International Law. Two years later he remained chairman when the name of the committee was changed to the Committee on the Development of International Law through International Conferences. He also became a member of the Section's Committee on the Restatement of International Law.

From time to time, Dr. Scott represented the American Bar Association before other professional gatherings. For instance, in May 1926 he was a delegate of the Association to the meeting of the American Academy of Political and Social Science, at Phila-

---

[16] See the Report by Wm. D. Guthrie, chairman of the A.B.A. Subcommittee, entitled "Visit of A.B.A. to Paris, July 1924" published in the A.B.A. Journal (1924) and the manuscript of the Report, Scott Papers.
[17] A.B.A. Report, 1933, p. 103.

delphia, where on 15 May he delivered an address on "Disarmament Through International Organization".[18] On 12 July of the same year he represented the American Bar Association at the celebration of the 150th anniversary of the Virginia Bill of Rights at Williamsburg, Virginia, where he delivered a tribute to George Mason. On Christmas Eve of 1937 he was a member of the Committee of the American Bar Association which attended the burial service at the Washington Cathedral for Frank B. Kellogg, former Secretary of State and former President of the Association.

---

[18] The address was printed in the Annals of the Philadelphia Association for July 1926.

10

[Fragments]

Robert E. Lee and the War Between the States

Among the literati of Washington who met at the Round Table Club of the capital on 25 February 1914 were James Brown Scott and Charles Francis Adams. The next day Mr. Adams wrote to Dr. Scott: "I yesterday derived much satisfaction from our meeting and I should be very glad to improve our acquaintance". Dr. Scott eagerly took advantage of the opportunity to exchange views on historical and current public questions with his distinguished acquaintance. This took place in the course of an interesting correspondence and of several personal meetings at informal dinner-table symposiums attended by a very limited number of selected guests invited by Mr. Adams.

In acknowledging receipt of some of Mr. Adams' addresses and lectures, Dr. Scott referred to the form of acknowledgement used by Disraeli, who, he said, "was accustomed to say, when he received books or pamphlets, that he would lose no time in reading them"; but, Dr. Scott was quick to assure Mr. Adams, "the time spent in reading your publications could not in any way be considered wasted". In the same letter Dr. Scott put in writing his views toward the south in its conflict with the North during the War between the States. He had expressed them in a previous conversation with Mr. Adams, and repeated them as follows:

> While still a student at Harvard and learning American history from Professor Hart, who, as you know, was then if not now a somewhat bitter partisan of the North in matters Southern, I could not overcome the feeling that the war between the States was deeper and more fundamental than a question of property and that, although the desire to retain and to protect slavery may have been the immediate cause of the resort to arms, slavery was merely the pretext for the assertion of a right on the part of the

Southern States to withdraw from the Union whenever it seemed to them that the Union worked to their disadvantage, as they had joined the Union in the first instance merely because it seemed to each State in so joining – witness the refusal of North Carolina and Rhode Island to ratify the Constitution – to be beneficial to it. I am, of course, aware that this is the historical argument or view, and that it is opposed to the national view, which fortunately triumphed; but in any fair interpretation we cannot exclude history, and even in construing a contract, a statute, or a constitution, we must, I believe, carefully consider, weigh, and balance the reasons which influenced the parties to enter into the contract, to pass the statute, or to frame the constitution.

The immediate approach was the impeachment proceedings against President Johnson, and from an examination of his policy and the Acts of Congress from which the Southern States were excluded, I came to the conclusion that, however just the criticism of intemperate utterance might be as applied to him, his views as to reconstruction and his acts in regard thereto were wise and statesmanlike, and that the success of the impeachment proceedings would have been a blunder, which, we are assured on high authority, is worse than a crime . . .

Turning to the address 'Tis Sixty Years Since', which you were good enough to send me with an inscription in your own handwriting, I find on page 52 a passage which strongly appeals to me, confirming as it does the thoughts and impressions of youth. 'In the Andrew Johnson impeachment', you say, 'was it not better that things were as they were?'

Passing now to your various utterances on the South, and especially to your work entitled 'Lee at Appomatox and Other Papers', and to the Oxford Lectures, entitled 'Trans-Atlantic Historical Solidarity', and which formed the subject matter of our conversation Wednesday last, I take the liberty of asserting that, so far as I understand the course of your events, your statements are not only literally but spiritually true, and that you have rendered no less service to the nation by your pen than you did in the four trying years of the Civil War with sword in hand. I am unable to understand how in a Republic, founded upon successful revolution, the action of a man who claimed and exercised the right of revolution should be questioned, unless it be that we draw the distinction between successful revolution, on the one hand, and unsuccessful revolt, on the other. When we look at the motives of Lee, we must perforce admit that they were as pure and high-minded as were the motives of any man of whom history takes note; that his character, subjected to the most rigid and partisan criticism, fails to disclose a flaw; that judged by the standard of actual achievement he does not suffer by comparison with the great of any time or country; and that the Virginian was indeed an American of whom his fellow countrymen may be proud and only too happy if they may approach his standard of moral elevation, intellectual poise, and devotion to duty as God gave it to him to see his duty. I was much touched by the passage in the Oxford Lectures ('Trans-Atlantic Historical Solidarity', page 105) in which you say, 'I add as the result of mature reflection that under exactly similar conditions I would myself have done as Lee did'.

I am a Northerner by birth and education, and I too would humbly ask that, while I regret his attitude, I cannot blame or criticize him for it, and in your statement that Lee was, with Washington, Franklin, and Lincoln, one of the four great 'world celebrities' which America has produced, I concur, although my knowledge of him, of his associates, and of the essentials of 'world celebrities' may be insufficient to enable me to defend the thesis which you proclaim.

You will pardon me for writing you this long letter, in reply to a very short one from you; but my heart is full and, as a devoted lover of his country, who in a minor capacity has served it in the field, I wish to thank you for what you have written and spoken of Lee and of the South, for to me, as to you, Lee is an American and the South is a part of the United States.[1]

Paris Notes on Reparation, 22 January 1919

At the office, Mr. Miller and I took up the question of German Responsibility where we had left it. I read aloud and commented on the Boxer Incident as set forth in Moore's *Digest* and we were strengthened by our examination of it that it was not only worth citing, but that it was persuasive when not or if not actually in point. Eleven nations solemnly held China liable for civil damages to foreigners and their property, and Chinese officials responsible individually for "crimes unprecedented in human history, crimes against the law of nations, against the laws of humanity and against

[1] Copy of letter from Dr. Scott to Charles Francis Adams, 28 February 1914, in Scott Papers.

civilization, [which] were committed under peculiarly odious circumstances".

Reparation was to be made for the murder of the German Minister von Ketteler and the murder of the Japanese Counsellor of Legation; "maintenance, under conditions to be settled between the Powers, of the prohibition of the importation of Arms, as well as of material used exclusively for the manufacture of arms and ammunition" and huge indemnities were agreed on to be paid to the subjects and citizens of the various countries. All this was set forth in general terms in the note of the Powers signed 22 December 1900 to which Germany, Austria-Hungary, Belgium, Spain, Netherlands, and Russia were parties. This agreement was put into more formal form in a Protocol of 7 September 1901 to which the same Powers were signatories, accompanied by Annexes setting forth specifically and in detail what was to be done in each case.

It is interesting to note in the matter of punishment—that one En Hai, the Chinese officer in the immediate command of the Chinese soldiers who fired upon and killed von Ketteler, himself firing with the others, was publicly beheaded on 31 December 1900 "by the German military authorities, on the spot where the crime was committed". That crime was a crime against International Law and sauce for the goose would seem to be sauce for the gander.

Here we have the nations whose interests had suffered by crimes and violations of international law exacting penalties from Chinese and exacting punishment of Chinese civil and military officials for violation of the Law of Nations.

China was the executioner in the matter of penal punishment except in Ketteler's case, where the Germans not inappropriately stepped in as the butcher.

What nine signatory powers did in 1900, the same or larger members can do in 1919. But the Boxer case is precedent for punishment of violators of International Law by Chinese, i.e., national authority. The Wirz case is a precedent for capital punishment for violation of laws of war by a Commission appointed by the victor. Prof. Hershey, pursuant to our direction, looked up the case, finding elaborate reference in Rhode's *History of the United States* (1864-66), V, p. 608, note. "The Trial of Henry Wirz" there listed was a Congressional Document. After some discussion as to its whereabouts, I suggested the Bibliothéque Nationale. It was there, some eight hundred pages long, but could not be removed. However, we could examine it on the spot and take notes, which Professor Hershey was directed to do.

We were anxious for the French Report which Mr. Clemenceau had promised on Saturday to send to the various delegations in the hope that it would facilitate their labors. When it came I do not know, but it reached us late in the afternoon. I laid my hands on it and read it through the evening. We were to have dinner out with Colonel Delano, but he put it off till tomorrow and we were invited to the reception of the President and Mrs. Wilson after the Lansing dinner. We begged off on account of a prior engagement before we knew that the Delano affair was to be postponed and after this we did not feel like opening up the matter of the reception. The President and his wife had to pass the evening without us, whom they would barely have seen or noticed had we been there, and I passed the evening with the Kaiser and his crimes.

But I should say that Mr. Davis, our Ambassador to Great Britain, wanted to call on me if I were not too busy, and as Mrs. S. was resting, she telephoned me that I come over and entertain the distinguished gentleman in the Hotel parlor. This I did, going directly to him instead of having him come to me. We chatted about his embassy and life in England. He said that he had spoken twice in public, that the *Times* gave his first speech in full, his second in part as the novelty had worn off, and that they would probably only mention his third and succeeding performances. He said that he was much worried over the next to be delivered on Washington's Birthday, as it was hard to say anything new on this day and subject. I asked him if he had ever thought of Washington as a peaceful settlement man and that he could take advantage of the occasion of the Peace Conference in Paris to speak of Washington's views on a League of American States created by the Conference of American States in Philadelphia in 1787, of which he was Chairman and the Soul. I also said that the General had first proposed a Prize Court for the States in the War of Independence as far back as November 1775, when he was in Cambridge in command of the raw troops then besieging Boston, and that in submitting Jay's Report of 1785 to the First Session of the First Congress under the Constitution, he proposed not only peaceable settlement with Great Britain but with others, saying "In my opinion it is desirable that all questions between this and other nations be speedily and amicably settled". I also called his attention to General Grant's famous declaration in favor of peace through justice administered by an International

Tribunal. So that the new ideas were old ones with us and had the added force of coming from the two Commanders in Chief of the Army elected to the Presidency.

He said this was just what he wanted, and I promised to get extracts from Washington's letters and official papers and the passage from General Grant.

Just here A. came in and we returned to the Embassy as A. very properly asked him how he found his swell friends and expressed pleasure that he should care to see *us* after consorting with them. He said he was doing his share to make the world safe for democracy, but he admitted he was getting along fairly well with the other side – pulling out a letter from the Princess Beatrice written in her own fair hand. The lady had been bitter against the Germans as a good loyal English woman should be and appeared to be anxious to show him that not all German Princelings, meaning herself and her English relatives, were bad. In the course of the conversation she had referred to an article in the *Edinburgh Review* on German atrocities and sent it to him to read, and he in returning it sent Morgenthau's onset. This brought the letter in reply headed "Dear Davis" and signed Beatrice. There was, however, no especial affection in it; it is just Royalty's way of addressing a commoner even although he happens to be an Ambassador of a foreign and friendly country.

The French memo is capitally written, but it is conceived and executed in the interest of the thesis that Germany and German Emperor are responsible and punishable for outbreak of war, that the German Emperor is responsible personally and criminally for its excesses triable before an International Tribunal to be instituted by the Allied and Associated Powers, that the Emperor, a refugee in Holland, is extraditable and that if Holland should refuse, his extradition can be forced.

The truth is war is permissible as the law stands today and by the Hague Conventions it only needed to be declared before beginning it or by ultimatum with time limit. This was followed in summer of 1914. It is therefore legal to prepare for a permissible action and for this purpose alliances may be contracted. It may be true that in municipal law a conspiracy to do a lawful act may be criminal and indictable, but the law of nations is a stranger to such subtlety.

The case may well be different in violations of the laws of war in the conduct of hostilities. The invasion of Belgium was admittedly a violation of international law as it was using neutral territory to attack France. The Chancellor admitted the illegality of the act and promised reparation when the military purpose they had in mind was accomplished. Germany is liable for the consequences of the war so far as Belgium is concerned. Insofar as the war, which Germany declared against Belgium in the teeth of the treaty, was concerned, the Kaiser is personally responsible for any excesses he may have ordered, but not for ordinary acts.

In the case of France, the declaration of war was legal and only illegality consists in excess of laws of war. Here the Kaiser can only be responsible for action contrary to International Law. The declaration of war vests Generals with all usual war powers and they are agents of the Supreme War Lord. In excess of laws of war, they are not his agents without direct command on his part to commit acts complained of and if he gives such commands they obey them at their peril as the Kaiser only possessed war powers allowed by International Law and any command beyond and inconsistent with the law of war is null and void and is no defense to agent claiming its protection. The mere fact that illegal acts have been committed does not tax Kaiser as many acts have no doubt been committed by U.S. soldiers for which President Wilson cannot be responsible.

Reports are exaggerated as they always have been in the past and the Kaiser is not to blame if he refused to believe them. They must be brought home to him to make him criminally liable and a latter stating that he must wage war without attention to the claims of humanity in order that the war shall be short and successful can only condemn him morally, not legally, unless it be shown that the acts complained of were done, were ordered generally or specifically by him. The thing to do is to appoint a Commission to examine acts and to connect the Kaiser or officers with them, and then to try them according to the law of the case. It will be difficult, perhaps impossible, to connect the Kaiser with them, but doubtless officers can be taxed with responsibility. If so, military commissions as in the Wirz case can be constituted.

In any event, extradition should not lie inasmuch as the duty to extradite does not exist without treaty; and only for offenses specified by the treaty, and even than acts criminal in themselves, committed for a public purpose, not for private gain, are political, not personal crimes for which extradition does not lie.

At least this is the way the case seems at present. Tomorrow may bring more light.

Neutrality

Throughout Dr. Scott's life, an official attitude of impartiality – or neutrality – in the wars of other nations, especially of Europe, was not only the traditional policy of the Government of the United States, but it was sanctioned by penal statutes. At the outbreak of every war to which the United States was not a party, the President issued a proclamation declaring the neutrality of the Government, calling attention to the neutrality laws of the United States, and warning everyone within the jurisdiction of the United States of the penalties which would be incurred for the violation of those laws.

The doctrine that supplying the enemy with means of warfare is a participation in the war dates from Antiquity. As Dr. Scott pointed out, Demosthenes said "that person, whoever he be, who prepares and provides the means for my destruction, he makes war upon me, though he have never cast a javelin or drawn a bow against me". To the same effect, but expressed in a different way, Dr. Scott quoted Lord Grenville: "If I have wrested my enemy's sword from his hands, the bystander who furnishes him with a fresh weapon can have no pretense to be considered as a neutral in the contest".

Neutrality was formerly regarded as a privilege, not a right, as it came to be recognized under the stimulus of American policy as formulated by President Washington and Secretary of State Jefferson. As a privilege, the status of neutrality was expressly conferred by treaty. Belligerents claimed and exercised the right to prevent all commerce with the enemy, and the privilege of trading with the enemy, a trade which the United States proclaims to be a fundamental right, was formerly likewise a concession by treaty.

The development of the law of neutrality from its ancient origins up to the time when Dr. Scott presided over the United States Neutrality Board from August 1914 to April 1917 was succinctly summarized in an opinion of that board rendered to the Department of State:

In the long struggle between belligerent and neutral, the neutral seems to have obtained the upper hand, and to such an extent that what formerly was a privilege accorded to the neutral has become a right, and what was a right on the part of the belligerent to prevent trade has become a privilege. Trade with the enemy is, therefore, free to neutral subjects and citizens unless the privilege of belligerents be exercised. Trade with the enemy is, therefore, free to neutral subjects and citizens unless the privilege of belligerents be exercised. It is not *ipso facto* illegal, that is to say, it is only illegal in a limited sense – illegal as toward the enemy of the belligerent with which the trade is carried on, and then only when the trade is in goods that are contraband, or in case of blockade, when the trade is attempted through a blockaded port.

The trade may be prevented in two ways. A belligerent may declare the ports of his enemy blockaded—indeed, the entire coast, as in the case of the American Civil War—and, if he can make entrance or departure from the ports or coast dangerous by the presence of vessels of war, or if he can make the blockade effective, to use the technical term, he may prevent commerce of all kinds from any part of the world and from any neutral from entering or from leaving the enemy country. In the absence of a declaration of blockade, trade with the enemy country is not illegal. As, however, the question of blockade is not involved in the present discussion, it will not be further considered.

The other privilege possessed by the belligerent is to prevent neutral commerce of certain kinds, specified by the belligerent in advance or upon the outbreak of war, from reaching the enemy country or the enemy forces, either directly or circuitously. Articles exclusively of a warlike use—commonly called absolute contraband—may be captured and confiscated if directed to the enemy country. Articles useful in times of peace, but intended for hostile use in time of war, variously termed conditional or relative, accidental or occasional contraband, are said to be exempt from capture if they are not directed to the enemy government, an enemy agent, the armed forces of the enemy, or ports of naval or military equipment. If they are really intended to be delivered to any one of these, they may be captured and confiscated, and the interposition of a neutral port in order to disguise the real and ultimate destination does not avail the neutral shipper. It is thus seen that all trade may be expressly forbidden, if the belligerent can render a blockade effective; and that neutral

> articles of commerce of certain specified classes, or with certain destination, are subject to capture, with or without blockade.[2]

The need for a national policy of neutrality was thrust upon the Government of the United States during the wars of the French Revolution, if the young Republic were to be spared a repetition of the experiences of the colonies during the colonial wars in America preceding the American Revolution. By its conduct as a neutral in the European wars in Washington's administration, the United States laid the basis of the modern law of neutrality. A leading English writer on international law, reviewing in the retrospect of a century the development of that branch of the law, concluded that "the policy of the United States in 1793 constitutes an epoch in the development of the usages of neutrality. There can be no doubt that it was intended and believed to give effect to the obligations then incumbent upon neutrals. But it represented by far the most advanced existing opinions as to what those obligations were; and in some points it even went further than authoritative international custom has up to the present time advanced. In the main, however, it is identical with the standard of conduct which is now adopted by the community of nations".[3]

The code of municipal law drafted unilaterally by the United States on the subject of neutrality was confirmed and expanded from time to time by the practice and legislation of other nations, so that when the Hague Peace Conferences meet in 1899 and 1907, several international conventions of a multilateral character were ripe for adoption on various phases of neutrality during war on land and sea. Dr. Scott's experiences as a delegate to the second of those conferences and his writings as an historian of both of them provided him with an exceptionally valuable background for his services to the United States Government as Chairman of its Neutral Board when the war broke out in Europe in 1914.

---

[2] Duplicate manuscript opinion of the Board, No. 57, 23 December 1914 in Scott Papers.

[3] W. Hall, *International Law* (4th ed.; Oxford, 1895), sec. 213, p. 616.

Canada and the United States

In a letter written to Dr. Scott by an English colleague in London in 1915, the latter contrasted the neighborly relations existing between the United States and Canada with the unneighborly attitude of Germany toward England. "If", he wrote, "your country had been bent, scheming for it in open and underhand ways, on annexation of Canada, what a time this would be for the blow. Not only are our hands full, but Canada is depleting itself of its fighting population. You are trusted because you are neighborly". Dr. Scott was long, as was often the case, in replying to his correspondent, but when he did, his answer left nothing to be desired. "It is gratifying to hear what you say about Canada. Of course we would like it", he admitted. "We would be very glad if the ripened apple would fall in our lap. We would like to see one Government and one People from the Gulf of Mexico to the Arctic, but we have no intention, not even during a storm, to give the tree an extra shake. If the apple would only drop in our lap, as I said before, we would be very happy, but if it will not, why, that's the end of it, and I am of the opinion that the apple is likely to cling to the tree. The trunk is pretty strong and the branches show no signs of giving way.

You do not need to fear us. We evacuated Cuba twice, when Europe expected us to stay in the little island. We gave back the unexpended portion of the Chinese indemnity, but no other country followed our example. We make mistakes – all people do – and we acknowledge them, thereby freeing our conscience, as happened in the Mexican war, when we paid for the territory we conquered – if I were not writing to a foreigner, I would say, robbed. But, after all, you are not a foreigner, and therefore I shall say, stolen. However, we try to be as honorable as circumstances will permit, and in the present instance you can take every mother's son away from Canada without fear of invasion.

The Best Friend of Cuba

A friend is a person with whom I may be sincere. Before him, I may think aloud.[4]

---

[4] Quoted from Cosme de la Torriente, "La Obra del Major Amigo de Cuba", in *Cuba y los Estados Unidos* (Habana, 1929), p. 233.

President McKinley's message to Congress of 11 April 1898 recommending that the United States intervene in Cuba disclaimed any purpose of acquiring territory by conquest, and the joint resolution of Congress of 20 April 1898 demanding that Spain withdraw from the island committed the United States to the independence of Cuba.

In Article 1 of the treaty of peace between Spain and the United States, signed at Paris 10 December 1898, Spain relinquished "all claim of sovereignty over and title to Cuba". The island was not ceded to, although it was occupied by the United States, which felt itself bound by the terms of the resolution declaring war against Spain to turn the island over to its people. This declaration of intention was not a contract, but it was properly regarded as creating an equitable estoppels against the United States in favor of the Cubans who had aided it in driving the Spanish forces from the island. The United States occupied Cuba, and during its occupation prepared it for self-government, to be turned over to its people when that time should have come. On 20 May 1902 the world saw the unwonted spectacle of a country living up to its solemn promise and turning over a coveted possession to the inhabitants thereof in pursuance of a solemnly declared purpose, the hauling down of the American flag, the symbol of sovereignty during the occupation, and the unenforced, voluntary evacuation of Cuba Libre by the American troops.

Mr. Root's task as Secretary of War, from the time of the relinquishment of Cuba under the treaty and its release to its people, was to prepare Cuba for self-government and to determine the relations between Cuba and the United States.

The solution of the problem recommended by Mr. Root and adopted and put into effect by the Government of the United States is described in Mr. Root's reports as Secretary of War. The solution was:

> 1. Not to sail away and leave the island to disorder and probable anarchy and bloodshed, but to remain long enough to create a complete civil government composed of Cubans trained to the performance of their duties, and to turn the island over to the Cuban people with that government in operation as a going concern.
>
> 2. To require from the Cubans guarantees for the conduct of their government and to prevent the island from falling into the hands of any other nation so that the United States would not be placed in a worse position than before by reason of turning Spain out of the island. This was accomplished by including in the Cu-

ban constitution and in the legislation of the United States and in a treaty between the United States and Cuba the provisions known as the Platt Amendment.

These provisions were presented to the Cuban Constitutional Convention pursuant to Mr. Root's instructions to the military governor of Cuba dated 9 February 1901. They had previously been approved by President McKinley and his Cabinet.

It appearing desirable to incorporate the above provisions in the statutes of the United States, Mr. Root's instructions to the military governor of Cuba were later introduced in the Senate by Senator Orville H. Platt at the request of President McKinley and Mr. Root, and were adopted as an amendment to the Army Appropriate Bill of 2 March 1901, thus becoming known as the Platt Amendment. The Platt Amendment was subsequently incorporated in identical terms in the Cuban constitution and in the treaty of 1 July 1904 between Cuba and the United States.

In that portion of the instructions to the Military Governor of Cuba which became Article 3 of the Platt Amendment, Mr. Root said that:

> Upon the transfer of the control of Cuba to the government established under the new constitution, Cuba consents that the United States reserve and retain the right of intervention for the preservation of Cuban independence and maintenance of a stable government, adequately protecting life, property, and individual liberty, and discharging the obligations with respect to Cuba imposed by the Treaty of Paris on the United States and now assumed and undertaken by the Government of Cuba.

As the reservation of the right of intervention seemed to cause some uneasiness in the Cuban constitutional convention, it was thought advisable to interpret the sense in which the United States understood the right to intervene and the circumstances which would justify and require it. It was necessary that the right and the circumstances should be understood in the same sense by Cuba. Therefore, Mr. Root put the interpretation of the Government of the United States upon this article in his telegram to the Military Governor dated 3 April 1902, directing him at the same time to lay the telegram before the Cuban constitutional convention, which was then in session, in order that the article should be adopted with the interpretation which the United States had placed upon it. The telegram which the Military Governor laid before the convention, pursuant to instructions, was thus worded:

> You are authorized to state officially that in the view of the President the intervention described in the third clause of the Platt Amendment is not synonymous with intermeddling or interference with the affairs of the Cuban Government, but the formal action of the Government of the United States, based upon just and substantial grounds, for the preservation of Cuban independence, and the maintenance of a government adequate for the protection of life, property, and individual liberty, and adequate for discharging the obligations with respect to Cuba imposed by the Treaty of Paris on the United States.

The Cuban Government, as previously stated, was turned over to the people of the island on 20 May 1902. Trouble broke out in the island in 1906, and, exercising the right of intervention contained in the statutes of the United States, President Roosevelt intervened. A provisional governor was appointed for Cuba and various officials were selected to aid in the work of reorganization. American troops were sent to the island and the necessary measures taken to restore and maintain order. Upon the accomplishment of the purposes of the occupation, the United States, on 31 March 1909, again withdrew from the island (Cir. No. 92, War Department, 31 December 1909), leaving Cuba for the second time to its newly elected and duly constituted authorities (See *Foreign Relations of the United States*, 1906, I, pp. 480 et seq.).

This chapter of Cuban history is, it is believed, a unique chapter in the world's history, and it reflects great credit upon the Republic which adopted the policy and upon the wisdom and constructive ability of the statesman who devised it.[5]

---

[5] Adapted from Dr. Scott's headnote to the chapter on Cuba in Elihu Root, *The Military and Colonial Policy of the United States: Addresses and Reports by Elihu Root* (Cambridge, Mass., Harvard University Press, 1916), pp. 185–188.

NOTES ON PRINCIPAL PERSONAE

Set out below are concise biographical details on some of the principal individuals mentioned in Finch's biography of James Brown Scott to assist the reader. Details given are those that may be especially relevant to Scott. – [WEB].

ALVAREZ, ALEJANDRO (1868–1960), Chilean jurist and spiritual father of the concept of an American International Law. Member of the International Court of Justice from 1946 to 1955.

BACON, ROBERT (1860–1919), diplomat, served briefly as Secretary of State in early 1909, during which time he secured Senate advice and consent for the Panama Canal treaties with Panama and Colombia and was Ambassador to France from 1909 to 1912. Worked assiduously to improve relations with Latin America.

BARRETT, JOHN (1866–1938), diplomat. Served as Minister to Argentina, Panama, and Colombia. Appointed 1907 to what became the Pan American Union and presided over the Pan American Scientific Congress (1916).

BIEBERSTEIN, ADOLF MARSCHALL VON (1842–1912), German jurist and diplomat, Secretary of State of the Foreign Office of the German Empire. Representative of Germany to Second Hague Peace Conference.

BLAINE, JAMES GILLESPIE (1830–1893), politician. Served in House of Representatives and Senate of the United States and twice was appointed Secretary of State. His foreign policy strongly oriented towards Latin America.

BOURGEOIS, LEON VICTOR AUGUSTE (1851–1925), French statesman, jurist, and diplomat, delegate to First and Second Hague Peace Conferences and to Paris Peace Conference. Member (1903) of Permanent Court of International Arbitration; President of Council of League of Nations. Laureat of Nobel Peace Prize (1920).

BREWER, DAVID JOSIAH (1837–1910), jurist. Associate Justice of the United States Supreme Court for twenty years; President of the United States Commission on the Boundary between Venezuela and British Guiana in 1895.

BRYAN, WILLIAM JENNINGS (1860–1925), jurist and politician, unsuccessful candidate for the Presidency of the United States. Secretary of State under President Woodrow Wilson. Negotiated 28 arbitration treaties.

BUSTAMANTE Y SIRVEN, ANTONIO SANCHEZ (1865–1951), Cuban jurist. Member of the Permanent Court of International Justice (1922-1944). Delegate to the Paris Peace Conference; member of Hague Permanent Court of Arbitration. President of Pan American Congress (1928); author of Bustamante Code of Private International Law.

BUTLER, CHARLES HENRY (1859–1940), diplomat and jurist, tenth reporter of the decisions of the United States Supreme Court (1902-1916), and author of work on *Treaty Making Power of the United States* (1902). Delegate of the United States to the Second Hague Peace Conference.

BUTLER, NICHOLAS MURRAY (1862–1947), President of Columbia University from 1901 to 1945 and a close friend and confidant of James Brown Scott and Elihu Root. Laureate of the Nobel Peace Prize in 1931. Active in Republic politics, ran as candidate for Vice President of the United States in 1912. Served as President of the Lake Mohonk Conferences on International Arbitration from 1907 to 1912. Helped persuade Andrew Carnegie to found the Carnegie Endowment and served as President from 1925 to 1945.

CARNEGIE, ANDREW (1835–1919), American industrialist and philanthropist of Scottish origin who established, among others, the Carnegie Endowment for International Peace and secured the appointment of James Brown Scott to be Secretary and a division head of that institution. Carnegie played a significant role through his personal contacts and political influence in advancing the cause of international arbitration in American foreign policy and financed the construction of the Peace Palace in The Hague.

CECIL, LORD EDGAR ALGERNON ROBERT GASCOYNE, VISCOUNT (1864–1958), jurist and diplomat. Principal architect of the League of Nations. Laureate of the Nobel Peace Prize (1937).

CHOATE, JOSEPH HODGES (1832–1917), jurist and diplomat, served as Ambassador to the Court of St. James from 1899 to 1905 and was a member of the American Delegation to the Second Hague Peace Conference. Noted litigator and former President of the American Bar Association.

CREMER, SIR WILLIAM RANDAL (1828–1908), British liberal politician and Nobel Laureate (1903) of humble origins who played a leading role in establishing the International Arbitration League and was a great influence upon Andrew Carnegie.

CROWDER, ENOCH HERBERT (1859–1932), jurist and career military officer. Delegate to Fourth Pan American Congress (1910). Served as Judge Advocate General for twelve years. Ambassador to Cuba from 1923 to 1927; then entered private law practice.

CROWE, SIR EYRE (1864–1925), diplomat; assistant undersecretary of State for foreign affairs from 1912 and delegate to the Versailles Peace Conference.

DAY, WILLIAM RUFUS (1849–1923), diplomat and jurist. Associate Justice of the United States Supreme Court from 1903 to 1922. Served several months as Secretary of State before becoming head of the United States Peace Commission to settle the Spanish-American War.

DONWORTH, GEORGE (1861–1947), jurist and judge. Served from 1909 to 1912 on the United States District Court for the Western District of Washington and then remained in private practice for the rest of his life.

DRAPER, ANDREW SLOAN (1848–1913), President and Regent of the University of Illinois from 1894 to 1904; served as arbitrator on the *Alabama* Claims arbitration; Commissioner of Education of the State of New York from 1904.

FAUCHILLE, PAUL AUGUSTE JOSEPH (1858–1926), international lawyer; member of the Institute of International Law and author of a fundamental treatise on the subject.

FRY, SIR EDWARD (1827–1918), jurist and judge. Member of the Permanent Court of International Arbitration; British legal assessor to investigate Dogger Bank incident; delegate to Second Hague Peace Conference.

FULLER, MELVILLE WESTON (1833–1910), jurist. Eighth Chief Justice of the United States Supreme Court from 1888 to 1910.

GLADSTONE, WILLIAM EWART (1809–1898), politician, served four times as Chancellor of the Exchequer and Prime Minister of the United Kingdom.

GREY, SIR EDWARD, FIRST VISCOUNT GREY OF FALLODON (1862–1933), statesman. Foreign Secretary from 1905 to 1916. Ambassador to the United States from 1919 to 1920 and later Leader of the Liberal Party in the House of Lords.

GRIGGS, JOHN WILLIAM (1849–1927), jurist; Governor of New Jersey and United States Attorney General. Among first members appointed to Permanent Court of Arbitration at The Hague, serving from 1901 to 1912.

HAY, JOHN MILTON (1838–1905), jurist, diplomat, Ambassador of the United States to the Court of St. James (1897–1898), Secretary of State of the United States from 1898 until his death in 1905. Negotiated the Treaty of Paris in 1898 to end the Spanish-American War. Noted also as former private secretary to Abraham Lincoln.

HERSHEY, AMOS SHARTLE (1867–1933), jurist and international lawyer. Professor of Political Science at the University of Indiana. Staff member of American Commission to Negotiate Peace from 1918 to 1919.

HILL, DAVID JAYNE (1850–1932), historian and diplomat, university president. Served as Assistant Secretary of State from 1898 to

1903, and the as Minister to Switzerland and the Netherlands, later Ambassador to Germany. Member of the American Delegation to the Second Hague Peace Conference.

HOOVER, HERBERT (1874–1964), mining engineer. 31st President of the United States from 1929 to 1933. Mediated while President a territorial dispute between Chile and Peru and did much to improve Latin American relations with the United States.

HUDSON, MANLEY OTTMER (1886–1960), Professor of International Law at Harvard Law School from 1919 to his retirement in 1954; member of the Permanent Court of International Justice; first Chairman of the United Nations International Law Commission; Director of Harvard Research in International Law; Associate, Institute of International Law; twice nominated for the Nobel Peace Prize.

HUGHES, CHARLES EVANS (1862–1948), jurist and diplomat. Governor of New York, Associate (1910–1916) and Chief (1930–1941) Justice of the United States Supreme Court, and Secretary of State from 1921 to 1925. Convened the Washington Naval Conference in 1921.

HULL, CORDELL (1871–1955), jurist and Congressman. Served as Secretary of State from 1933 to 1944. Laureate of the Nobel Peace Prize in 1945.

JAY, JOHN (1745–1829), American statesman, jurist, and diplomat who negotiated a peace treaty with the United Kingdom in 1794 and was a co-author of *The Federalist Papers*. Served as the first Chief Justice of the United States Supreme Court from 1789 to 1795.

KELLOGG, FRANK BILLINGS (1856–1937), jurist. United States Senator from Minnesota. Served as Secretary of State from 1925 to 1929. Co-author of the Kellogg-Briand Pact, a treaty which laid the foundations of the modern system of international security. Laureate of the Nobel Peace Prize in 1929. Member of the Permanent Court of International Justice from 1930 to 1935.

KIRCHWEY, GEORGE WASHINGTON (1855–1942), Professor of Law and Dean at Columbia of University from 1891 to 1916; pioneer in developing the American casebook; co-founder of the New York

Peace Society in 1906 and President of the American Peace Society in 1917.

KNOX, PHILANDER CHASE (1853–1921), jurist and diplomat; Attorney General of and Senator from Pennsylvania, and Secretary of State from 1909 to 1913. Achieved settlement of the Bering Sea and North Atlantic fisheries disputes.

LANSING, ROBERT (1864–1928), jurist and diplomat; legal adviser to the Department of State and Secretary of State from 1915 to 1920. Strong proponent of neutrality in First World War. Member of American Delegation to Versailles Peace Conference.

LAPRADELLE, ALBERT GEOUFFRE DE (1871–1955), international lawyer who taught at Grenoble and Paris and wrote extensively on the law of the sea, disarmament, and arbitration.

LIEBER, FRANCIS (1800–1872), American jurist of German origin especially noted for preparing the *Code for Government of the Armies in the Field* (1863) during the American Civil War. Among his academic appointments was Professor of Political Science at Columbia Law School from 1860 until his death.

MCKINLEY, WILLIAM (1843–1901), jurist, 25th President of the United States from 1897 to 1901, led the United States into the Spanish-American War.

MARBURG, THEODORE (1862–1946), active supporter of American membership in the League of Nations.

MARTENS, FEDOR FEDOROVICH (1845–1909), jurist, diplomat, and professor of international law at St. Petersburg University; author of numerous treatises and treaty collections. Advisor to Russian Ministry of Foreign Affairs. Russian delegate to First and Second Hague Peace Conferences.

MORROW, WILLIAM W. (1843–1929), jurist; Congressman from California. Served as special attorney before the United States-France Claims Commission, 1881–1883, and *Alabama* Claims Commission, 1882–1885.

NELIDOV, COUNT ALEKSANDR (1838–1910), Russian diplomat and President of the Second Hague Peace Conference.

OLNEY, RICHARD (1835–1917), jurist and diplomat. Attorney General of the United States and Secretary of State from 1895 to 1897 under Grover Cleveland.

PASSY, FRÉDÉRIC (1822–1912), jurist and economist, strong proponent of disarmament and international arbitration, laureate of the Nobel Peace Prize in 1901. Significantly influenced by the views and activities of W. R. Cremer (q.v.).

PAUNCEFOTE, JULIAN, FIRST BARON PAUNCEFOTE (1828–1902), jurist, judge, diplomat. Ambassador to the United States from 1893 to 1902. Negotiated the Hay-Pauncefote Treaty in 1899 to replace the Clayton-Bulwer Treaty of 1850 and enable the United States to build the Panama Canal.

PESSAO, EPITÁCIO LINDOLFO DA SILVA (1865–1942), Brazilian jurist and politician. Chief of Brazilian delegation to Versailles Peace Conference and member of Permanent Court of International Justice.

REEVES, JESSE SIDDALL (1872–1942), historian and political scientist. Professor at the University of Michigan for 32 years.

RENAULT, LOUIS (1843–1918), professor of international law at the University of Paris and legal advisor to the French Ministry of Foreign Affairs; delegate to the First and Second Hague Peace Conferences and the London Naval Conference (1908–1909). Laureate of the Nobel Peace Prize (1907).

ROLIN-JAEQUEMYNS, GUSTAVE HENRI ANGE HIPPOLYTE (1835–1902), Belgian international lawyer and among the founders of the Institute of International Law in 1873 and a co-founder of the *Revue de droit international et de législation comparée*.

ROOSEVELT, THEODORE (1858–1919), 26th President of the United States from 1901 to 1909, politician, naturalist, explorer, author, soldier. Laureate of the Nobel Peace Prize (1906).

ROOT, ELIHU (1845–1937), New York lawyer who acted as Secretary of War (1899–1904); Secretary of State (1905–1909); Senator from the state of New York in the Senate of the United States (1909–1915); Ambassador to Russia (1917); First President of the Carnegie Endowment; Laureate of the Nobel Peace Prize (1912); Founding Chairman, Council on Foreign Relations (1918); co-founder, American Society of International Law (1905); American Law Institute (1923); served on Commission of Jurists which founded the Permanent Court of International Justice; served as Vice President, American Peace Society.

ROWE, LEO STANTON (1871–1946), jurist. Director General of the Pan American Union from 1920 to 1946; among the founders of The Brookings Institution.

ROZHESTVENSKII, ZINOVII PETROVICH (1848–1909), Admiral of the Imperial Russian Navy in command of the Second Pacific Fleet at the Battle of Tsushima, who was also involved in the Dogger Bank Incident that led to a celebrated inquiry.

STEVENS, DORIS CAROLINE (1888–1963), suffragist. Active in National Woman's Party and chairman from 1928 to 1939 of Inter-American Commission on Women, an advisory group attached to the Pan American Union. Close friend of James Brown Scott. Attended his lectures at Georgetown University on international law from 1925 to 1931. Elected to the American Law Institute.

WHITE, ANDREW DICKSON (1832–1918), historian, diplomat, university educator. First President of Cornell University; Ambassador to Germany and Russia. President of American Delegation to First Hague Peace Conference.

WICKERSHAM, GEORGE WOODWARD (1858–1936), Attorney General of the United States from 1909 to 1913 and President of the Council on Foreign Relations from 1933 to 1936.

WIGMORE, JOHN HENRY (1863–1943), jurist. Professor and Dean at Northwestern Law School. Pre-eminent comparatist, with special reference to Japanese law. Author of leading treatise on the law of evidence.

WILSON, THOMAS WOODROW (1856–1924), jurist and historian; 28th President of the United States. Strong supporter of the League of Nations and architect of American policies at the Versailles Peace Conference.

INDEX OF NAMES

www.ingramcontent.com/pod-product-compliance
Ingram Content Group UK Ltd.
Pitfield, Milton Keynes, MK11 3LW, UK
UKHW041851031026
15587UKWH00005B/1166/J

9 781616 191658